John Knox

John Knox

An Introduction to His Life and Works

RICHARD G. KYLE
AND
DALE W. JOHNSON

WIPF & STOCK · Eugene, Oregon

JOHN KNOX
An Introduction to His Life and Works

Wipf & Stock
A Division of Wipf and Stock Publishers
199 W. 8th Ave., Suite 3
Eugene, OR 97401
www.wipfandstock.com

ISBN 13: 9781498252362

Manufactured in the U.S.A.

To Joyce, Brent, Susan, and Taylor

Contents

Preface

AS GRADUATE STUDENTS, WE developed an interest in John Knox. This fascination drove our early academic careers—producing two dissertations, two books, and many articles. But through the years, we took leave from John Knox, moving into other areas of research. Still, we could not get Knox completely out of our systems. In knowing that there existed a gap in Knoxian studies—specifically, an analysis of his writings—we moved in that direction.

This volume traces the life and thought of John Knox by examining his writings. A number of biographies tell the story of the famous Scottish reformer. But we have taken the reader in a different direction, offering an interpretation of his writings. We take a chronological approach to his writings, allowing them to speak for themselves. In doing so, Knox's writings partially tell the story of his life and ideas.

Chapter one, "The Man and His Times," introduces the Europe of John Knox and his life. Chapter two, "The Mind of John Knox," summarizes his major ideas from a thematic perspective. The next six chapters analyze his writings through distinct chronological periods—his early life, his exile, and his return to Scotland.

Chapter three, "The Reformer in Training (1547–54)," examines Knox's writings in his early years. They record his thoughts while on a French galley and in England. Subjects such as justification by faith, idolatry, the Lord's Supper, and prayer are addressed. In addition, Knox's pastoral side is demonstrated in his letters to Mrs. Bowes. The next chapter, "The Exile Years (1554–56)," describes Knox's mind-set during his early exile on the Continent. While he addressed several subjects, his major concern was idolatry, which he interpreted to be Catholicism, and how the faithful should respond to idolatrous rulers.

For several years Knox had been inching toward resistance against idolatrous monarchs. Chapter five, "The Outburst Against Idolatrous Rulers (1556-59)," describes how Knox stepped over the line. He articulated a full blown theory of resistance to Catholic rulers. In four pamphlets published prior to August 1558, Knox spelled out his ideas regarding government and religion—that is, the rights of subjects against idolatrous and oppressive sovereigns.

Despite Knox's preoccupation with resistance to idolatrous monarchs, he took time to address other subjects, namely, Anabaptism and predestination. While his great enemy was the Catholic Church, recognized by law and backed by the power of the state, he was not about to be outflanked by more radical groups on the left wing of the Reformation. So he vehemently opposed the Anabaptists, and in doing so he also elaborated upon his doctrine of predestination. These subjects are addressed in chapter six, "Confronting the Anabaptists and Defending Predestination (1557–60)."

Upon returning to Scotland in 1559, Knox began writing his *History of the Reformation in Scotland*, a task that would last until 1571. This substantial work occupied the better part of two volumes and tells us much that is known about Knox. Perhaps more important is that it opens another window to his worldview—a subject noted in chapter seven, "History Through the Eyes of John Knox (1559–71)."

Upon his return to Scotland, Knox did more than write his history. He played an important role in bringing about the Scottish Reformation and solidifying Protestantism in Scotland. This story is told in chapter eight, "Knox in Zion: The Reformation in Scotland (1559–72)." Most of Knox's writings during this time focus on the issue of securing the Reformed faith in Scotland. The last chapter, "Views of Knox: Extreme Makeover," examines the ways Knox has been regarded over time. These perspectives have covered a wide spectrum: adulation, severe criticism, and even ignoring Knox's role in the Scottish Reformation.

No one writes a book alone. In the time this book has been in gestation, we have accumulated debts to several individuals and institutions. We hope our memories are not short in this regard and that we do not inadvertently omit any thanks that are due. Appreciation must go to the library staffs of Tabor College and Erskine Seminary for arranging the acquisition of many books and articles through interlibrary loan. Without these sources, our work would not have been possible. Gratitude is due to Provost Lawrence Ressler of Tabor College for providing financial assistance through the Hope Scholars Grant for work on this study. Thanks must go to Joe Hall, James Edward McGoldrick, Brian Armstrong, and Donald Sullivan for directing our earlier study of John Knox.

Many debts have been incurred in the production of this book. We especially thank Ellie Rempel for her work in putting this manuscript in its final form. Appreciation must be offered to Carrol Ediger for editing an early version of the manuscript. Academic publishing presents many challenges. Therefore, much thanks must go to the staff of Wipf and Stock for publishing this volume—especially to its production editor Heather Carraher, assistant managing editor Christian Amondson, and typesetter Tina Campbell Owens. Finally, our gratitude goes to two individuals who were involved only indirectly with the writing and publishing process—our wives Joyce Kyle and Susan Johnson. Without their support and patience, our publishing endeavors and professional activities would not have been possible.

Richard Kyle
Dale Johnson
Hillsboro, Kansas
Due West, South Carolina

1

The Man and His Times

REVOLUTIONARY OR SERVANT OF God? Thundering prophet or con-
summate politician? Nasty old man or spiritual pastor? Ardently
loved or passionately despised? Will the real John Knox please stand up?
John Knox indeed was a complex and contradictory figure. To be sure, he
displayed several faces and wore many hats.

The Scottish reformer, therefore, has been the subject of many inter-
pretations—some wildly different. Knox was a controversial figure in his
day. And he continues to be so down to the present. He has been both loved
and hated by his contemporaries and historians through the centuries.
No sixteenth-century reformer has aroused such a range of emotions and
opinions. Few people have taken a neutral stance in regard to John Knox.

These differing opinions largely concern several related questions:
What was Knox's role or vocation? How did he perform this role or voca-
tion? What kind of person was John Knox? How important was he to the
Scottish Reformation? Historians have expressed different views regarding
Knox's role or vocation—prophet, pastor, preacher, reformer, statesman,
revolutionary, and more.[1] Actually, most modern scholars have focused

1. Different writers have emphasized the roles that Knox played. For some examples,
see the following: Jasper Ridley, *John Knox* (New York: Oxford University Press, 1968);
W. Stanford Reid, *Trumpeter of God* (New York: Scribner's, 1974); E. Russell, "John
Knox as Statesman," *The Princeton Theological Review* 6, (January 1908): 1–29; Dale
W. Johnson, "Prophecy, Rhetoric and Diplomacy: John Knox and the Struggle for the
Soul of Scotland," Ph.D. diss. Georgia State University, 1995; J. Douglas MacMillan,
"John Knox—Preacher of the Word," *Reformed Theological Journal* (November 1987):
5–19; W. Stanford Reid, "John Knox, Pastor of Souls." *Westminster Theological Journal*
40, no. 1 (1977): 1–21; Stewart D. Gill, "He made my tongue a trumpet . . ." John Knox,
The Preacher," *The Reformed Theological Review* 51 (1992): 102–10. See also James Kirk,
"John Knox and the Historians," in *John Knox and the British Reformations* ed. Roger A.
Mason (Aldershot, UK: Ashgate, 1998), 7–26; Richard Kyle, *The Ministry of John Knox:*

on two aspects of one general subject: Knox's political ideas, especially his theory of resistance, and his attitudes toward female rulers.[2]

In respect to evaluating Knox, W. Stanford Reid divided the reformer into three camps: his supporters, his opponents, and those in the middle.[3] Knox's advocates have seen him as the "right man for the right time in Scotland." Some of these admirers see little fault in Knox. In their eyes, Knox has no warts and may have even been "St. John."[4]

But the Scottish reformer has had his fierce opponents—both in his day and today. In his time, of course, the leading Catholics denounced him.

Pastor, Preacher, and Prophet (Lewiston, NY: The Edwin Mellen Press, 2002); Richard Kyle, "The Thundering Scot: John Knox the Preacher, *Westminster Theological Journal* 64, no. 1 (2002): 135–49; Richard Kyle, "Prophet of God: John Knox's Self Awareness," *Reformed Theological Review* 61, no. 2 (2002): 85–101; Richard Kyle, "John Knox and the Care of Souls," *Calvin Theological Journal* 38, no. 1 (2003): 133–44.

2. A partial list would include the following writings: Roger A. Mason, ed. *John Knox: On Rebellion* (Cambridge, UK: Cambridge University Press, 1994); Amanda Shephard, *Gender and Authority in Sixteenth Century England* (Keele, UK: Keele University Press, 1994); Marvin A. Breslow, ed. *The Political Writings of John Knox* (Cranbury, NJ: Associated University Presses, 1985); Roger A. Mason, "Knox, Resistance and the Moral Imperative," *History of Political Thought* 1 (1980–1981): 411–36; John R. Gray, "The Political Theory of John Knox," *Church History* 8 (June 1939): 132–47; Jane E. Dawson, "The Two John Knoxes: England, Scotland and the 1558 Tracts," *Journal of Ecclesiastical History* 42, no. 4 (1991): 555–76; John Cassidy, "The Quest for Godly Rule: The Development of Resistance Theory in Reformation Scotland," *Scottish Tradition*, 14 (1988): 1–10; W. Stanford Reid, "John Knox's Theology of Political Government," *Sixteenth Century Journal* 19, no. 4 (1988): 529–40; K. M. Brown, "In Search of the Godly Magistrate in Reformation Scotland," *Journal of Ecclesiastical History* 40, no 4 (1989): 553–81; Robert M. Healey, "Waiting for Deborah: John Knox and Four Ruling Queens," *Sixteenth Century Journal* 25, no. 2 (1994): 371–86; Richard Kyle, *The Mind of John Knox* (Lawrence, KS: Coronado Press, 1984), 241–305; J. H. Burns, "The Political Ideas of the Scottish Reformation," *Aberdeen University Review* 36 (1955–1956): 251–68; Richard L. Greaves, "Calvinism, Democracy and the Political Thought of John Knox," *Occasional Papers of the American Society for Reformation Research* 1 (1978): 81–92; Richard L. Greaves, "John Knox, The Reformed Tradition, and the Development of Resistance Theory," *The Journal of Modern History* 58 (September 1976): 1–31.

3. W. Stanford Reid, "John Knox and his Interpretaters," *Renaissance and Reformation* 10, no. 1 (1974): 14, 15; Reid, *Trumpeter of God*, 285–86.

4. Views supporting Knox range from near hero worship to a positive attitude. Some examples include the following: Richard Bannatyne, *A Journal of Transactions in Scotland* (Edinburgh: Bannatyne Club, 1836); Thomas Carlyle, *On Heroes, Hero Worship and the Heroic in History* (London: Chapman and Hall, 1897); Thomas M'Crie, *The Life of John Knox* 2 vols. (Edinburgh: William Blackwood, 1818); Joannes Spotiswoode, *The History of the Church and State of Scotland* (London: R. Roystan, 1677); Reid, *Trumpeter of God*; J. A. Froude, *The Reign of Edward VI* (London: J.M. Dent, 1909).

So did the more secular Protestants who opposed his program. In our day, some biographers and historians have criticized Knox's attitude toward Queen Mary, his outlook regarding female rulers, his advocacy of violence, or minimized his role in the Scottish Reformation.[5] The film *Mary Queen of Scots* portrays Knox as a strange man with a long black beard who jumps out from behind a bush and berates the queen. "The image of John Knox as a cross between Ian Paisley and the Ayatollah Khomeini" seems to be "lodged in the popular mind," says Stewart Lamont.[6]

Fortunately, some observers have taken the middle ground. They do not go overboard in either their praise or condemnation of Knox. Instead, they have sought a measure of objectivity. They regard Knox as a leading figure in the Scottish Reformation, but not the only force. There would have been a reformation without Knox. Still, he helped chart its course. Some observers in this camp have even become somewhat indifferent toward the Scottish reformer.[7]

Whether one views Knox positively or negatively, he certainly pursued his vocation with great vigor. His vocation was to preach the gospel, not to be a writer nor an ecclesiastical organizer or official. His main duty

5. In various degrees, the following writers have taken a critical view of Knox. Andrew Lang, *John Knox and the Reformation* (London: Longmans, Green and Co., 1905); Ridley, *John Knox*; Antonia Fraser, *Mary Queen of Scots* (New York: Delacorte Press, 1969); H. Trevor-Roper, "John Knox," *The Listener* 80 (1968): 745f.; Gordon Donaldson, "Knox the Man," *in John Knox: A Quatercentenary Reappraisal* ed. Duncan Shaw (Edinburgh: St. Andrew Press, 1975); John Durkan, "Scottish Reformers: The Less Than Golden Legend," *The Innes Review* 45, no. 1 (1994): 1–28.

6. Stewart Lamont, *The Swordbearer: John Knox and the European Reformation* (London: Hodder and Stoughton, 1991). Ian Paisley regards Knox as the model for his career. See Martha Abele MacIver, "Ian Paisley and the Reformed Tradition," *Political Studies* 35 (September 1987): 360–61.

7. Some examples of this somewhat vague category include the following: Pierre Janton, *John Knox: L'homme et l'oeuvre* (Paris: Didier, 1967); Pierre Janton, *Concepts et Sentiment De L'Eglise Chez John Knox: le reformateur ecossais* (Paris: Presses Universitarieres De France, 1972); W. C. Dickinson, "Introduction," in *History of the Reformation in Scotland* 2 vols. by John Knox (Edinburgh: Thomas Nelson and Sons Ltd., 1949); Geddes MacGregor, *The Thundering Scot: A Portrait of John Knox* (Philadelphia: Westminster Press, 1975); Elizabeth Whitley, *Plain Mr. Knox* (Richmond: John Knox Press, 1960); James S. McEwen, *The Faith of John Knox* (Richmond: John Knox Press, 1961); Richard L. Greaves, *Theology and Revolution in the Scottish Reformation* (Grand Rapids: Christian University Press, 1980); Kyle, *Mind of Knox*; Ian B. Cowan, "John Knox and the Making of the Scottish Reformation," *Proceedings of the Conference on Scottish Studies* 1 (1979): 22–30; Lord Eustace Percy, *John Knox* (Richmond: John Knox Press, 1966); P. Hume Brown, *John Knox* 2 vols. (London: Adam and Charles Black, 1894).

in life was, as he expressed it frequently, "to blow my master's trumpet." He saw himself as a preaching, rather than a writing, prophet proclaiming the gospel of God's grace in Jesus Christ: "For considering myself rather called by God to instruct the ignorant, comfort the sorrowful, confirm the weak, and rebuke the proud by lively voice in these most corrupt days, then to compose books for the age to come . . . ."[8]

Knox expressed his vocation in three overlapping roles—preacher, pastor, and prophet. He served as the pastor or minister of congregations in Scotland, England, and the Continent. Unlike our time, the minister's primary function was to preach God's Word. Thus the roles of pastor and preacher must be regarded as inseparable. As a minister, however, Knox did more than preach. He pastored or shepherded the flock, instructing and comforting them in their trials and tribulations. Still, when Knox preached, he often thundered like an Old Testament prophet—rebuking the proud and corrupt by a lively voice. His vocation focused on individuals, congregations, and entire nations. When attempting to reform religion on the national level, Knox often adopted the role and rhetoric of an Old Testament prophet.

In working out his vocation as a prophet, Knox can legitimately be seen as a revolutionary, a political figure, and the reformer of religion on a national level. But he also functioned as a pastor. And in doing so, a softer, more caring John Knox emerged. He could, of course, roar like a lion from the pulpit, denouncing both individual and corporate sins. But when performing his pastoral functions and dealing with individual problems, a gentler John Knox came to the forefront—not the bluebeard that many have portrayed him to be.

THE EUROPE OF JOHN KNOX

Knox did not blow his master's trumpet in a vacuum. He bellowed his sermons against the background and culture of his day. His denunciation of Catholicism must be seen in the context of the larger events—especially the perception of corruption in the Catholic Church and the ongoing Protestant Reformation. Knox wrote his treatises and letters in response to specific situations and problems, often persecution and moral lapses. Such

---

8. John Knox, *The Works of John Knox*, 6 *Vols.* ed. David Laing (Edinburgh: Printed for the Bannatyne Club, 1846–1864): 6: 229. Hereafter this collection will be cited as *Works* followed by the appropriate volume and page number. Also, the quotations from Laing's edition have been modernized to contemporary spelling.

writings were not abstract theological treatises. He offered counseling and spiritual advice to individuals with specific problems—usually issues encountered by first generation Protestants. What's more, his prophetic role must be seen against the backdrop of European events. Protestantism and Catholicism were locked in a cosmic struggle, and Knox saw himself on God's side pitted against the forces of Satan.

Political Factors

As the sixteenth century dawned, Europe stood on the brink of fundamental political change. The medieval, feudal world dominated by the papacy and the Holy Roman Empire came under challenge. To the south and east, Christian Europe faced a hostile Islamic power. But to the west, the discovery of the New World presented many new opportunities—plus a few challenges. All of this was occurring as the Reformation shattered the religious unity of Europe, dividing it into two antagonistic camps.

In such goings on, the major players were Spain, France, England, the papacy, and the Holy Roman Empire. Spain had extensive colonies in the New World and tremendous possibilities for trade and the acquisition of wealth. As yet, England and France possessed no colonies. So they sought to finance their wars and expansion elsewhere—usually from the coffers of the mercantile class. Traditionally weak rulers sat as the Holy Roman Emperor. But when Charles I of Spain became Emperor Charles V (1516–1556), circumstances changed. Charles created a huge power bloc, which ranged from the Netherlands and the German states to Spain. With the help of the Pope, Charles threatened to corner the French.

Sixteenth-century Europe witnessed constant warfare. To a large extent, these conflicts stemmed from the incessant rivalry between the Hapsburgs, who ruled Spain and the Holy Roman Empire, and the Valois, the ruling family of France. For the most part, England and Scotland stood on the sideline as such conflicts transpired. But when they did enter the fray, they usually did so according to their old alliances. Because of its age-old conflicts with France, England normally sided with Spain. Conversely, fear of England often drove the Scots into the arms of the French—the so-called "auld alliance."

Marriage between these royal houses created new alliances and served to complicate these dynastic rivalries. In 1509, Henry VIII of England (1509–1547) married Catherine of Aragon, thus cementing a union with Spain, the Emperor, and the pope against France. The French countered with their own blood alliances. Mary of Guise married James V of Scotland (1513–1542). The daughter of Henry II of France united with the Spanish royal line; their son Francis I (1559–1560) married Mary Queen of Scots, the daughter of James V and Mary of Guise. Scotland stood on the perimeter of European society. Still, such marriage alliances pushed Scotland into the European power game—sometimes as a key player but more often as a pawn.

As the century wore on, religious conflicts compounded these dynastic tensions. By the 1550s, Europe stood on the brink of the period of terrible religious wars. The forces of the Counter Reformation were on the march, threatening to engulf Protestantism. All of this produced an apocalyptic atmosphere. Violence and conflict were in the air and could be detected in the writings of many reformers, including John Knox.

In all of these events, Scotland and John Knox would play a role—a development that was not obvious at the start of the sixteenth century. At this time, Scotland was a poor, primitive, and remote part of Christendom. Political motives drove the developments of the Scottish Reformation. From James I to James V, the Stewart kings and the great nobles constantly struggled for power. Scotland still lived under feudal anarchy. In the 100 years prior to the birth of John Knox, every king of Scotland had met his death by violence. Only one had been as old as 15 at accession, and none survived beyond the age of 42. Without a doubt, royal power was weak. Both the king and nobility administered such order and discipline as existed. Many vassals considered the lord, not the king, as their sovereign. Both justice and military organization were feudal, contributing to the complexity and instability of society.

By the reign of James V (1513–1542), the conflict between crown and nobility began to have religious implications. King James attempted to assert royal authority. In doing so, he alienated many of his temporal lords, thus forcing him to turn to the ecclesiastical lords for support. This alliance produced two results. First, hostilities developed between factions of the nobility and the church leaders who were acquiring power. Second, some of the estranged nobles turned to England for support. For centuries, Scottish nobles had pursued this practice. But now the time appeared more opportune—Henry VIII had turned against the Pope and was reducing the power of the great churchmen in England.

As the secular lords turned to England, the ecclesiastics embraced Scotland's traditional ally, France. France supported Cardinal Beaton, the leader of the Scottish Church, even as England subsidized the "Assured Lords"—Scottish nobles in the pay of England. Beaton became influential in both the Scottish and French courts and was thus in a position to use Scotland as an instrument for France. The church's threefold policy of loyalty to the crown, hostility to England, and friendship with France seemed patriotic to the average Scot. With such an attitude prevalent, a widespread movement toward the "English religion" seemed remote. The church, therefore, sporadically exacted measures from the crown for the suppression of the Protestant heresy. Yet attempts to quell heresy did not succeed. And this failure—added to the disastrous results of Beaton's rash anti-English policy—tarnished the church's French alliance.

It gradually dawned on many Scots that French dominance threatened Scotland's independence more than any menace from England. Revulsion against the church and France produced an inevitable by-product; namely, a rising attitude of favor for Protestantism and England. The Scottish mind hardly distinguished between religious and political alliances. Then, in 1560, following a treaty between England and the Scottish lords, an English expeditionary force ejected the French military from Scotland. Scotland's future now lay with Protestantism and England.

In August 1560, the Scottish Parliament abolished Catholicism and made Protestantism officially the religion of the land. Still, Protestantism was not secure. Parliament ratified the *Scots Confession,* approving the Reformed faith in Scotland. But it failed to take more concrete steps. It rejected the *Book of Discipline,* which would have established Protestantism financially. To complicate matters, during the personal rule of Mary Stewart (1561–1567), Protestant Scotland had a Catholic queen. Mary's policies focused primary on diplomatic objectives, but they also presented a threat to Protestantism. These six years witnessed plots, assassinations, and political and religious conflicts. But more important, Mary's personal escapades doomed whatever chances her policies had for success. In July 1567, a coalition of lords forced Mary to abdicate during the same month the infant James VI was crowned king of Scotland. Parliament now established Protestantism on a more substantial basis.

In all of these developments, international politics played an important, if not decisive role. On one hand, foreign events determined the outcome of the Scottish Reformation. Would England continue to aid the Protestant party in Scotland? Would Mary Queen of Scots marry a Protestant or Catholic? Would France and Spain intervene in Scotland to crush the Protestant heresy? Indeed, the Scottish Reformation hinged not only on events in Scotland, but on decisions made in London, Paris, and Madrid.

On the other hand, the survival of Protestantism in England and perhaps even on the Continent depended in part on the success or failure of the Reformation in Scotland. If Protestantism failed in Scotland, would England—ruled by vacillating Elizabeth—retain Protestantism? What's more, if England had returned to Catholicism, Protestantism might have been in jeopardy all over Europe. John Knox understood the importance of such events. He was not just a backward Scot. Rather, he had lived in England and traveled extensively on the Continent. Such experiences helped Knox to think in European terms and to connect political and religious issues.[9]

Social and Economic Factors

Like the twentieth century, the sixteenth century witnessed sweeping economic and social changes—transformations that dramatically influenced the reformation of religion in Europe. Old medieval patterns disintegrated. Trade and industry accelerated at a rapid pace. Gold and silver poured in from the New World. New business methods stimulated the economy. The economy experienced its ups and downs with the low point occurring in the late 1550s. Such economic developments dramatically affected the entire fabric of European society. On the whole, the aristocracy came on hard times while the urban bourgeoisie rose in wealth and power. All of

---

9. This background information regarding the political situation in Europe and Scotland has been drawn from a number of general sources. Ridley, *John Knox*, 1–12; Reid, *Trumpeter of God*, 1–13; J. H. Burns, "The Political Background of the Reformation, 1513–1625," in *Essays on the Scottish Reformation* ed. David McRoberts (Glasgow: John S. Burns and Sons, 1962), 1–23; Lamont, *The Swordbearer*, 13–16; McEwen, *Faith of Knox*, 1–13; Henry Thomas Buckle, *On Scotland and the Scotch Intellect* (Chicago: University of Chicago Press, 1970), 68–91; Gordon Donaldson, *Scotland: James V to James VII* (Edinburgh: Oliver and Boyd, 1965), 3–106; Ian B. Cowan, *The Scottish Reformation: Church and Society in Sixteenth-Century Scotland* (New York: St. Martin's Press, 1982), 1–26; Michael Lynch, *Edinburgh and the Reformation* (Edinburgh: John Donald Publishers Ltd., 1981), 68–86; Jenny Wormald, *Court, Kirk, and Community: Scotland 1470–1625* (Toronto: University of Toronto Press, 1982), 3–26; Kyle, *Mind of Knox*, 1–3; Richard Bonney, *The European Dynastic States*, 1494–1660 (New York: Oxford University Press, 1991), 79–187.

this influenced the evolution of the middle class, which in turn impacted the reformation of religion.[10]

On the eve of the Scottish Reformation, the established church did not command extensive loyalty in any of the social classes. The nobility at the top of the social ladder not only desired to evict the church leaders from influential government positions, but also envied the church's wealth. The aristocracy, frequently wealthy in land but short in cash, significantly felt the impact of the century's far-reaching economic changes. No longer indispensable to the national governments as either soldiers or officials, they often had to seek income elsewhere. This transition the upper nobility could make by obtaining positions at court or by acquiring church revenues. The upper echelons of society, therefore, blatantly attempted to control church revenues by any means possible.[11] But the gentry, or lower aristocracy, faced a more difficult situation—one that often led them into competition with the aristocracy for lucrative positions and into conflict with their tenants who resisted their demands for increased rents or services. Frequently, the gentry's main hope was the bourgeoisie, or wealthy element in the towns, who could provide them with loans or lucrative marriage arrangements [12]

The increasing importance of the lesser lords (or lairds) and burgher class provided a major social factor leading to the Scottish Reformation. While the feudal nobility generally experienced a decline, the middle group acquired wealth in trade. Paralleling this expansion of trade came the growth of the Scottish town. The middle class moved in two directions: they formed an alliance with the nobility and became the leaders of the lower classes. Schooled by commercial activity to make shrewd

10. See H. G. Koenigsberger, George L. Mosse, and G. Q. Bowler, *Europe in the Sixteenth Century* 2nd ed. (New York: Longman, 1989), 28–64; Reid, *Trumpeter of God*, 2–3; L. W. Cowie, *Sixteenth-Century Europe* (Edinburgh: Oliver and Boyd, 1977), 79–93; Lewis W. Spitz, *The Protestant Reformation 1517–1559* (New York: Harper and Row, 1985), 18–34.

11. The aristocracy's desire to retain a sizeable share of the ecclesiastical wealth, among other motives, prompted them to reject the *Book of Discipline*. This document would have used the wealth of the old church to support the new Reformed church, thus depriving the nobility of church revenue. Knox strongly disapproved of the plan to divide up the wealth of the Catholic Church. See *Works*, 2:310; Reid, *Trumpeter of God*, 205–7; James K. Cameron, "The Historical Background," in *The First Book of Discipline* ed. James K. Cameron (Edinburgh: St. Andrew Press, 1972), 3–13; Ridley, *John Knox,*, 388–401; Donaldson, *Scotland: James V to James VII*, 105, 111, 144.

12. Kyle, *Mind of Knox*, 3.

judgments of people and events, the burghers became hardheaded and rationalistic. They also received at least a smattering of education and, in some cases, a good one. To cap it all, the Scottish bourgeoisie were nationalistic.

By the early sixteenth century, therefore, the middle group was prepared for a reformation. With its growing intellectual interests, the burger class increasingly criticized the church. Indeed, the gross maladministration of the church, its notorious immorality and corruption, and strong support for France offended the instincts and nationalism of this class. So when a rival faith came on the scene, the middle class turned its back on the old church. The Reformed Church gave this class a means of fulfilling some of its ambitions. Thus the burghers not only welcomed the Reformation, they took steps to support it. In fact, of all the social groups, the middle class did the most to further the cause of the reformation in Scotland. To a large extent, the Scottish Reformation's success and direction came from the burgher class. From this group emerged John Knox (1514–1572).[13]

The poor, at the bottom of the social scale, experienced very hard times. At best, life was difficult. And far from relieving this burden, the church exacted more revenues from them. In countries that experienced better church administration, the monasteries often befriended the poor. Not so in Scotland. Here, maladministration and corruption rendered the monasteries incapable of aiding the poor either spiritually or materially. Merciless absentee abbots and lay leaders appropriated money designed for the poor into their own pockets.

Even Bishop John Leslie, an ardent Catholic whose historical writings sought to support the Catholic cause, painted a bleak picture of monastic life in Scotland. Abbot Quintin Kennedy and Ninian Winzet, two Catholic apologists, criticized clerical corruption more severely than did the Protestants. Indeed, the parish clergy existed in poverty while the ecclesiastical prelates misused the church's wealth. Such a contrast contributed to the decline of the medieval Catholic Church. Thus when the Reformation brought the downfall of the monasteries and the old church,

---

13. W. Stanford Reid, "The Middle Class Factor in the Scottish Reformation," *Church History* 16, no.3 (1947): 137–53. See also Kyle, *Mind of Knox*, 3–4; McEwen, *Faith of Knox*, 13–14; Lynch, *Edinburgh and the Reformation*, 49–55.

it did not alter the life of the poor for the worse. However, unlike the English, the Scots staged no mass uprising in its defense.[14]

Religious Factors

Political, economic, and social developments conditioned Europe for the Reformation. Still, the sixteenth-century Reformation must be seen primarily as a revival of religion. But such a renewal had its roots in the late Middle Ages. In addition to sweeping economic, political, and social changes, the late medieval world witnessed a severe crisis in religious values. The Great Schism, conciliarism, ecclesiastical corruption, anticlericalism, new intellectual movements, and more, all challenged the Catholic Church.

Indeed, to borrow a phrase from Steven Ozment, these "late medieval developments were a threshold as well as a foothold" for the sixteenth-century reformations.[15] And such religious unfoldings reached Scotland. Aside from the corrupt state of the Catholic Church in Scotland, the Scottish Reformation must not be regarded as an "indigenous movement" says Reid. Rather, it was an aspect of the larger religious revival taking place on the Continent.[15]

Religious discontent—often manifesting itself as heresy—appeared in Scotland toward the end of the Great Papal Schism (1378–1415).[17] The years of the Papal Schism were a spiritual disaster for the Scottish church. In impoverished Scotland, the church provided the only path to wealth, and the crown and nobility attempted to capitalize on this situation. By 1550, half of the real estate in Scotland belonged to the church. What's more, sources estimate ecclesiastical revenues about that time to have been approximately £300,000 (Scots) compared to a beggarly £17,000 for

14. David Laing, ed., *The Miscellany of the Wodrow Society*, Vol. 1 (Edinburgh: Printed for the Wodrow Society, 1847), 89–168, 263–68; Matthew Mahoney, "The Scottish Hierarchy, 1513–1565," in *Essays on the Scottish Reformation*, 60; McEwen, *Faith of Knox*, 14, Kyle, *Mind of Knox*, 4; Cowan, *Scottish Reformation*, 68–71.

15. Steven Ozment, *The Reformation in the Cities* (New Haven, CN: Yale University Press, 1975), 118.

16. W. Stanford Reid, "Reformation in France and Scotland: A Case Study in Sixteenth-Century Communication," in *Later Calvinism* ed. W. Fred Graham (Kirksville, MO: Sixteenth-Century—Essays and Studies, 1994), 197.

17. The Papal Schism began in 1378 and lasted until 1415. In Scotland, it lasted until 1418 because the Scots were slow in withdrawing allegiance from the last surviving antipope.

the crown. During the schism years, the proportion could not have been much different.[18]

Therefore, these years saw rival popes bid for Scottish support, granting dispensations for all sorts of irregular appointments to ecclesiastical living. Such dispensations not only violated canonical law, but also made a mockery of common decency and morality. Wealthy benefices went to the crown and nobility as rewards to favorites. As a result, spiritually-degenerate men with little administrative ability rose to high ecclesiastical positions. Such a practice had two results—church discipline tragically declined and the lower clergy fell into miserable poverty. The years following the Papal Schism saw no general improvement. While it should not be exaggerated, ecclesiastical corruption also touched upon other areas of church life—that is, clerical immorality, financial abuse, monastic laxity, and the neglect of religious duties. Despite temporary and local improvements, corruption and laxity continued until the Reformation.[19]

Into this spiritual void came a number of reform movements. The fifteenth century witnessed Lollard activity in Scotland. Bible reading and anticlerical beliefs thrived—to the extent that in 1425, Parliament passed legislation against heretics. Lollardy indeed penetrated southwest Scotland, so much so that Knox devoted the opening pages of his *History* to their activities. Yet Lollardy could not reform Scotland. It was largely a negative movement, and reformations need more than negations to succeed. Moreover, Lollardy had no one central positive doctrine—such as Luther's justification by faith—to serve as a focal point.[20]

Popular piety, however, could still exist within the official framework of the church. The Mendicant Orders, the Dominicans, and the observant branch of the Franciscans experienced a revival on the Continent early in the fifteenth century and were well established by mid-century. Austerity and purity of life, a small restoration in learning, and a great emphasis on preaching characterized this revival. In Scotland, this awakening lasted

---

18. Gordon Donaldson, *The Scottish Reformation* (Cambridge, UK: Cambridge University Press, 1960), 35–37; Reid, *Trumpeter of God*, 6–7; Gordon Donaldson, ed., *Accounts of the Collectors of the Thirds of Benefices 1561–1572* (Edinburgh: Scottish History Society, 1949), xv.

19. Wormald, *Court, Kirk, and Community*, 79–81; Kyle, *Mind of Knox*, 5; Donaldson, *Scottish Reformation*, 12–17.

20. *Works*, 1: 5–12; W. Stanford Reid, "The Lollards in Pre-Reformation Scotland," *Westminster Theological Journal* 11 (1942): 269–83; Wormald, *Court, Kirk, and Community*, 79–94.

approximately one generation, but even this brief revival helped. Many of the regular ecclesiastics, however, hampered the Observants. Still, James IV believed that the salvation of Scotland lay in their hands and strongly supported them.[21]

Before the Reformation could come, however, Scotland needed a new doctrine of grace and the sacraments. About the time the Observant movement declined, Lutheranism began to enter Scotland, and some of the best friars embraced it. Lutheranism's central tenet, justification by faith, broke from the sacramental concept of salvation. Piety began to move outside the official church. Conditions in Scotland and especially in the church made the country ripe for Lutheranism. The teachings of Luther penetrated eastern Scotland to the extent that in 1525 Parliament banned the importation of Lutheran books.[22]

Yet this proscription and other measures proved ineffectual. In 1528, officials convicted Patrick Hamilton of the Lutheran heresy, and Archbishop Beaton ordered him burned at the stake. The archbishop may have silenced one man—but he could not stop the spread of Luther's views. William Tyndale's *New Testament* had arrived in Scotland, allowing people to compare the claims of the old church with the teachings of the Word of God.[23]

We should not underestimate the influence of Lutheranism upon the Scottish Reformation. Though Calvinism ultimately triumphed over the Catholic Church in Scotland, Lutheran ideas continued. The emphasis upon justification by faith—so characteristic of Scottish Reformed teaching—may be partially attributed to the persistence of Lutheran influence. Many of those who afterward became leaders in the Reformation—in-

21. McEwen, *Faith of Knox*, 20, 21; Kyle, *Mind of Knox*, 5–6; Wormald, *Court, Kirk, and Community*, 90–93; Anthony Ross, "Some Notes on the Religious Orders in Pre-Reformation Scotland," in *Essays on the Scottish Reformation*, 185–233.

22. W. Stanford Reid, "Lutheranism in the Scottish Reformation," *Westminster Theological Journal* 6 (1944–1945):91–111; McEwen, *Faith of Knox*, 19–20, 55–58; Cowan, *Scottish Reformation*, 89–90; Maurice Taylor, "The Conflicting Doctrines of the Scottish Reformation," in *Essays on the Scottish Reformation*, 245–46.

23. James Edward McGoldrick, "Patrick Hamilton: Luther's Scottish Disciple," *Sixteenth Century Journal* 17 (1986): 81–88; James Edward McGoldrick, *Luther's Scottish Connection* (Cranbury, NJ: Associated University Presses, 1989); 48–50. See Peter Lorimer, *Patrick Hamilton, the First Preacher of the Scottish Reformation* (Edinburgh: Thomas Constable and Co. 1857).

cluding Balnaves, Erskine of Dun, and probably Knox himself—received their early nurture from the Lutheran faith.[24]

Despite Lutheranism's importance in Scotland, it failed to bring about a reformation. Why? First, an anti-English attitude prevailed during the reign of James V. England embraced Protestantism, and any form of it was unacceptable in Scotland at this time. Second, Lutheranism was politically quiescent. Lutheran reformations never succeeded except under the guiding hand of a favorable sovereign, and Scotland had no such prince.[25]

Still, we should not assume that the Scottish Reformation took a leap from Luther to Calvin without the influence of Zurich from the 1530s onward. The effect of Zwinglianism in the years prior to the success of Protestantism needs further research. It must be noted that Lutheranism was a blanket expression covering the views of various continental reformers—including Zwingli and Bullinger, and on occasions, those of John Wycliffe's followers.[26] Knox succeeded in Scotland with a generally Calvinistic theology. Would this triumph have been possible without considerable preparation? Hardly! Evidence indicates that Lutheranism alone could not have paved the way for such a development. Rather, Zwinglianism must have been widespread in Scotland, and along with Calvinism, contributed significantly to the success of the Reformed faith.[27]

But the Catholic Church was not finished. Before the triumph of the Reformed faith, the Scottish Church made one last abortive attempt to reform itself and thus prevent a reformation. Archbishop Hamilton, Beaton's successor, issued a series of statutes designed to reform the church. Published in 1552 as the *Catechism of Archbishop Hamilton,* these

---

24. See Reid, "Lutheranism in the Scottish Reformation," 91–111; McEwen, *Faith of Knox,* 19–20, 55–58; Kyle, *Mind of Knox,* 6; McGoldrick, *Luther's Scottish Connection,* 55–73; Iain R. Torrance, "Patrick Hamilton and John Knox: A Study in the Doctrine of Justification by Faith." *Archiv für Reformationgeschicte* 65 (1974): 171–84; James K. Cameron., "Aspects of the Lutheran Contribution to the Scottish Reformation, 1528–1552," *Lutheran Theological Journal* 19 (1985): 12–20.

25. Kyle, *Mind of Knox,* 6–7.

26. Duncan Shaw, "Zwinglian Influences on the Scottish Reformation," *Records of the Scottish Church History Society* 22, pt. 2 (1985): 119–39; Duncan Shaw, "Foreword, Zwingli Research—the Chasm in British Reformation Studies," in *Zwingli's Thought: New Perspectives* by Gottfried W. Locher (Leiden: E. J. Brill, 1981), ix–xvii.

27. Shaw, "Zwinglian Influences on the Scottish Reformation," 119–39; Shaw, "Foreword, Zwingli Research," ix–xvii.

statutes represented an attempt by the Scottish Church at a crucial moment in its life to give a complete, though brief, account of what Catholics believed and, in particular, to instruct ignorant priests in the faith. This reform, however, came too late and had little effect. By then, the church could not produce an alternative to reformation.[28]

By 1546, Zwinglian reforming thought had made its way to Scotland, largely through the efforts of George Wishart, a Scottish reformer. Zwingli rejected all forms of worship not expressly commanded by Scripture. Hence, the Swiss version of Protestantism was more uncompromising and separatist than Lutheranism. From such a background, the Reformed Church of Scotland began to emerge as a coherent force.

Although John Knox began his public ministry in 1547, until 1559, he spent little time in Scotland. But during this time, Protestantism in Scotland progressed politically as well as spiritually. In 1559, Knox returned home at a critical time; plans existed to utilize French military aid to strengthen Catholicism and eradicate Protestantism among the Scots. Thanks to an English alliance and a turn of events, however, Scotland embraced the Reformed faith. Yet the Reformation of 1560 only partially established Protestantism. Mary Queen of Scots nearly undid the work of the Reformation, but in 1567, the Scots deposed her and Protestantism was secure. In these events, John Knox played an important role.[29]

KNOX THE MAN

First impressions carry much weight. How we meet someone often determines our opinion of them. How did the various Protestant reformers make their debut? Jasper Ridley describes their entrance: Calvin can be seen at his desk writing a scholarly work. Cranmer is first seen searching Scripture for texts to justify Henry VIII's divorce and remarriage. Luther is more vigorous—we find him nailing his theses on a door in Wittenberg.

---

28. Mahoney, "The Scottish Hierarchy 1513–1565," 73–75; Donaldson, *Scottish Reformation*, 33–35; Taylor, "Conflicting Doctrines of the Scottish Reformation," 252–53; Cowan, *Scottish Reformation*, 77–78.

29. Taylor, "Conflicting Doctrines of the Scottish Reformation," 254–55; Reid, *Trumpeter of God*, 1–14; McEwen, *Faith of Knox*, 22; Kyle, *Mind of Knox*, 7–8. For more on the events prior to the Reformation, see J. H. S. Burleigh, *A Church History of Scotland* (London: Oxford University Press, 1960); Ridley, *John Knox*, 314–34; Cowan, *Scottish Reformation*, 89–138; and Knox's own account in *Works*, 1.

But "Knox is the only one who enters carrying a two-handed sword."[30] Whatever else this might say, it tells us that of all the reformers, Knox was a man of action—a characteristic that is evident throughout his life.

His Life

Knox's early life is shrouded in obscurity. Born near Haddington about 1514,[31] he was educated at St. Andrews, probably under the conciliarist and scholastic John Major. In 1536, the Bishop of Dunblane ordained Knox into the priesthood. Due to an oversupply of priests, he may not have obtained a parish and thus served as a notary and a private tutor. Exactly when Knox became a Protestant, we do not know. But Thomas Guilliame appears to have been instrumental in his conversion, and he subsequently came under the influence of John Rough and George Wishart, a follower of the Swiss reformers. Knox probably acquired his sense of a prophetic vocation from Wishart.[32]

In 1547, after Wishart's martyrdom, Knox went to St. Andrews. Here, he received a call to preach the gospel. When the castle fell, Knox became a prisoner and spent the next 19 months in a French galley ship. During this time, he penned a summary of Henry Balnaves' compendium of Protestant thought based on Luther's commentary on Galatians. In this early work, Knox demonstrated his acceptance of Luther's doctrine of justification.

After his release in 1549, Knox went to England where he stayed until 1554. The English authorities appointed him preacher at Berwick and Newcastle, two frontier towns in northern England. Here, his attack on the Mass as idolatry caused him to be called before the Council of the North in 1550 to answer for his views. His sermons in the North drew the attention of the authorities in London. In 1551, they made him a chaplain to Edward VI. As such, Knox assisted in the revision of the *Book of Common Prayer*. He criticized the provision that called for kneeling during Communion. While Thomas Cranmer largely had his way on

---

30. Ridley, *John Knox*, 40.

31. Ridley, *John Knox*, 529–34; J. Wilkinson, "The Medical History of John Knox," *Proceedings of the Royal College of Physicians of Edinburgh* 28 (1998): 83. There is some question as to the date of Knox's birth, but modern research indicates that 1514 is the most probable year. See appendix in Ridley's biography for a discussion.

32. Biographies of Knox are numerous. We have counted about 25; the most recent is by Stewart Lamont (1991). Among the most noteworthy are those by W. Stanford Reid, Jasper Ridley, Pierre Janton, Lord Eustace Percy, P. Hume Brown, and Thomas M'Crie.

this issue, Knox appears to have been chiefly responsible for the inclusion of the Black Rubric—a declaration explaining that kneeling at the Lord's Supper does not signify adoration to either the bread or wine. The English authorities also offered Knox the bishopric of Rochester, which he refused for reasons that are not completely clear. Though he criticized the details of English ecclesiastical policy, he generally approved of the religious climate that prevailed in Edwardian England. But things would soon change.

Edward died and the Catholic Mary Tudor came to the throne of England—a move that would turn English religion upside down. By January 1554, events drove Knox into exile. From this time until the deposition of Mary Stewart in Scotland some 13 years later, he more or less occupied himself with the problem of idolatry—that is, Catholicism. When confronted by idolatry, how should the "the faithful Christian" respond? Should they obey or disobey an "idolatrous" sovereign?

Shortly after arriving at Dieppe, France, Knox completed *An Admonition or Warning*, urging "true Christians" not to participate in idolatrous Catholicism. He then moved to Switzerland. Here, he met with Calvin, Bullinger, and other Reformed leaders, posing questions on rebellion against idolatrous monarchs and female sovereigns. Knox returned to Dieppe for a short while where he wrote *A Faithful Admonition*—a long publication which attacked Mary Tudor directly, and argued that England was repeating the idolatrous history of Israel.

In 1554, Knox left for Geneva, but at Calvin's urging, he headed for Frankfurt where he became a pastor to the English congregation. A nasty dispute over the *Book of Common Prayer* led to his departure and return to Geneva in 1555. But he did not stay long, returning the same year to Scotland. Here, he openly preached Protestant doctrine with considerable success. Thus the Catholic Church summoned Knox to appear in Edinburgh in May 1556 on a charge of heresy. In an attempt to gain the support of the Protestant nobles, however, Mary of Guise intervened and quashed the summons. Still, the continuing persecution of Protestants in Scotland led Knox to accept a call to the English church at Geneva.

In Geneva, he published several tracts concerning problems in Scotland and England. Though he addressed several subjects, political issues received the most attention. In four pamphlets published in 1558, the reformer clearly set forth his views on the rights of subjects against idolatrous and oppressive rulers. *The First Blast of the Trumpet*

Against the Monstrous Regiment of Women—in which Knox argued that female sovereignty contravened natural and divine law—startled Europe. Subsequent tracts—*The Appellation* and *Letter to the Commonalty*—went even further. Using Old Testament models, Knox urged both the nobles and common people to compel their rulers to make religious reforms.

In these tracts, Knox stated unequivocally some earthshaking propositions: the nobles had the right to remove an unrepentant monarch, while the commonality could set up their own reformed kirk if their rulers failed to act. It was, however, *The First Blast* that gained for Knox a reputation among his contemporaries of being a revolutionary. He primarily targeted *The First Blast* at Mary Tudor. But shortly after its appearance, she died and Elizabeth became Queen of England, making Knox's name odious in her court. During his sojourn in Geneva, Knox also addressed other subjects, especially predestination. In *An Answer*, his longest writing, he defended Calvin's teaching on predestination against an attack by an Anabaptist. In doing so, he focused on the practical necessity of predestination to his view of salvation.

Yet the Protestant Lords of the Congregation sought Knox's return to Scotland and he arrived in May 1559—a critical moment for the Reformation's success. After becoming a minister in Edinburgh and a leader of the Reforming party, he devoted himself to preaching and to procuring money and troops from England. The secular lords, nevertheless, did more to acquire aid from England than did Knox. And in respect to political affairs, Knox became somewhat of a liability, so he tended to focus more on religious matters. After the death of Mary of Guise, Knox and other leaders drew up the *Scots Confession*, which Parliament approved in 1560. The confession abolished the authority of the Pope and proscribed the celebration of the Mass. Knox and five others also drafted the *Book of Discipline*, which spelled out the practical and financial aspects of Knox's reform program.

After Mary Stewart's return to Scotland in 1561, Knox came into repeated conflicts with the Queen over her desire to practice the Mass and the worldliness of her court. During 1561–1562, he engaged in a controversy over ordination with Ninan Winzet, a Catholic priest and educator. Although he lacked the miracles to prove it, Knox claimed an extraordinary calling—like that of Amos and John the Baptist. Knox also disputed with Quintin Kennedy, Abbot of Crossraguel, regarding the Mass.

Meanwhile, the conflict with Mary reached its conclusion. She had her husband, Lord Darnley, murdered. After this deed, she was captured and Knox demanded her execution. Following her abdication, he preached at the coronation of her son, James VI. Knox now became closely connected with the regent, James Stewart, the Earl of Moray. After Moray's murder in 1570, Knox's political clout diminished, though his fundamental cause triumphed.[33]

His Personality

This brief summary outlines the events that shaped Knox's life and, in turn, his ministry. But what about the inner man? What about his personality? These subjects are more speculative and difficult to document. They, too, have also shaped Knox's ministry and career as a reformer.

Knox has justifiably been described as a "contradictory and complex character—at once unpredictable and yet so unflinchingly single-minded.[34] One side of Knox could be charismatic, hateful, forceful, courageous, and intimidating. To be sure, a cannon at Edinburgh Castle is aptly nicknamed John Knox.[35]

But Knox had another side. On Sunday, this "great voiced, bearded man of God" could beat the pulpit. On Monday, however, he would sit with his parishioners and weep with them over their trials and temptations. While he castigated female rulers (usually Catholics), he could be warm and tender to other women. At times Knox had the courage of a lion. On other occasions, he prudently protected his life, fleeing danger as the need arose. He promoted godly living—but not excessive Puritanism. He was less austere than supposed.[36]

What events forged Knox's personality—contradictions and all? Any answer to this question must be largely speculation. The sources of Knox's

33. We have drawn this brief outline of Knox's life from several sources. Most directly, it came from two of our earlier summaries of Knox's life. See Richard Kyle, "John Knox," in *Dictionary of Scottish Church History and Theology* ed. Nigel M. de S. Cameron (Edinburgh: T and T Clark, 1993), 465–66; Richard Kyle, "John Knox," in *Encyclopedia of the Reformed Faith* ed. Donald K. McKim (Louisville: Westminister/John Knox Press, 1992), 208–9.

34. David D. Murison, "Knox the Writer," in *John Knox: A Quatercentenary Reappraisal* 33 (quote); Kirk, "Knox and the Historians," 16, 22.

35. E. G. Rupp, "The Europe of John Knox," in *John Knox: A Quatercentenary Reappraisal*, 14.

36. Donaldson, "Knox the Man," 18–22; Kirk, "Knox and the Historians," 18, 22–23.

anger and hatred are more easily identified. He abhorred Catholicism—which he equated with idolatry—and anyone or anything that promoted it. A short list would include "idolatrous" sovereigns and the French establishment.

Why hate Catholicism? Undoubtedly, the two driving forces include his belief that Scripture condemned idolatry and his calling to be God's mouthpiece. Still, other factors cannot be ignored. Knox's social background pointed him in that direction. He was one of the "middling sort," the social class which tended to be most critical of the church. Knox spent 19 months as a prisoner on a French galley—an experience that intensified his hatred for Catholicism and the French. Moreover, he spent much of his life as a refugee, fleeing three female sovereigns. Without a doubt, such an ordeal fueled his anger toward female rulers. Even the volcanic mood of Europe contributed to Knox's personality. "Knox lived in a world where martyr and apostate were a grim polarity," says E. G. Rupp. In such an uncompromising environment, Knox saw himself as a prophet proclaiming God's judgment.[37]

But what about Knox's gentle and prudent side? This is more difficult to explain. He did have a conversion experience, one that shaped his life. Knox was a deeply spiritual man, one who took seriously the New Testament emphasis on love and compassion. This characteristic tempered Knox's harsher tendencies. What's more, the reformer must not be regarded as a backward Scot. He traveled extensively, living in several European countries. He spoke French fluently and understood French society. Of considerable importance, his sojourn in Calvin's Geneva left a deep impression on the reformer. Such factors may have helped forge the "other" John Knox.[38]

How then should we view Knox? He has often been seen in "either . . . or" terms—either as a hero or a villain. To interpret his life in such exclusive categories is a mistake. Rather, a more pluralistic approach to Knox should be adopted. He can be better viewed from a "both . . . and" framework. Depending on the context, he can be regarded as both compassionate and unforgiving, tolerant and uncompromising, etc. And these opposites are not easily reconciled.

37. Gordon Rupp, "The World of John Knox," in *John Knox; A Quatercentenary Reappraisal*, 8–10; Reid, "John Knox and His Interpreters," 15–20; Donaldson, "Knox the Man," 18–24; Carol Edington, "John Knox and the Castilians," in *John Knox and the British Reformations*, 46–48.

38. See Reid, *Trumpeter of God*, 1–3, 24–27; Reid, "John Knox: Pastor of Souls," 1–21; Donaldson, "Knox the Man," 26–29.

2

The Mind of John Knox

JOHN KNOX FIRST STEPPED onto the pages of history carrying a two-edged sword—a fitting posture for the dramatic life he would lead. For the rest of his life, he brandished a double-edged sword—not literally, but his tongue and pen served as such. No wonder scholars have correctly identified Knox as a man of action—a doer—and not a thinker. Indeed, Knox himself denied being a "speculative theologian."

Still, ideas drove Knox's actions. He was a pastor, a preacher, and he regarded himself as a prophet—God's spokesman. As such, religious conviction moved him to action. Knox had charisma with a cause—and the cause was driven by his beliefs. The reformer possessed a theology, but not a systematic one. The closest thing Knox wrote to a specific work on theology per se was his treatise concerning predestination. Nearly all of his tracts, pamphlets, letters, books, or sermons were in response to a concrete problem. Yet these expressions contained an implicit theology—one that provided the basis for his ministry.[1] And to have a proper understanding of Knox as a pastor, preacher, and prophet, some understanding of this theology is necessary.

Moreover, Knox fully comprehended the big picture: he clearly recognized that the Reformation rested on a new theology. Along with the other reformers, Knox believed that this new belief system had produced a new religious order. It had caused the break with Catholicism; it gave Protestantism purpose, direction, and depth. At heart, the Reformation was a spiritual revival, but one driven by a set of beliefs.[2]

---

1. Richard Kyle, *The Mind of John Knox* (Lawrence, KS: Coronado Press, 1984), 8–9; Thomas F. Torrence, *Scottish Theology* (Edinburgh: T and T Clark, 1996), 2–3.

2. R. A. Finlayson, "John Knox: His Theology," *The Bulwark* (March/April 1975): 2.

INTELLECTUAL INFLUENCES

As we have seen, real life experiences shaped Knox's beliefs and actions—his middle class background, his stay on a galley ship, his calling to the ministry, opposition from female rulers, and more. Still, many intellectual influences also molded Knox's thinking. Scripture heads any such list; it dwarfed all other influences. Coupled with his call to preach went his conviction that the Bible was the Word of God. Though other men shaped his interpretation of Scripture, Knox was, first and foremost, a man of the Bible. In particular, his Old Testament emphasis dominated his thought.[3]

Few people go to the Bible without some guidance, and Knox certainly did not. The list of intellectual influences on Knox is substantial. Yet any tabulation must be headed by John Calvin. Scholars sharply disagree over the matter of Calvin's impact on Knox, however. That Calvin held considerable sway over Knox's thought is a view generally accepted and need not be argued here. But questions still remain. When did Calvin influence Knox? In what areas did this influence come? To what extent did Calvin's theology dominate Knox's thinking?

In regard to these questions, three general trends emerge. The first category consists of those who, in varying degrees, place a strong emphasis upon Calvin's spell over Knox. They believe that Calvin influenced Knox early—before their meeting in Geneva—and very thoroughly over a wide range of theology. Traditionally, this interpretation has held sway in academic circles, but it has not gone unchallenged.[4]

---

3. See Richard Kyle, The Hermeneutical Patterns in John Knox's Use of Scripture," *Pacific Theological Review* 17, no. 3 (1984): 19–23; Richard Kyle, "John Knox's Methods of Biblical Interpretation: An Important Source of His Intellectual Radicalness," *Journal of Religious Studies* 12, no. 2 (1985): 57–59; Richard Kyle, "John Knox: A Man of the Old Testament," *Westminster Theological Journal* 54, no. 2 (1992): 65–78; Richard Greaves, *Theology and Revolution in the Scottish Reformation* (Grand Rapids: Christian University Press, 1980), 4–6; Richard Greaves, "The Nature of Authority in the Writings of John Knox," *Fides et Historia* 10, no. 2 (Spring 1978): 30–31.

4. Examples of this position include W. Stanford Reid, *Trumpeter of God* (New York: Charles Scribner's, 1974); V. E. D'Assonville, *John Knox and the Institutes of Calvin* (Durban: Drakensberg Press, 1968); Pierre Janton, *John Knox: L'homme et l'oeuvre* (Paris: Didier, 1967); Edwin Muir, *John Knox: Portrait of a Calvinist* (Edinburgh: J. and J. Gray, 1929); Henry Cowan, *John Knox: The Hero of the Scottish Reformation* (New York: Knickerbocker Press, 1905); D. Macmillan, *John Knox* (London: Andrew Melrose, 1905); William Hastie, *The Theology of the Reformed Church in Its Fundamental Principles* (Edinburgh: T.&T. Clark, 1904); James Kirk, ed. *The Second Book of Discipline* (Edinburgh: St. Andrew Press, 1980); W. Stanford Reid, "John Calvin, John Knox, and the Scottish Reformation," in

A second category acknowledges Calvin's influence on Knox, but not before 1554. Until the Scottish reformer went to Geneva in 1554, he continued in the general Lutheran tradition of the previous Scottish Protestants. After this time, one can explicitly see Calvin's impact on Knox's thought.[5] A third category less easily identified consists of those who question the degree of Knox's dependence on Calvin. Rather, they often emphasize the non-Calvinistic influences on the Scottish reformer.[6]

We contend that Calvin influenced Knox early, at least by 1553, and perhaps earlier. Knox read some of Calvin's writings by 1553. Evidence also seems to indicate that he had read Calvin's *Institutes of Christian Religion* prior to this date. Moreover, though Calvin's influence varied according to the subject, on the whole, it was substantial. Yet Calvin's relationship to Knox was not one of master and disciple. Not only did they live in different historical circumstances, but non-Calvinistic currents influenced Knox considerably. And on certain issues, the Scottish reformer clearly differed from Calvin.[7]

Besides Calvin, other Reformed leaders also had an important influence on Knox. The list would include George Wishart, Huldrych Zwingli, Heinrich Bullinger, Theodore Beza, Martin Bucer, and Pierre Viret. In some areas—especially justification by faith—Luther had a lasting impact. The church fathers, particularly Augustine, also guided Knox's interpretation of Scripture. Nor can secular ideology be discounted, especially in regard to political theory. Perhaps Greek philosophy and medieval political thought as channeled primarily through John Major influenced Knox's thought. Knox also read the Magdeburg *Bekenntnis*, a Lutheran political treatise. Even his colleagues Christopher Goodman and John Willock may have affected him.[8]

Church, Word and Spirit eds. James E. Bradley and Richard Muller (Grand Rapids: Wm Eerdmans, 1987), 141–51.

5. An example of this position is Maurice Taylor, "The Conflicting Doctrines of the Scottish Reformation," in *Essays on the Scottish Reformation* ed. David McRoberts (Glasgow: John S. Burns and Sons. 1962).

6. Examples of this position would be Richard Greaves, *Theology and Reformation*; James McEwen, *The Faith of John Knox* (Richmond: John Knox Press, 1961); Gordon Donaldson, *The Scottish Reformation* (London: Cambridge University Press. 1960).

7. Kyle, *Mind of Knox*, 18.

8. Greaves, *Theology and Revolution*, 14–16, 42–43, 64, 94, 144, 213, 218; Duncan Shaw, "Zwinglian Influences on the Scottish Reformation," *Records of the Scottish Church History Society* 22, pt. 2 (1985): 119–39; James K. Cameron, "Aspects of the Lutheran Contribution

SOME MAIN THEMES

As a pastor, preacher, and a prophet, Knox dealt with real life issues. His writings and sermons focused on tangible objectives—not abstract theological or political constructs. The reformer's thought came in response to everyday situations. His method of presentation, if not his content, resembled the Pauline epistles, which were written to the churches for the purpose of practical instruction. Still, Knox had much to say about theological subjects. And from his polemical writings, it is possible to formulate his ideas on authority, God, Christ, the church, the covenant, the sacraments, salvation, human nature, Satan, the antichrist, Christ's return, and resistance to political rulers.[9]

We will only note the subjects closely related to his role as a reformer of religion. Some topics connect better with Knox the pastor; others relate best with his roles as a preacher and prophet. These focal themes include Knox's notions regarding reform, authority, methods of interpreting Scripture, divine immutability and sovereignty, the church, the purification of religion, salvation, and resistance to idolatrous rulers.

Concept of Reform

The word "reform" means to correct what is wrong and to restore to a former and better condition. Knox wished to correct the religious abuses which he termed to be the "dregs of papistry"—the Roman Catholic Mass and everything related to it. Essentially, he strove for a corporate return of Scottish religion to the ideal of spiritual Israel. By no means did Knox ignore individual salvation and worship. Yet he emphasized primarily corporate religion and Old Testament instructions.[10]

---

to the Scottish Reformation 1528–1552, "*Records of the Scottish Church History Society* 22, pt.1 (1984): 1–12; James Edward McGoldrick, *Luther's Scottish Connection* (Cranbury, NJ: Associated University Presses, 1989), 70–73; Iain R. Torrance, "Patrick Hamilton and John Knox: A Study in the Doctrine of Justification by Faith," *Archiv für Reformationsgeschicte* 65 (1974): 171–84; Kyle, *Mind of Knox*, 19; W. Stanford Reid, "Lutheranism in the Scottish Reformation," *Westminster Theological Journal* 7 (1944–1945): 91–111; David F. Wright, "John Knox and the Early Church Fathers," in *John Knox and the British Reformations* ed. Roger A. Mason (Aldershot, UK: Ashgate, 1998), 99–115.

9. See Richard Kyle, "John Knox: The Main Themes of His Thought," *Princeton Seminary Bulletin* 4, no. 2 (1983): 101–2; Kyle, *Mind of Knox*, 16–17.

10. John Knox, *The Works of John Knox* 6 Vols. ed. David Laing (Edinburgh: Printed for the Bannatyne Club, 1846–1864), 3:74, 143, 190–91, 193–94; 4:123, 187, 489–90, 501, 505, 539–40; 2:372–73; 5:265, 484, 517.

Many static concepts ran through Knox's mind. The reformer stressed divine immutability, and had little sense of progressive revelation and historical change. Consequently, he saw sixteenth-century Scotland as a mirror of ancient Israel. Knox even viewed himself as a model of a Hebrew prophet—therefore, demanding that the doctrine and worship of the Scottish church be restored to the purity that God had commanded of Israel.[11] The Scottish reformer seldom succeeded in completely actualizing this concept of reform, yet its imprint bore indelibly on his thought.

Every reformation needs a means to implement its objectives. Knox planned to use the Christian Commonwealth as the primary instrument for restoring the purity of Scottish religion. As Knox's concept of reform reflected his Old Testament orientation, so did his vehicle of reform—the Christian Commonwealth.[12] Knox and the other authors of the *Book of Discipline* described the Christian Commonwealth as a country in which both the civil and ecclesiastical powers cooperated in the cultivation of what they believed to be "true" religion. They accepted the idea that government had a responsibility for establishing "true" religion and for abolishing all held to be contrary to it. Still, in effecting such a religious reformation the civil power had strict limits. The rulers had no authority to admit anything in religion not approved by Scripture. Given this understanding between the two powers, a problem arose—Knox could not accept a Catholic queen as sovereign and maintain, at the same time, the Reformed Church.[13]

Scripture: Its Authority and Interpretation

As is commonly known, John Knox advocated some ideas that were controversial for his time. Perhaps the most radical of his positions concerned the purification of worship and resistance to idolatrous rulers. For these

---

11. Ibid. 3:171, 191; 4:399; 6:408.

12. See Richard Kyle, "The Christian Commonwealth: John Knox's Vision for Scotland," *The Journal of Religious History* 16, no. 3 (1991): 247–59; Richard Kyle, "The Church-State Patterns in the Thought of John Knox," *Journal of Church and State* 30, no.1 (Winter 1988): 72–81; Roger A. Mason, "Knox, Resistance and Royal Supremacy," in *John Knox and the British Reformations*, 156–64.

13. *Works*, 3:183f.; James K. Cameron, "Introduction," in *The First Book of Discipline* ed. James K. Cameron (Edinburgh: St. Andrew Press, 1972), 67.

notions, Knox drew from many sources—both secular and religious. But foremost were his methods of interpreting Scripture.[14]

Knox believed the Word of God to be primarily the canonical Scriptures found in the Old and New Testaments. Yet he did not limit the Word of God to the text of Scripture; to him the Word was also a vibrant, living power. Occasionally, he equated the Word with the person of Christ, the power of God, and the gospel message.[15] For the most part, John Knox made God's Word, as revealed in Scripture, his sole authority. In questions pertaining to the faith, the reformer subordinated all other authorities—whether they be the Church of Rome, church councils, tradition, individual conscience, majority opinion, or even princes and parliaments to God's Word.[16]

But the source of Knox's radicalness and uniqueness did not lie in his views on the nature of God's Word or its authority. In these respects, he did not differ greatly from the mainstream Protestant reformers. Rather, Knox's theological trademark devolved from two features of his biblical interpretation—an overemphasis on the Old Testament and pronounced literalness.[17]

Between the Old and New Testaments, there exists both a large degree of continuity and discontinuity. Jesus Christ himself illustrated this. He demonstrated continuity in his insistence that he came to fulfill the law. Yet the fulfillment of such became discontinuity—largely because Christ proceeded to give a deeper, more searching meaning to God's moral law. In respect to overemphasizing continuity at the expense of discontinuity, Knox experienced some problems.[18]

Two dangers exist regarding the relationship between the Old and New Testament: they are either stated to be identical or to differ substantially. John Calvin's solution was to recognize the unity of substance between

---

14. See Kyle, "John Knox's Methods of Biblical Interpretation," 57–70; Kyle, "Hermeneutical Patterns in John Knox's Use of Scripture," 20.

15. *Works*, 2:145; 5:420. See also Pierre Janton, *Concept et Sentiment De L'Eglise Chez John Knox: the reformateur ecossaise* (Paris: Presses Universitaire de France, 1972), 174; Kyle, *Mind of Knox*, 24–30; D'Assonville, *Knox and the Institutes*, 69.

16. *Works*, 1:194, 196–97; 3:166; 4:80, 133–38, 231, 446, 469–70, 478; 5:59, 93, 96, 112, 310, 421, 516; 2:93, 112; 3:75, 351; 4:446.

17. See Kyle, "John Knox's Methods of Biblical Interpretation," 57–70; Richard Kyle, "John Knox" in *Dictionary of Biblical Interpretation* ed. John Hayes, 2 vols. (Nashville: Abingdon Press, 1999), 2:34.

18. McEwen, *Faith of Knox*, 39–40; D'Assonville, *Knox and the Institutes*, 73–75.

the two testaments while pointing to the difference in administration.[19] As we come to Knox, he not only agreed with Calvin concerning the lack of difference in substance between the Old and New Testaments, but he overemphasized this. His failure to recognize a discontinuity between the testaments led to an over-identification of the Old with the New Testament. Knox believed the Old Testament foreshadowed the things revealed in the New. Still, he did not see the New as superseding the Old—except in regards to matters such as the atonement or the new covenant.[20]

More specifically, Knox's major premise, drawn from Deuteronomy 12:32, dominated his view of Scripture. At the onset of his public ministry in St. Andrews, he quoted from it: "All that the Lord thy God commands thee to do, that do thou to the Lord thy God: add nothing to it; diminish nothing from it! By this rule, think I, that the Kirk of Christ will measure God's religion, and not by that which seems good in their eyes."[21] Because John Knox made this verse the focal point of his biblical interpretation, his theology acquired its own trademark. The consequences of his literal Old Testament hermeneutic, with its starting point in Deuteronomy 12:32, manifested itself clearly in Knox's drive to purify religion. This, in turn, provided the motivation for Knox's notions of resistance to idolatrous rulers.[22]

Pronounced literalness became the second trait of Knox's biblical interpretation. All of the major reformers—Luther, Calvin, and Zwingli—employed in varying degrees the literal method of interpreting Scripture. But they modified their literalness in several ways. Luther insisted that Scripture must be interpreted through the perspective of the gospel and is thus Christocentric. Also, if they enhanced one's faith, Luther permitted certain liturgical practices—e.g., church hymns and stained glass windows—even if they had no specific scriptural warrant.[23] Calvin placed an

---

19. Adrien Mezger, *John Knox et ses rapports avec Calvin* (Montauban: Imprimerie Cooperative, 1905), 76–77; D'Assonville, *Knox and the Institutes*, 71–73.

20. *Works*, 2:111; Richard Greaves, "The Nature of Authority in the Writings of John Knox," *Fides et Historia* 10, no. 2 (Spring 1978): 45–46; McEwen, *Faith of Knox*, 39–40.

21. *Works*, 1:197.

22. See Richard Kyle, "John Knox and the Purification of Religion: The Intellectual Aspects of His Crusade Against Idolatry," *Archiv für Reformationsgeschicte* 77 (1986): 265–80; Kyle, "John Knox's Methods of Biblical Interpretation," 57–70.

23. Paul Althaus, *The Theology of Martin Luther* (Philadelphia: Fortress Press, 1966), 76–80. Luther regarded the Book of Romans as the key to the whole Word of God. By gospel, Luther did not mean the four gospels—Matthew, Mark, Luke, and John—but the message of the gospel.

emphasis on the interior witness of the Holy Spirit as a means of assisting in the interpretation of Scripture.[24] However, Knox did not have Luther's Christ-centeredness or Calvin's interior witness to modify the rigidity of his literalness.

Biblical interpretation can emphasize the substantive content of Scripture or the literal form of the Bible. On several occasions, Luther accentuated the substance of the Bible over the literal form of Scriptures. On the other hand, Calvin maintained a healthy balance between the substance and the letter of Scriptures. Unlike Luther and Calvin, but somewhat like Zwingli, Knox placed the literal forms of Scripture above its substantive content. This can be seen especially in the Scottish reformer's crusade against idolatry and theory of resistance to rulers.[25] In fact, Knox often transferred people and events from the Old and New Testaments to his own time so literally that historical repetition appeared to occur. He constantly drew parallels between Israel and Scotland and Israel and England—parallels that often went beyond analogies or lessons and seemed to become historical equations.[26]

Divine Immutability and Sovereignty

Central to Knox's thinking—particularly with his political thought—was his concept of God. In his *History of the Reformation in Scotland,* the reformer clearly rejected the concept that limited God to heaven or had him inactive in the world.[27] Rather, the God of John Knox intervened in human affairs; nothing transpired in history that God had not ordained because his providence encompassed all events. As the sovereignty of God dominated Calvin's thought, divine immutability ruled Knox's. Immutability must be seen as an aspect of divine sovereignty. Still, such a modification can be seen as a shift in emphasis between Knox and Calvin. And as one

24. Francois Wendel, *Calvin: The Origins and Development of His Religious Thought* (New York: Harper and Row, 1963), 157–59; Ruport E. Davies, *The Problem of Authority in the Continental Reformers* (London: Epworth Press, 1946), 118; H. Jackson Forstman, *Word and Spirit* (Stanford: Stanford University Press, 1962).

25. *Works*, 4:232, 437, 468; 3:34–38, 280; 5:516; 2:446.

26. D'Assonville, *Knox and the Institutes*, 74–75. Did history become another source of revelation for Knox as it appears to have become for Puritans such as Thomas Beard who wrote *Theatre of God's Judgments*? See Ronald J. Vander Molen, "Providence as Mystery, Providence as Revelation: Puritan and Anglican Modifications of John Calvin's Doctrine of Providence," *Church History* 47, no. 1 (March 1978): 27–47, especially 40.

27. *Works*, 1:12; Torrance, *Scottish Theology*, 8.

reads Knox's writings, the immutability of God pervades every aspect of his thought.[28]

Without divine immutability, Knox's thought on history, predestination, providence, idolatry, the punishment of sin, political thought, and virtually everything else had little basis. Indeed, as Knox noted often, the law of God never changes. So God must respond to sin in the same manner in Scotland as he did at Sodom and Gomorrah or anywhere. The justice of God is infinite and immutable, and what he damned in one place cannot be excused in another.[29] In fact, the Scottish reformer saw God as responding to a situation in the same way at all times, and consequently somewhat of a prisoner of his own nature.

This stress on divine immutability influenced Knox's thought in several ways. It led him to demand that God's law be upheld in the Commonwealth of Scotland as if it were Old Testament Israel. Next, it inclined Knox to parallel events and people from the Old and New Testaments with events and people of his time so literally that history seemed to be reenacted. Finally, God's immutability played a central role in Knox's scheme of salvation. The reformer declared that God's love toward his elect—those predestined to eternal salvation—is immutable. Consequently, those elected can never fall out of divine love nor be eternally lost. Election had taken place in God's eternal and immutable council and could not change.[30]

In Knox's mind, the omnipotence and sovereignty of God ranked second only to his immutability.[31] These attributes emerge most often in the context of his predestination tract. Here, Knox declared that God demonstrated his omnipotence in the battle with Satan, whose purpose God constantly frustrates. What seems at times as a victory for Satan is only an appearance, "for God is omnipotent, and is compelled to suffer nothing which he hath not appointed in His eternal counsel."[32] The re-

---

28. See Richard Kyle, "The Divine Attributes in John Knox's Concept of God," *Westminster Theological Journal* 48, no. 1 (1986): 163–66.

29. *Works*, 3:171, 191; 4:399; 6:408; Kyle, "Divine Attributes," 165–66.

30. *Works*, 5:44–51.

31. *Works*, 1:23; 3:5–8, 54; 5:33, 133, 390; 6:415. See Richard Kyle, "John Knox's Concept of Divine Providence and Its Influence on His Thought," *Albion* 18, no. 3 (1986): 395–410.

32. *Works*, 5:193. In the same context, Knox said that the Godhead is free from passions. God is omnipotent and when the Holy Ghost used phrases such as "God suffers" or

former believed that all events are ordained by an omnipotent, immutable God whose eternal will and purpose cannot be frustrated by any creature—whether human or angelic. Knox apparently did not use the word "sovereign" in reference to God. But in the political arena, the reformer implied nothing less for he desired God's sovereignty to be established in a real sense in Scotland.[33]

Knox's concept of history virtually depended upon his concept of God. Utterly convinced of the sovereignty of God over all history, the reformer thus believed all occurrences—from the largest to the smallest—to be decreed by God for reasons known only to himself.[34] Knox tended to transfer events from biblical times to his day. He saw the story of the Old Testament being replayed in Scotland with himself as Isaiah, Moses, Daniel, and Jeremiah all combined in one. In his *History*, Knox did not portray the struggles—"Protestantism versus Catholicism, church versus state, monarch versus people"—in a political sense. Rather, his *History* depicted a holy war "between the saints of God and these bloody wolves who claim themselves the title of clergy." In this dramatic struggle, which Knox's *History* described in epic fashion, God's hand manifested itself in all events.[35]

The Church and Sacraments

The primary objective of Knox's career was the establishment of "true" religion (the Reformed faith) in Scotland, and to a large extent, this endeavor could be achieved through the vehicle of the church. Thus Knox placed great importance on the church. He did not, however, reveal any strikingly new ideas in this regard. Rather, Knox's originality rests not in the invention

---

"sorrows," God was simply subjecting himself to human language in order to help human understanding.

33. *Works,* 2:283; Kyle, "Knox's Concept of Divine Providence," 406–7.

34. See Richard Kyle, "John Knox's Concept of History: A Focus on the Providential and Apocalyptic Aspects of His Religious Faith," *Fides et Historia* 18, no. 2 (1986): 19–20; Torrance, *Scottish Theology*, 10–12.

35. *Works,* 1:4, (quote) 6, 131–32, 223, 351; 2:417; 1:89, 205, 220, 270–72; E. G. Rupp, "The Europe of John Knox," in *John Knox: A Quatercentenary Reappraisal* ed. Duncan Shaw (Edinburgh: St. Andrew Press, 1975), 4–5; David Murison, "Knox the Writer," in *John Knox: A Quatercentenary Reappraisal*, 43 (quote). See Richard Kyle, "John Knox and Apocalyptic Thought," *The Sixteenth Century Journal* 15, no. 4 (1984): 460–62.

of new concepts but in the degree and manner in which he applied common ideas—especially the purification of worship in the church.[36]

The church of John Knox wore many faces. Alternately and even simultaneously, as historical circumstances dictated, Knox's church was invisible and visible, universal and local, a small flock and a national organization, a true church and an antichurch. Moreover, he tended to confound church and nation.[37] But most relevant to Knox's ministry were his notions regarding the invisible church and the visible body in its small flock and national manifestations.

In conformity with the Reformed tradition, Knox accorded much importance to the invisible or spiritual aspect of the church. The very essence of his church was its invisible form, for this church, known only to God, contains the elect of all ages. The invisible church emerged in particular historical circumstances, especially in the context of predestination and when the holiness of the visible kirk came under question. He spoke of the invisible church as containing the elect of all time and thus being universal, spanning all periods of history. Also, when the national Scottish church experienced tensions and struggles, Knox spoke of the invisible church—a church pure and indestructible.[38]

For Knox, the visible church came in several forms—most relevant being the small flock and national kirk. At times, he spoke of a small flock elected by God but persecuted by Catholicism. When Protestantism became established in 1560, it was a national church. These two aspects of the church had their own responsibilities. When but a small remnant, the church only had to maintain the integrity of its faith. But when Protestantism had been established and gained sufficient numbers, Knox insisted that it must suppress idolatry.[39]

Like his ideas on the church, Knox's thoughts concerning the sacraments broke no new turf. He accepted two sacraments, baptism and the Lord's Supper, which he regarded as two of the marks of the visible church. The reformer said that the sacraments "are ordained to be seals of the justice of faith, so are they also a declaration of our profession before the

36. Janton, *Concept et Sentiment*, 111; Richard Kyle, "The Nature of the Church in the Thought of John Knox," *Scottish Journal of Theology* 37, no. 4 (1984): 485.

37. Kyle, "The Nature of the Church," 485; Torrance, *Scottish Theology*, 18, 27.

38. Janton, *Concept et Sentiment*, 164; Kyle, "The Nature of the Church," 486–87.

39. *Works*, 2:442–43.

world."[40] He regarded the sacraments as signs and seals of God's promise. But along with Calvin and Bucer, Knox insisted that they are more than this confirmation. He considered baptism as primarily a sign. Not so with the Lord's Supper, which he envisioned as a continuous process by which the benefits of Christ's death nourish the soul of the elect. The sacraments held no magical power, nor are they merely bare signs, but rather they spiritually feed the believer's faith.[41]

The Purification of Religion

Knox regarded the church and the sacraments as important, but his greatest anxiety was idolatry, which he equated with Catholicism. To be a Catholic was to be an idolater. The fight against the "idolatrous" Mass so dominated his thinking that virtually no major area of his thought was free from it. Knox's anti-idolatry theme stemmed from his Old Testament hermeneutic and permeated his thought—his political ideas, doctrine of salvation, sacramental and ecclesiastical thought, view of church discipline, and even his perception of Christ's office as high priest.[42]

The fight against the "idolatrous" Mass—along with its counterpart, the establishment of "true" worship—can be seen as the great motive of Knox's career. In pursuit of this objective, Knox exceeded the vigor of his Reformed colleagues. Perhaps in this excess, he displayed his most unique trait. The consequences of his literal Old Testament hermeneutic—with its starting point in Deuteronomy 12:32—manifested itself clearly in the fight against idolatry. From the very onset of his public career, to his death in 1572, Knox maintained great hostility toward the "idolatrous" Mass.[43]

The crusade against idolatry, starting with Knox's first sermon in 1547, pervaded most of his writings. Still, its logic is largely repetitious and can be illustrated by a selected passage. After Knox returned from a duration on a French galley in 1549, he denounced the Mass from his pulpit in northern England. From his defense of this denunciation came

40. *Works*, 5:120, 125; Kyle, *Mind of Knox*, 160.

41. *Works*, 5:172; 2:114–15; Wendel, *Calvin*, 315.

42. *Works*, 3:34–35, 38, 44, 46, 48–49, 51–52, 54–61; 4:373–420, 433–59, 467–520, 523–38; 5:502–22.

43. Kyle, "Knox and the Purification of Religion," 265; Lord Eustace Percy, *John Knox* (Richmond: John Knox Press, 1966), 116.

A Vindication of the Doctrine That the Sacrifice of the Mass Is Idolatry (1550)—Knox's most direct attack on idolatry.[44]

The reformer's approach came in the form of two syllogisms. In these syllogisms—based on Deuteronomy 12:32—one can see the key to Knox's crusade against idolatry, and perhaps to his thinking in general. In *A Vindication*, he did not define idolatry in the strict literal sense of substituting a false god for a true god. Rather, he interpreted idolatry in the widest sense possible—for idolatry, as he said, entails not only the worship of that which is not God, but also to trust in anything besides God. And to honor anything in religion contrary to God's Word is to lean on something other than God—and is therefore idolatry.[45]

Knox's crusade against idolatry certainly did not wane after his major work on the subject. The reformer, of course, did not again attack idolatry so logically or so directly as he did in *A Vindication*. Yet the theme, anchored in his Old Testament hermeneutic, continued to dominate his thought.[46] During his exile (1554–1559), the crusade intensified but took different paths. In one place, Knox comforted believers who were being persecuted by the papists and warned them to separate from idolatry. In another, he denounced nations for their breaking of the covenant and for corporate idolatry. But increasingly, Knox developed his anti-idolatry theme in a political context and as a springboard to resistance. His reasoning, however, is largely a reiteration of that found in *A Vindication*.[47]

The Path to Salvation

The question, *What must I do to be saved?* has evoked a variety of responses throughout history. On this question, Knox stood with the other Protestant reformers—namely Luther, Zwingli, and Calvin. They declared the twin pillars of salvation to be justification by faith and predestination.

The doctrine of justification came early in Knox's ministry and underwent few changes. It was more pronounced in his earlier ministry, but he retained it in a living sense throughout his life. The Bible teaches justi-

---

44. *Works*, 3:29–70; Kyle, "Knox and the Purification of Religion," 266.

45. *Works*, 3:34–35, 38, 44, 46, 52, 54.

46. Kyle, "Knox and the Purification of Religion," 268; Kyle, *Mind of Knox*, 178.

47. Kyle, "Knox and the Purification of Religion," 268–69; Kyle, "Main Themes of His Thought," 107.

fication by faith.[48] Still, the strong Lutheran influence in the early years of the Scottish Reformation must have helped point John Knox to the doctrine of justification as found in the Bible. As time progressed, however, he closely identified justification with a more complete doctrine of salvation including predestination and sanctification.[49]

What were Knox's views on justification? The gist of this doctrine emerged fully in his 1548 *Summary of Balnaves on Justification by Faith*. He stated the substance of justification is "to cleave fast unto God, by Jesus Christ, and not by ourself, nor yet by our works."[50] Here, one encounters a typically strong Lutheran rejection of works as a means of salvation. The Scottish reformer asserted that the wicked believe works to be a part of salvation, but a true preacher must exclude them from justification as did Christ and the prophets.[51] Yet Knox did not condemn good works. Like Luther, he held them to be a fruit of justification, but not the cause of it.

Very similar to rejecting justification by works was the repudiation of the law as an instrument of salvation. Since neither good works nor obeying the law suffices, one must seek justice from Christ whom the law could not accuse.[52] According to Knox, Scripture clearly teaches that faith in Christ is the only vehicle for apprehending justification and the mercy of God. Moreover, Knox possessed the New Testament faith. How did this faith relate to that in the Old Testament? They were one and the same, he said. The patriarchs stood in God's favor in the future promised seed, and Knox stood in God's grace by faith in the seed that had already been revealed.[53]

Predestination did not stand at the center of Knox's thought world. Yet the doctrine was not just a theoretical matter for Knox. It had practical importance, revealing a mainspring of his thinking and action.[54] Knox's writings concerning predestination primarily span from 1552 to 1560. The best sources are Knox's writings to his mother-in-law Mrs. Bowes,

---

48. The best illustrations are Romans 3, 4, and 5 and Ephesians 2:8–9. Knox drew his doctrine of justification from Scripture. See *Works*, 3:16–17, 20, 22; 4:467.

49. See McGoldrick, *Luther's Scottish Connection*, 70–73; Kyle, *Mind of Knox*, 101–2; Torrance, "Hamilton and Knox," 171–84.

50. *Works*, 3:15.

51. Kyle, *Mind of Knox*, 98.

52. *Works*, 3:18–19.

53. Ibid., 3:20.

54. Reid, *Trumpeter of God*, 152.

An Answer, A Faithful Admonition, and letters to his Scottish brethren. Otherwise, the reformer made few references to the subject.[55]

Knox adopted a practical approach to predestination—shaped by historical circumstances. He tended to emphasize predestination, as he did the small flock concept of the church, during troubled times and prior to the establishment of the Reformation in Scotland. The 1550s were indeed difficult times for Knox—the return of Catholicism to England, the exile years, and more.[56] More specifically, Knox's practical approach to predestination had a pastoral inclination. The troubled Mrs. Bowes doubted her salvation and Knox used predestination toward this end.[57] Of great importance, Knox personalized the doctrine of predestination. He had no doubt that he was numbered among God's elect.[58]

On the whole Knox followed Calvin in respect to predestination. Yet he apparently deviated from Calvin at two points: confusion between double and single predestination and a different emphasis on the cause of reprobation. According to Reformed theology, the decree of reprobation comprises two elements: preterition (the determination to pass by some people) and condemnation (the determination to punish those who are passed by for their sins).[59] Being a man of action and not a theologian, Knox often confused such fine points. But on the whole, he seemed to follow Augustine and Zwingli in accentuating a more passive approach to reprobation—not Calvin's active condemnation.[60]

The Theory of Resistance

Why look at Knox's political ideas in a study of his ministry? How do they connect? In his role as preacher and prophet, Knox constantly warned individuals and nations to resist idolatrous Catholicism. And his admonitions often had political overtones—even the call to outright rebellion.

---

55. See Richard Kyle, "The Concept of Predestination in the Thought of John Knox," *Westminster Theological Journal* 46, no. 1 (1984): 54. However, *An Answer* was not an insignificant work. It ranged about 170,000 words. See *Works* volume 5.

56. Janton, *Concept et Sentiment*, 91, 105–6; Kyle, "Concept of Predestination," 54.

57. *Works*, 3:337–402.

58. Ibid, 6:639, 643, 659.

59. Louis Berkhof, *The History of Christian Doctrines* (Carlisle, PA: Banner of Truth, 1937), 136; Wendel, *Calvin*, 280.

60. *Works*, 5:125–26. Kyle, "Concept of Predestination," 70–71.

Moreover, his political ideas must be seen as an outgrowth of his basic theological concepts.

Was Knox a political theorist? No more than he was a speculative theologian. In fact, Knox would have denied having political thought as such. His one purpose in life was to perform God's work—namely, the reformation of religion. Therefore, to divide Knox's thought into rigid religious and political categories would be rather artificial. Knox, of course, sought the reformation of religion rather than the adjustment of political grievances. Yet one should not separate religious development from the secular realities of an era. So Knox's reform efforts cannot be divorced from the political milieu of Europe and Scotland.[61]

Knox desired the reformation of religion in Scotland, and in his mind, this meant returning the Christian religion to the ideal of spiritual Israel. However, the power of the Catholic Church—established by law and promoted by the civil power—stood in opposition to such reform. For any reforming movement to succeed, it must somewhere find the power to effect the changes it desires. The early Protestant reformers found that power in the temporal state. Unlike the principalities of Luther's Germany or Edward VI's England, Scotland did not have any sovereigns favorable to Protestantism.[62] Thus for a Scottish Reformation to triumph, its proponents must advocate certain political measures: the overthrow of established temporal authority, the seizure of political power, and the use of that power to bring down the Roman Church. In such a setting, Knox's thought turned to a resistance theory.

---

61. Our contention that Knox was fundamentally concerned with the reformation of religion does not go unchallenged. Those who also present a religious emphasis include the following: John R. Gray, "The Political Theory of John Knox," *Church History* 8 (June 1939): 132–47; W. J. Vesey, "The Sources of the Idea of Active Resistance in the Political Theory of John Knox," Ph.D. diss. Boston University, 1961, 44; Michael Walzer, *The Revolution of the Saints: A Study in the Origins of Radical Politics* (New York: Atheneum, 1973), 92–113; W. Stanford Reid, "John Knox's Theology of Political Government," *Sixteenth Century Journal* 19, no. 4 (1988): 529–40. Those emphasizing Knox primarily as a political thinker largely isolated from his religious thought are the following: E. Russell, "John Knox as a Statesman," *The Princeton Theological Review* 6 (January 1908): 1–28; J. H. Burns, "John Knox and Revolution," *History Today* 8 (August 1958): 565–73. To some extent, others lean in this direction. See Jasper Ridley, *John Knox* (Oxford University Press, 1968); Lord Eustace Percy, *John Knox* (Richmond: John Knox Press, 1966); Paul M. Little, "John Knox and English Social Prophecy," *Presbyterian Historical Society of England* 14 (1968–1972): 117–27.

62. Kyle, "Main Themes of His Thought," 109; Kyle, *Mind of Knox*, 246.

John Knox did not develop his theory of resistance in a vacuum. Both the sequence of events and the thought of his time influenced it. For its very success, the Scottish Reformation depended on resistance to political authorities—namely, the Regent, Mary of Guise, and the Queen, Mary Stewart. The intellectual milieu of the exile years and Knox's consultation with other Reformed ministers played no small part. Nor is it entirely accurate to view Knox's notions of opposition to rulers as entirely religious and nonpolitical.

Knox was a religious reformer and as such his resistance theory must largely be seen as a means to an end—the end being the reformation of religion in Scotland. Knox, of course, drew on several sources for his notions on rebellion. But the Bible—especially the Old Testament and the way he interpreted it—must be regarded as the wellspring of his resistance theory.[63] Events and ideology not withstanding, Knox's thought on rebellion could have little rational basis without his concepts of God, sin, idolatry, and the covenant.

Most directly, John Knox connected his notion of political resistance to his belief in active resistance to sin. As he stated in his debate with Maitland of Lethington when in a minority, the faithful must only separate themselves from idolatry. When in a dominant position and reasonably unified, however, they must not simply separate from idolatry—they must abolish it.[64] And if exterminating idolatry meant overthrowing a Catholic sovereign, then so be it. For this active resistance to idolatry and its political consequences, Knox adduced considerable support from the Old Testament.[65]

Knox adopted the role and rhetoric of an Old Testament prophet and may have even integrated his personality into that of a Hebrew prophet. His resistance theory rested on religious grounds, but not exclusively. As Paul Little points out, Knox did not assail Mary Tudor solely as an idolater. Rather, he displayed concern for the entire fabric of English society. For example, in *A Faithful Admonition* (1554), he attacked her on the ground of endangering national independence.[66] In transforming religion, Knox

63. Vesey, "The Sources of Knox's Political Theory," 47–227. The argument of Vesey's dissertation is that Knox derived his theory of resistance from the Old Testament.

64. *Works*, 2:442–43.

65. *Works*, 3:165–216, 263–330; 4:170, 234, 245, 281, 377–402; 2:372, 432–33; Vesey, "The Sources of Knox's Political Theory," 47–227.

66. *Works*, 3:295; Little, "John Knox and English Social Prophecy," 122–25.

did not intend to bypass the existing political structure—monarch, nobility, and estates. Instead, he sought to animate the structure with a religious purpose. When Knox found no monarch to reform religion, he turned to the nobility. Only when the sovereign and the nobility failed to purify religion did Knox advocate going outside the structure. The Scottish Reformation, indeed, intermingled religious and political motives. Though religion dominated Knox's thought, as a typical sixteenth-century man, he could not separate the two.[67]

When did Knox advocate rebellion to constituted political authority? Scholars debate this point.[68] He waited until the spring of 1558 to explicitly reveal a full-blown doctrine of resistance. Still, Knox had been inching toward such a theory by 1554, and perhaps even earlier. Several writings between 1554 and 1557—*A Godly Letter, A Faithful Admonition,* and *Letters to the Brethren*—signaled the outburst that would come.[69]

The radical break came in 1558. Knox wrote four revolutionary pamphlets—which together advocated popular rebellion and regicide. *The First Blast* declared female rule over a kingdom to be against both the law of God and nature. All ranks of sixteenth-century society accepted both in theory and practice the inferiority and subjection of women to men. Paradoxically, society considered women ineligible for any public office except that of head of state. In *The First Blast*, Knox exposed the

67. *Works,* 3:295; 4:373–420; 1:272; Little, "Knox and English Social Prophecy," 122–25; J. H. Burns, "The Political Ideas of the Scottish Reformation," *Aberdeen University Review* 42 (1955–1956): 251–68; Burns, "John Knox and Revolution," 565, 567–68.

68. J. H. Burns believes that Knox held to passive obedience until 1558 when he advocated armed resistance. See Burns, "Political Ideas of the Scottish Reformation." 251–60; Burns, "Knox and Revolution," 565–73. Ronald Vander Molen says that while Knox issued no clear call for rebellion in 1554, his writings by that time certainly implied such and were interpreted as seditious by Cox's Anglican group at Frankfurt. See Ronald J. Vander Molen, "Anglican Against Puritan: Ideological Origins During the Marian Exile," *Church History* 42 (March 1973): 54f. Richard Greaves contends that Knox demonstrated a practical belief in the right to rebellion as early as 1547. See Richard Greaves, "John Knox, the Reformed Tradition, and the Development of Resistance Theory," *The Journal of Modern History* 58 (September 1976): 1:31, especially 1–3, 14. Little and Ridley also seem to favor a date earlier than 1558. See Little, "Knox and English Social Prophecy," 117; Ridley, *John Knox,* 171, 174. Roger Mason also notes that while Knox clearly articulated a theory of rebellion in 1558, such ideas could be detected much earlier. See Mason, "Knox, Resistance and Royal Supremacy," 160–65; Roger Mason, *Kingship and the Commonweal* (East Lothian, UK: Tuckwell Press, 1998), 143–50.

69. *Works,* 1:177, 272; 3:166, 168, 170, 175, 178, 184–88, 190–94, 221–26, 274–75, 282–83, 308–9; 4:262–86.

illogical nature of this system. And in so doing, he attacked the special position of the crown.[70] Knox's premise—that female rule had subverted both the divine and natural order—did not seem so startling. But his conclusion certainly alarmed Europe: the faithful, if afflicted by a female sovereign, "ought to remove from honor and authority that monster in nature," and if any support her, they ought "execute against them the sentence of death."[71]

By the summer of 1558, Knox published three tracts putting forward his doctrine of revolution even more clearly. He wrote one to Mary of Guise, one to the nobility, and the third to the common people of Scotland—that is, the middle group. In addition, he attached the abortive *Second Blast* to his last tract. In these works, Knox denounced Tyndale's doctrine of Christian obedience as sinful. Most sixteenth-century theologians instructed the people to obey the king—not from fear of earthly punishment but from fear of God. Knox now reversed this. If people obeyed the unjust commands of evil rulers, they would receive a far more terrible punishment from God than any sovereign could inflict upon them for treason. In earlier works, Knox implied the right of resistance. He now imposed upon the nobility, estates, and the common people the duty of armed resistance to a Catholic sovereign.[72]

In the four pamphlets published before August 1558, Knox set forth very clearly his views on the matter of government and the rights of subjects against oppressive and idolatrous rulers. He touched upon most of these matters in *The First Blast*, but spelled them out in the later letters. He first called upon the Queen Regent to reform the church. Then he followed with an appeal to the nobles to force such reforms and a summons to the commonalty to pressure the rulers toward the same end. He stated unequivocally that the nobles had the right to remove an unrepentant monarch. And the commonalty could set up their own "reformed church" if their rulers failed to act. After this 1558 outburst, Knox more or less elaborated upon or modified the same themes for the duration of his career.[73]

70. Ridley, *John Knox*, 269–70.

71. *Works*, 4:415–16.

72. Kyle, *Mind of Knox*, 270–71.

73. *Works*, 4:469–70, 483–87, 495–501, 505–7.

3

The Reformer in Training
(1547–1554)

FOR HUNDREDS OF YEARS, biographers of John Knox listed his birth date near Haddington, Scotland as 1505. They based this date on Theodore Beza's book of famous reformers titled, *Icones*, published in 1580. In 1904—as scholars prepared biographies to commemorate the reformer's four hundredth birthday—Professor D. Hay Fleming of St. Andrews proved convincingly that Knox was more likely born in 1514. Fleming traced the error to David Buchanan's 1644 edition of Knox's *History of the Reformation in Scotland* and Buchanan's misreading of Beza.[1]

SAINT ANDREWS, THE FRENCH GALLEY
AND ENGLAND

Unfortunately, we possess few solid facts regarding Knox's early life and education. Knox studied at the University of St. Andrews and not Glasgow as an earlier generation of scholars argued. He was ordained into the priesthood April 15, 1536 and became a papal notary in 1540.[2] His rejec-

1. *Scottish Historical Review* 1, "When Was Knox Born?" (1904): 467. See also D. Hay Fleming, "The Date of Knox's Birth," *The Bookman* 28 (September 1905): 193–96. Jasper Ridley also deals with this topic in an appendix of his biography, *John Knox*, (New York: Oxford University Press, 1968): 531–34, and Henry Cowan, "When Was John Knox Born?" *Records of the Scottish Church History Society* 1 (1926): 217–28.

2. Theodore Beza, *Icones*, Geneva, 1580), cited by Ridley, *John Knox*, 17. Ridley also discusses this in an appendix number II titled, "Knox's University," *John Knox*, 535. See also W. Stanford Reid, *Trumpeter of God: A Biography of John Knox* (New York: Charles Scribner's Sons, 1974), 16. Reid admits that no documentary evidence directly supports this view, but he cites the overlap of dates of Knox and Major, the proximity of St. Andrews to Knox's home, and the similarity of views between Knox and Major as his evidence that Knox studied under Major. On Knox's ordination see, J. Shearman, *et al*, "The Ordination of John Knox: A Symposium," *Innes Review* 6 (1955): 42f.

tion of Roman Catholicism and subsequent evangelical conversion came from his personal study and through his association with Protestant lairds in the area of his birth. Sir Hugh Douglass of Longniddry, a gentleman of East Lothian who had accepted Lutheran doctrines, gave Knox the charge of tutoring his two sons. Douglas and other lairds of East Lothian—including Alexander Crichton and John Cockburn of Ormiston—were among those who provided the Protestant preacher George Wishart protection during his preaching tour of Scotland in 1544–1545.[3] Wishart's preaching drew large crowds in Montrose, Dundee, and Leith and attracted the attention of Cardinal David Beaton's agents.[4]

Given his association with such gentlemen, it is entirely reasonable to place Wishart within the context of the "assured Scot" movement. In this development, the Scottish lairds traded their support for an English union in exchange for pensions and protection from the incursions of English troops in Scotland. King Henry VIII and later Regent Somerset employed this tactic effectively in Scotland. The assured Scot phenomenon also held implications for religion.[5] For King Henry a reformation of religion took a moderate tone. It included independence from Rome, despoiling the monasteries for the royal treasury, and at least temporarily, a vernacular Bible chained to each pulpit. Henry also promoted the linkage of the two realms through a dynastic marriage between Prince Edward and Mary Stewart, the infant daughter of James V. The proposed marriage alliance—called the Greenwich Treaties—was signed in 1543, but never enforced. For the purpose of advancing reformed principles in Scotland,

3. Ridley, *John Knox*, 26. See also Thomas M'Crie, *The Life of John Knox* (Edinburgh, 1812) abridged reprint edition, (Glasgow: Free Presbyterian Publications, 1976), 21. M'Crie takes an uncritical view of Knox, but he thoroughly researched his topic. See also Edwin Muir, *John Knox Portrait of a Calvinist* (London, 1929); reprint ed., (Port Washington, NY, 1972), 14 and James Edward McGoldrick, *Luther's Scottish Connection* (Rutherford, NJ: Farleigh Dickinson University Press, 1989), 23, cites an act of the 1496 Scottish Parliament which required Latin instruction for sons of nobles and freeholders. See Gordon Donaldson, ed. *Scottish Historical Documents* (New York: Barnes & Noble, Inc., 1970), 92–93 and Ridley, *John Knox*, 39–40.

4. John Knox, *History of the Reformation in Scotland*, trans. William C. Dickinson, 2 vols., (New York: Philosophical Library, 1950), 1:69, hereafter cited as *History*. Ridley on page 44 says that if Knox had stayed with Wishart nine more hours he would have died with Wishart.

5. Marcus H. Merriman, "The Assured Scots: Scottish Collaborators with England during the Rough Wooing," *Scottish Historical Review* 47 (April 1968): 10–34.

with what Clare Kellar has called a "unmistakably Protestant flavour," at least some of the assured Scots promoted the cause of "assurance."[6]

John Knox tells us in his *History* that he accompanied Wishart and a party of about fifty bodyguards armed with a two-handled sword, a traditional Scottish weapon. The large crowds attracted by Wishart alarmed Catholic officials, and Cardinal David Beaton ordered his arrest. Sensing that his capture was imminent, Wishart ordered Knox to flee for his own safety. One by one the lairds began to abandon Wishart. After five weeks of constant association, Knox obeyed Wishart's command and returned to his pupils.[7] Albeit brief, Knox's association with Wishart changed his life and shaped his ministry. Knox witnessed the power of God on Wishart's life and the courage that he drew from it. Following Cardinal Beaton's orders, Catholic officials keen to stamp out Lutheran heresies arrested, tried, strangled, and burned Wishart early in 1546.[8]

Historian Lord Percy has described Cardinal Beaton as a kind of Italian Renaissance figure—a "tyrant, statesman, inquisitor, sumptuous and ruthless."[9] Beaton at one time positioned himself for election to the papal office. Had he triumphed he would have fit comfortably with a long line of Renaissance popes, more passionate about aesthetics and patronage of grand art and architecture than the spiritual duties as the Vicar of Christ. The father of many illegitimate children, Cardinal Beaton was widely despised for his immorality and for his murder of George Wishart. Some radical Protestants, seeking to avenge Wishart's murder, executed their own brand of justice and murdered Beaton in St. Andrews Castle on May 29, 1546. Knox took no part in the bloodshed and called it "gangsterism." Yet at the same time, he rejoiced over Beaton's death in his *History*: "these things we write merrily . . . these are the works of God, whereby He would admonish tyrants of this earth."[10]

The radical Protestants, who murdered Beaton, held his home in St. Andrews' Castle for a year—during which time they preached openly throughout the area. Knox joined the so-called "Castilians" in April of 1547 because his employer and friends now lived there. Knox also sought

6. Clare Kellar, *Scotland, England, and the Reformation 1534–1561* (New York: Oxford University Press, 2003), 98.

7. Knox, *History*, 2:69.

8. Knox, *History*, 2:69–74; Ridley, *John Knox*, 44.

9. Lord Eustace Percy, *John Knox* (Richmond, VA: John Knox Press, 1966), 42.

10. Knox, *History*, 1:79.

refuge from Beaton's successor, Archbishop John Hamilton, who sought to kill him for his earlier association with Wishart.[11] The castle provided Knox protection, and it allowed him to continue teaching his pupils. Knox found the castle a hotbed of revolutionaries. Only a few of the men resident in the castle—such as Henry Balnaves and John Rough—possessed purely religious motives.[12] Favorably impressed by his exposition of John's Gospel at the parish church, Balnaves and Rough asked Knox to take charge of preaching in the castle.[13] Knox was overtaken by the enormity of their formal call and the obvious danger he would face if the castle returned to Catholic hands. Only after an outburst of tears and days of sequester in his room did Knox accept this unusual call to preach.[14]

The Castilians' hold on the castle was precarious despite a promise of help from the English crown.[15] In July of 1547 about twenty French ships sailed near the shore of St. Andrews. The Castilians surrendered to the French on July 30, 1547, after an effective cannon assault of a few weeks.[16] French officials arrested the Castilians and sailed for the coast of Normandy, loaded with Cardinal Beaton's property and the Scottish prisoners. Knox spent the next 19 months confined as a galley slave, fixed in irons and forced to row between Scotland and France with winters on the Loire River.[17] In this unlikely setting, Knox began his literary career. He wrote letters to his former "congregation" in St. Andrews and revised Henry Balnaves' treatise on the doctrine of justification by grace through faith. The details of Knox's release are not known, but it occurred in February of 1549 through the auspices of the English government. In 1551 all of the Scottish prisoners were freed. Of the 120 in the original group of Castilians, only one died in French hands and that of natural causes.[18]

11. Ibid., 1:82, and M'Crie, *The Life of John Knox*, 22.

12. Reid, *Trumpeter of God*, 44–46; Burleigh, *A Church History*, 129–30.

13. M'Crie, *A Life of John Knox*, 24; Knox, *History*, 1:82.

14. Knox, *History*, 1:83.

15. Reid, *Trumpeter of God*, 51; Ridley, *John Knox*, 60.

16. Reid, *Trumpeter of God*, 52–53. For details of the weapons used in the assault and defense of St. Andrews Castle see Gladys Dickinson, "Some Notes on the Scottish Army in the First Half of the Sixteenth Century," *Scottish Historical Review* 33 (April 1949): 141–42.

17. Knox, *History*, 1 96; M'Crie, *The Life of John Knox*, 33.

18. Ian Cowan, *The Scottish Reformation* (New York: St. Martin's Press, 1892),105. No consensus exists on the details of Knox's release. M'Crie, *The Life of John Knox*, 38 gives three possible explanations for his release. Ridley, *John Knox*, 38, thinks a prisoner

EPISTLE TO THE CONGREGATION
OF THE CASTLE OF ST. ANDREWS

While bound in irons in Rouen aboard a French galley named *Notre Dame*, Knox received a manuscript from Henry Balnaves on justification with a request that the Scottish reformer evaluate it. After a thorough restructuring of the manuscript, he attempted to have it sent to Scotland for publication. Along with this treatise, Knox wrote an epistle—titled, *An Epistle to the Congregation of St. Andrews* (1548)—intended to encourage his fellow prisoners. Knox used biblical examples to illustrate his assurance that good would triumph over evil, and God would frustrate the plans of Satan. The biblical Joseph was forced into slavery and carried into a strange country, mistreated and imprisoned, but in the end Satan's plans were frustrated. Through the providence of God, Joseph received high honors and served in Pharaoh's court. Furthermore, God honored the righteous faith of the prophet Daniel who survived the lion's den. Darius the King ordered that everyone worship the Lord God of Daniel, the only true and living God. Despite adversities—the stoning of Stephen and the dispersion and banishment of believers in the early church—the gospel of Christ was faithfully preached.

Knox's entire argument is that God is the God of irony. What Satan intended for evil, God intended for good. It was ironic, yet the scattering of Christians after Stephen's death ensured that the gospel penetrated into new cities. This short epistle thus established the pattern for Knox's worldview, which recurred in his writings for the next 25 years. His is a simple, yet profound confidence in the triumph of Christ over the forces of darkness. Christians were engaged in a cosmic struggle against Satan. Using the Bible as his new two-handled sword, Knox was convinced that we wrestle not against flesh and blood, but against principalities and powers. In Knox's words, "the head of Satan shall be trodden down, but the believer will surely triumph . . . though the battle appears strong, your Captain is . . . given all power in heaven and earth."[19]

---

exchange occurred between England and France through the mediation of the king of Denmark. Reid, *Trumpeter of God*, 84, says Protector Somerset worked diligently to obtain Knox's freedom.

19. John Knox, *The Works of John Knox*, David Laing, ed., 6 vols. (Edinburgh: Printed for the Bannatyne Club, 1846–1864), reprint ed., (New York: AMS Press, 1966), 3:10. Hereafter Laing is cited as *Works*.

SUMMARY OF BALNAVES ON JUSTIFICATION

Knox rearranged Balnaves' text into 28 chapters. Printed in full in volume three of Knox's *Works*, it runs over 100 pages.[20] Knox probably thought in pastoral terms as he considered how to best handle and disseminate this theological treatise. Length prohibited its wide distribution and readership. In an effort to place it in the hands of the people—for what he called "for the better memory of the reader"—Knox divided the treatise into chapters and wrote a summary of each chapter condensing the whole Confession into ten readable pages. (Readers should remember here that they are reading Balnaves, through the editorial lens of Knox). The Scottish reformer then arranged for it to be sent to Scotland for publication. Somehow the Confession was lost or misplaced. The Confession and Epistle were rediscovered and printed in 1584, some 12 years after Knox's death.

In his summary of Balnaves' treatise, Knox argues from history—especially biblical history and predominately from the Old Testament. God gave us the stories—of Adam, Cain and Abel, Seth, Ishmael, Isaac, Jacob, Esau, Noah, Moses, and Abraham—as examples of how a faithful follower of God must despair of their own righteousness and trust Christ. It is a *tour de force* against what Luther called "works righteousness." Satan is constantly deceiving human beings. This often occurs when they invent practices that the Scriptures did not ordain in order to achieve a right standing with God. Such practices abound, especially in the church, and are often related to Holy Communion. The degenerate genius of humanity has prostituted the sacred sacrifice of Christ into idolatry.

In chapter 12, Knox argues for what was at a later time called total depravity or the complete inability of humankind in a spiritual sense. Knox writes defending the federal headship of Adam: "for by the transgression of Adam, all his posterity became rebels to the law."[21] In chapter 13, Knox raises three questions that he proceeds to answer through the next several chapters. Why would God give the law if humankind could not keep it? Why should we perform good works when we see that by them we are not made just?[22] Thirdly, Knox posed the provocative question, how were the Patriarchs and Old Testament fathers made just? (Theologians should not press Knox too precisely here on the language of the last question. He un-

---

20. Ibid., 3:437–42.
21. Ibid., 3:18, cf. 3:467.
22. Ibid., 3:18.

derstood that we were not made righteous, but rather declared righteous by the finished work of Christ on our behalf. With his thorough condemnation of sinful human nature, Knox understood that ours is an alien righteousness, namely Christ's righteousness, and certainly not our own).

God gave us the law as a means of revealing himself and his nature to humankind. The law of God extends to the whole of creation whereby God is glorified. Why should we do good works? Works are an outward testimony of our faith in Christ. Echoing Luther Knox wrote, "as the good tree bears good fruit, so the just man works good works." Timing was everything. These "good works" were not performed for our justification, but as a result of our justification. "As the tree is good before the fruit, so that man is just before the work be good." According to Knox, our Old Testament fathers were justified because they believed in the promised seed which was to come. Knox then followed the trajectory of this faith in the promised seed. "We believe [he] is already come, and hath fulfilled all which was spoken of him in the Law and the Prophets." Seeking justification through one's own best effort spoiled "God of his glory" and "Christ of his office."

Knox is cutting in his references to scholastic theology and the theologians he calls "Sophists." In his summary of chapter 20, Knox condemns the notion of the Sophists who argue "that works preceding faith deserve the grace of God *de congruo*." Knox found this the equivalent of saying that our sin deserves the grace of God. He was arguing against the Scholastic tradition of the *via moderna* of William of Occam (c. 1285–1347) and Gabriel Biel (c.1420–1495)—who affirmed that humanity's best efforts obligated God to honor our good works. A congruence existed between the work of humankind and God. In short, humanitys' work merited the grace of God. In chapter 21 Knox attacked the excessive works of the saints and the hypocrites who would sell them to others. Without naming indulgences and the treasury of merit, Knox had these corrupt Roman practices clearly in mind.

Should we perform good works? Yes, of course, but with the full knowledge that "neither works preceding nor following faith justify." In the end, the work that we do is to "believe in Him whom he has sent."

A VINDICATION THAT THE MASS IS IDOLATRY

Protestant fortunes in Europe deteriorated during the months of Knox's captivity in France. Holy Roman Emperor Charles V finally used military force to settle the religious question in Germany. In April of 1547, a year after Luther's death, Charles and the Imperial army defeated the Protestant Schmalkaldic League at Muhlberg on the Elbe River in Saxony. *The Augsburg Interim* and the subsequent *Leipzig Interim* settled the religious question in Germany along Catholic lines. If Knox still considered study in Germany, the news of conditions on the Continent led him to reconsider. Between 1547–1549, Strasbourg, Constance, and Augsburg all fell into Catholic hands. Only Geneva, a few scattered principalities, and England offered safety to Protestants.

Prospects in England looked very favorable indeed for Protestants. Though not of one mind regarding theology, Protestants in England agreed on the need for more thorough reforms than the tepid measures introduced during the reign of Henry VIII. Archbishop Thomas Cranmer enjoyed new freedoms to reform the English church. Cranmer invited a number of experienced reformers from the Continent to come to England to teach, preach, and assist in the reformation of the church. A dozen men accepted Cranmer's offer while luminaries like John Calvin and Philip Melanchthon offered cordial regrets. We can count John Knox among this group of émigrés enlisted by the Archbishop to bring their gifts to England. He could not return to his native Scotland because a war raged between the French, English and Scots, and because his theological views were unwelcome.[23] Upon his release by the French, Knox received a job offer from the English Privy Council.

The state licensed the relatively inexperienced preacher to promote reformed ideas in Berwick, a rough border town in northeast England. In Berwick Knox perfected his preaching skills and demonstrated particular ability to reach soldiers with his forceful rhetoric and his references to military life. He also began to develop specific preferences for worship. His pulpit crusade against idolatry was aimed at the practice of kneeling while taking Communion and the sacrificial nature of the Roman Mass. His vehement attack on the Mass attracted the rage of Dr. Cuthbert

---

23. Reid, *Trumpeter of God*, 67–68 notes that the prisoners escaped to England because Scotland was not safe. If Knox had returned to Scotland, he would have faced heresy charges.

Tunstall, the Bishop of Durham. Officials in the Council of the North, acting on behalf of the Privy Council, summoned Knox to appear in April of 1550. If the Council intended to intimidate Knox, their strategy failed badly. Knox appeared before the Council in Newcastle on April 4 where he delivered his blunt speech titled, *A Vindication of the Doctrine That the Sacrifice of the Mass Is Idolatry.*

First Syllogism

Knox expressed his delight that eminent and learned men were present to hear his speech.[24] He realized the gravity of the issue. The Mass was in fact the foundation of the Roman religion, and Knox argued that he would dismantle it using Scripture. No doubt a legacy of his scholastic training, Knox structured his speech using two syllogisms. He used a scholastic method to destroy the foundation of scholastic, sacerdotal theology. The syllogism begins with a major premise, followed by a minor premise, and a logical conclusion. His first syllogism reads thus: "The Mass is idolatry. All worshiping honoring or service invented by the brain of man in the religion of God, without his express commandment, is idolatry. The Mass is invented by the brain of man without any commandment of God; therefore it is idolatry."[25]

Knox used the example of King Saul who disobeyed God when he failed to kill all the people and beasts of Amalek. Saul instead saved Agag the King and the fattest animals from slaughter. Saul offered these animals without the express warrant of God. Moreover, he was not a member of the tribe of the Levi and thus ineligible to occupy a priestly role. Samuel the prophet rebuked Saul for his disobedience to God and called it idolatry. Knox thus equated the invention of Saul with the sin of idolatry.

A further illuminating example came from papal history. Pope Gregory devised a litany using the invocation of saints for the purpose of honoring God. According to Knox, 80 priests died within an hour after they recited Pope Gregory's prayer. Catholic historians attributed this disaster to contagious air and the plague. Knox, however, saw it as a dramatic example of God's wrath poured out on those who without biblical warrant invented worship practices and thus introduced a false, diabolical religion into the church. Knox also concluded that the invocation of saints

24. *Works,* 3:33.
25. Ibid., 3:34f.

on the behalf of sinners detracted from the sacrifice of Christ by suggesting its insufficiency. Knox included a whole myriad of Roman practices including fasts, ceremonies, chastity of priests, vows, prayers of saints, and the Mass under the banner of gross idolatry. Satan and his brethren invented or inspired all of these idolatrous practices. Amazingly, they came to enjoy the blessing of the Roman Church as holy acts of piety!

Secondly, Knox took up his minor premise that the Mass is an invention of humanity and not rooted in Scripture. Some had defended the Mass as linked to the Hebrew word *Missa*, (the Latin name for the Mass), which signifies a gift or tribute from a servant to a master. Knox admitted his ignorance of Hebrew, but accepted the authority of the learned men who wrote that the word *Missa* had a Hebrew connection, but it is not a biblical word. Nowhere in Scripture is the biblical word *Missah* used as an oblation.

The Roman Church claims so but cannot prove Peter and James first celebrated the Mass. Knox argued that Pope Sixtus I instituted the altar of the Mass. From this point subsequent popes placed their own creative stamp on the Mass. Felix consecrated the altar, Pope Boniface commanded clean cloth on the altar, and Gregory the Great added candles and mandated that priests wear certain clothing. All of these developments flowed from the creative mind of humankind—hundreds of years after the Apostles—without the express warrant of Scripture. The Roman Church violates the clear teaching of Christ in the gospels when they reserve the cup only for themselves. Knox drove home his conclusion of the syllogism: despite good intentions, papists have added their opinions and inventions. The Mass is thus proven, Knox argued, to be idolatry.

Second Syllogism

After proving the logic of his proposition and subsequent conclusion (at least to his own satisfaction) Knox then preceded to his second syllogism. "All honoring, or service to God, whereunto is added a wicked opinion, is abomination. Unto the Mass is added a wicked opinion. Therefore it is abomination." Knox repeated several of his previous arguments with some slight nuance. He critiqued the Mass on the basis of its sacrificial nature. Citing Hebrews chapter ten, Knox argued Christ's sacrifice was perfect and need not be repeated. Convinced Paul wrote Hebrews, Knox attacked the Catholic retort that the Mass was not a sacrifice. He offered the following rebuttal: "A sacrifice for sin was never perfect until the beast offered was slain. If in your Mass you offer Jesus Christ for sin . . . then necessarily in your Mass must you need kill Jesus Christ."[26] Readers were left with the only conclusion: every Mass was a re-sacrifice of Christ.

Knox concluded his speech contrasting the Lord's Supper with the Mass. In the Supper we become eternal debtors to God. By contrast, in the Mass, God becomes a debtor to us for the sacrifice of Christ we repeatedly offer. Rome had profaned the Mass into a kind of lucky charm, attaching to it miraculous powers. Priests dress up with peculiar vestments and offer the Mass for rain, for peace, on behalf of sick animals, and even the relief of a toothache! After a thorough critique of the "papists" and the teaching of their "malignant kirk," Knox changes the tone and ends on a pastoral note. He claims that in his logical arguments, he is not trying to "trap men with words." His primary concern is truth. He promised to pray for his listeners and asks that they would in turn pray for him. He desires the blessing of the Spirit of God in order to speak the truth as a true messenger of God.

A SUMMARY OF THE LORD'S SUPPER

Between 1550 and 1553 Knox continued to develop his understanding of the reformation of worship according to Scripture. In Berwick, Knox instructed his congregation to remain seated during the Lord's Supper. He believed those who knelt while taking Communion might unwittingly "adore the elements and ascribe to them magical properties and thus commit idolatry." Both the Roman liturgy and the *First Book of Common Prayer* (1549) taught the "popish doctrine of the body presence of Christ in the Supper."[27] Fellow reformers John Hooper and John à Lasco concurred with Knox's opposition to kneeling. His strong opinions regarding worship would lead to periodic conflict throughout Knox's career.

If Knox wrote in a polemic tone in his critique of the Mass, his very brief summary of the meaning of the Lord's Supper is positive, affirming, and beautifully written. It would be hard to improve on Knox's elegant balance of the spiritual and mysterious versus the material and earthly

26. John Knox, *Selected Practical Writings of John Knox, Public, Epistles, Treatises, and Expositions to the Year 1559,* Kevin Reed, ed., (Dallas, Texas: Presbyterian Heritage Publications, 1995), 35. Hereafter cited as *Selected Writings.*

27. *Works,* 3:80.

nature of the Lord's Supper. First, the reformer urged people to "confess that it is a holy action, ordained of God, in . . . which the Lord Jesus by earthly and visible things set before us, lifts us up unto heavenly and invisible things." Afterwards "when [Christ] had prepared his spiritual banquet, he witnessed that he himself was the lively bread wherewith our souls are fed unto an everlasting life."[28]

Knox defended the idea of the spiritual presence of Christ in the Supper whereby our spirits are joined with the Spirit of God and elevated to commune with the Godhead. Feeding on Christ spiritually nourishes us as a means of our growth in godliness. It is also a means of uniting and strengthening the Church of Christ. In the last two paragraphs, Knox once again goes on the offensive citing Scripture and selected church fathers to prove that belief in transubstantiation will lead to eternal damnation. What God requires is faith in the finished work of Christ, which has "pacified his Father's wrath toward us."[29] Belief in the bread and wine as the transubstantiated body and blood of Christ as an article of faith will lead to eternal damnation.

A DECLARATION OF THE NATURE
AND OBJECT OF PRAYER

In the summer of 1551, on the strength of his preaching the crown transferred Knox from the relatively remote area of Berwick to the town of Newcastle. One year later the Privy Council promoted him again, this time to London as one of King Edward's six chaplains. Northumberland—the second Regent to the boy king Edward—soon recommended that Knox fill the vacant bishop's chair in Rochester and the pulpit of Allhallows in London.[30] Knox turned down both offers, apparently without any hint of gratitude. Historians generally interpret Northumberland's gesture as a political maneuver, intended to reduce Knox's influence on the impressionable King Edward VI at court.[31]

When King Edward's health began to fail, Northumberland grew increasingly fearful about his own security. Mary Tudor, Edward's half sister and a practicing Roman Catholic, was the rightful heir to the

28. Reed, *Selected Writings*, 67.

29. Ibid., 68–69.

30. *Works*, 3:79–88.

31. Ridley, *John Knox*, 115.

throne. Northumberland thought that he had placated Mary by tolerating her participation in the Mass. By contrast Knox denounced this practice of "idolatry" in the strongest terms—first in a Christmas sermon he preached at Newcastle and then before King Edward in the Lenten sermons of 1553.[32] From the time of his evangelical conversion until his death, Knox was relentless in his condemnation of the Roman Mass.

When Knox refused the second church offered to him, the Privy Council summoned him to appear. His refusal and lack of gratitude had naturally insulted Northumberland and others who labored on his behalf. The Council posed three questions for Knox. Why did he refuse the benefice offered to him? Did he find the rites and practices of the Church of England unacceptable? Was kneeling at the Lord's Table an indifferent practice or was it a serious matter? Knox did not say so, but he probably refused the offers knowing that King Edward's days were numbered. If Mary Tudor, a sincere Roman Catholic, became queen and found Knox in the position of bishop or rector of Allhallows he would have been considered a "marked man." He thought it safer to minister in a less prominent position.

Questions two and three were related. Knox found several rites of the Church of England, including kneeling, objectionable because they were not specifically mandated in Scripture. He answered that Christ did not kneel at the Supper, nor should we kneel. "Kneeling was man's addition or imagination." Instead, we should follow the example of Christ as we sit at the Lord's Table. It is notable that Knox did not repeat the inflammatory language of idolatry found in his treatise on the Mass. Both questions relate to the inventions of humankind, and neither follow the express warrant of Scripture. On this occasion Knox was remarkably dispassionate regarding a topic where his passions ran high. He pulled his punches here without drawing the conclusion that this invention of humanity, despite its expression of piety, in fact constituted idolatry.

On the occasion of King Edward's death at age sixteen on July 6, 1553, Knox wrote a very brief tribute and prayer he called a "Confession." Like Ezra in the Old Testament, Knox blames himself as well as others for the judgment of God that was likely to follow. He confessed that we have abused "thy most holy word . . . and despised thy mercies." "We have little regarded the voice of thy prophets; thy threatenings we have esteemed

---

32. Ibid., 117–18, 121–26.

vanity."[33] He implored the Lord, "take not from us the light of thy Evangel and suffer no papistry [to] prevail in this realm." Knox prayed for God to "illuminate the heart of our sovereign lady, Queen Mary, with pregnant gifts of thy Holy Ghost, and inflame the hearts of her council with thy true fear and love."[34]

For a few months Knox enjoyed the freedom to preach to large crowds, but with a wary eye towards Mary—the new Roman monarch in London who proclaimed a temporary toleration of religion.[35] She proceeded cautiously at first, but with an entourage of Roman officials from Spain as her counselors, Mary began to reverse the reforms of Archbishop Cranmer and the continental reformers. In Knox's words, God's wrath was kindled against England because she was moving (spiritually speaking) back into the superstition of Egyptian bondage. In this sermon in Buckinghamshire, Knox introduced an image he would later make famous in his *First Blast of the Trumpet*. England was ruled by a headless monster because its supposed "head," Mary, could not be considered a legitimate "head."

Instructions on Prayer

Under these dire circumstances, Knox began writing his treatise on prayer. Being forced to flee England, he arrived in Dieppe, on the north coast of France in January 1554 where he completed his treatise. The treatise was very practical and aimed at Christians living under desperate circumstances under a (headless) Roman sovereign. Knox asked, "for whom should we pray?" "Principally for such of the household of faith as suffer persecution, and for commonwealths tyrannically oppressed."[36]

Knox divided his treatise into forty subdivisions, but actually repeated about five points. He began by arguing that a person cannot have true faith apart from fervent prayer. "It is like a fire without heat or a burning lamp without light." He defined prayer as an "earnest and familiar talking with God, to whom we declare our miseries, and whose support and help we implore and desire in our adversaries and whom we laud and praise

---

33. *Works*, 3:166.
34. Ibid., 3:107.
35. Ibid., 3:87. See also Percy, *John Knox*, 132.
36. *Works*, 3:103.

for our benefits received."[37] When we pray we should keep in mind the majesty and might of the God to whom we pray. He is "the omnipotent Creator of heaven and earth."

Knox implored his readers to pray with a clear focus without the burdens of the world clouding their minds. We must be on guard because Satan works overtime when we attempt to pray. He diverts our attention and distorts our thinking. The Spirit of God, however, helps us battle our adversary. The Spirit does our bidding and gives us strength and courage in the face of adversity and confusion. It is the Spirit who prevents us from rambling and vain repetition, which only impedes what Knox calls "perfect prayer." Perfect prayer, Knox argued, demands that our hearts be inflamed with continual fear, honor, and love of God. We can come with confidence and offer our prayer because of the infinite goodness of God. God knows what is best and thus sometimes delays our childish craving for instant gratification.

"Perfect prayer" demands we come with clean hands and a pure heart because sin and a proud heart without repentance separate us from a holy God. Confession and repentance of our sins assured us that the rich mercy of God in Christ is ours. Fasting and alms deeds do not bribe God to answer our prayers, but reflect the depth of our sincerity. John Knox, Huldrych Zwingli, and Martin Bucer were among the reformers who promoted the practice of fasting. Professor W. Ian P. Hazlett suggests Knox may have learned this from George Wishart, who promoted it as a necessary component of Protestant piety.[38]

Knox took the precept, "pray without ceasing," not merely as prudent spiritual counsel, but as a command. Failure to pray in times of trouble is tantamount to denying God. It is also a command with a promise: Ask and you shall receive, seek and ye shall find. Just as a father loves to give his child a gift, so our heavenly father loves to shower his children with rich blessings.

Because of our fallen condition we are unable to appear before God, but our most merciful father has rescued us from our plight. Paraphrasing I Corinthians, I John and Hebrews, Knox reminds the believer of their right standing with God. Jesus Christ, our only mediator, has fully atoned for our offences. "We are clad that we may with boldness . . . appear before the

37. Ibid., 3:73.

38. Roger A. Mason, ed., *John Knox and the British Reformations* (Brookfield, VT: Ashgate Publishing Limited, 1998), 179f.

throne of God's mercy; doubting nothing but whatever we ask of our me-diator, we shall obtain most assuredly . . . ."[39] Knox quoted the Church Father Ambrose regarding the uniqueness of Christ: "For He alone is our mouth, by whom we speak to God. He is our eyes by whom we see God, and also our right hand by whom we offer anything unto the Father."[40]

Knox raised the question: do our prayers apply to spiritual benefits alone, or do they include material blessings? He answered that we can in-deed petition the Lord for material blessings, though he adds two caveats. First, we must check our conscience to ensure that we are at peace with God and depending on Christ alone. Secondly, we must acknowledge that gifts come only from God, not by chance, accident or the fruit of our own labor. Praying for and receiving the blessings of God give us a "taste of his sweetness" and are a means of our growth in grace and thanksgiving.

Knox used the occasion of his treatise on prayer to point out and ridicule common practices in both the Protestant and Roman Church. Knox specifically eliminated the prayers to saints and those to the Virgin Mary. Speaking on Matthew 18:20, "wherever two or three be gathered together in my name," Knox commented on the word "gathered." "I mean not to hear piping, singing, or playing; nor to patter upon beads or books whereof they have no understanding; nor to commit idolatry, honoring that for God which is no God indeed."[41]

The treatise ends on a note of triumph regarding the coming kingdom of God. We should not be surprised if judgment comes because it begins in the house of the Lord. Here Knox wrote not from a lofty ivory tower perch, but from genuine concern that Protestant Christians in England could expect persecution throughout the regime of Mary Tudor. When such persecution comes, he counseled, we must look with confidence to the future and the God who holds the future. Sin and death will end. God will defeat our enemies and deliver his people. Even in times of persecu-tion and trouble, all honor and praise belong to our Savior Jesus Christ.

EPISTLES TO MRS. BOWES

The letters of John Knox reveal a pastoral side of the reformer not evident in his theological treatises. About 50 of Knox's letters survive and nearly

39. *Works,* 3:94.
40. Ibid., 3:97.
41. Ibid., 3:73.

30 of them were written to Mrs. Elizabeth Bowes, a member of his con-gregation in Berwick.[42] In this parish, Knox met a woman who became a lifetime friend and spiritual counselor. Mrs. Bowes later became Knox's mother-in-law. In 1555 he married her daughter Marjory, despite the ob-jections of the family patriarch Sir Robert Bowes. Elizabeth Bowes lived in constant dread that she was not a genuine Christian. Most likely Knox played a significant role in Mrs. Bowes' conversion to the evangelical faith, but she suffered from a lack of assurance. Knox's letters certainly con-tributed to Mrs. Bowes' spiritual growth and served for her as a creative replacement of the Catholic confessional.

Knox's public writings demonstrate a man capable of abusive rheto-ric aimed at those engaged in idolatry. In private, however, Knox could show deep love, patience, profound respect, and empathy for women. The nineteenth-century writer, Robert Lewis Stevenson, had it right when he said Knox "was vehement in affection, as in doctrine." His sympathetic ear has earned him the label, "Pastor of Souls," from the late William Stanford Reid.[43] Knox demonstrated his deep sympathy and compassion for Mrs. Bowes. He informed her of his willingness to rearrange his schedule of prayer and study to help her. He told her privately he was a fellow com-panion in her spiritual troubles, and her letters pierced his heart. On rare occasions, Knox changed from compassionate Father confessor to stern prophet—warning of potential danger and mixing empathy and anger.

For many years biographers of Knox dismissed Mrs. Bowes as some-thing of a "religious hypochondriac."[44] The biography by Edwin Muir in 1929, however, represents a shift in the Bowes' historiography. While still in the shadow, the portrayal of Mrs. Bowes is much more balanced. Muir suggested the letters benefited both parties. Knox, Muir argued, needed Mrs. Bowes and the attention she gave him. "He needed a feminine in-timacy, an intimacy on the one side almost maternal . . . . Mrs. Bowes

---

42. A. Daniel Frankforter, "Correspondence with Women: The Case of John Knox," *Journal of Rocky Mt. Medieval and Renaissance Association* 6 (1985): 160.

43. W. Stanford Reid, "John Knox, Pastor of Souls," *The Westminster Theological Journal* 40 (Fall 1963):1f. Reid's comments on the pastoral side of Knox provide a help-ful balance to the negative assessment Knox often received. See also Richard Kyle, *The Ministry of John Knox: Pastor, Preacher, and Prophet* (Lewiston, New York: The Edwin Mellon Press, 2002).

44. Andrew Lang, *John Knox and the Reformation* (New York: Longmans, Green and Co., 1905), 43.

fulfilled the conditions to perfection."[45] A further shift occurred in the scholarship of Professor A. Daniel Frankforter in the 1960s. He emphasized the reciprocal benefits of the Knox-Bowes' correspondence. He found the letters valuable because they reveal "the subtle influence some ordinary women had on the famous man from whom they sought advice and reassurance."[46]

In Frankforter's research, Knox, not Mrs. Bowes is denigrated. The French scholar, Pierre Janton, suggested Knox suffered from a neurosis, a mother fixation.[47] Frankforter gave Mrs. Bowes a clean bill of health and saw her as developing and maturing. No longer an unstable neurotic or spiritual hypochondriac, she is now a colleague with Knox on a spiritual pilgrimage. "Despite her lack of theological training, Mrs. Bowes clearly saw the mysteries that lay at the center of Protestant preaching . . . . It was not simply as a model of Christian endurance that she inspired Knox, but more as a thinker whose questions keep pace with his own."[48] Colleague or not, the Knox-Bowes' correspondence is valuable on several levels. It reveals some of the general angst of the period; it demonstrates the challenges of faithful Christian living in a split family; and it shows a compassionate side of John Knox unfamiliar to many readers.[49]

45. Edwin Muir, *John Knox: Portrait of a Calvinist* (New York: Kennikat Press, 1929, reprint ed., 1972), 32.

46. Frankforter, "Correspondence with Women," 160. The reciprocal nature of this relationship is not as clear to other scholars. See for example, Diane Willen, "Godly Women in Early Modern Europe: Puritanism and Gender," *Journal of Ecclesiastical History* 43 (October 1992): 577 and note number 88. Some modern writers continue to refer to Mrs. Bowes as neurotic. See M. Charles Bell, *Calvin and Scottish Theology* (Edinburgh: The Handsel Press, 1985), 64, and endnote number 39.

47. Pierre Janton, *John Knox: L'homme et l'oeuvre* (Paris: Didier, 1967), 51, cited in Frankforter, "Correspondence with Women," 160.

48. A. Daniel Frankforter, "Elizabeth Bowes and John Knox: A Woman and Reformation Theology," *Church History* 56 (September 1987): 346–47.

49. Christine M. Newman, "The Reformation and Elizabeth Bowes: A Study of a Sixteenth Century Northern Gentlewoman," *Studies in Church History* 27 (1990): 328. Again, Diane Willen cautions readers against overuse of the notion of a brief feminist impulse in Tudor England, "Women and Religion in Early Modern England," in *Women in Reformation and Counter-Reformation Europe: Public and Private Worlds*, Sherrin Marshall ed., (Bloomington, IN: Indiana University Press, 1989), 141.

The Assurance of Salvation

The recurring spiritual problem faced by Mrs. Bowes involved her assurance of salvation. She wondered how she could be certain. Knox addressed her repeated questions with essentially the same Christocentric answer. Her security, like her salvation, did not depend on her performance or good behavior, but in the work of Christ. Employing Christian doctrine, Knox negated the notion that salvation depends on works. Mrs. Bowes committed the common error of making her sanctification the basis of her justification.

Some of Knox's clearest teaching on the doctrine of divine election can be found in his answers to Mrs. Bowes. It was not an arcane topic for pedantic theologians, but a very practical doctrine. The suffering she faced, Knox argued, clearly indicated she was one of the elect. "The elect of God suffer, as they have done from the beginning. And why shall we rejoice with them?" Knox explained, "Because it is a sure seal and testimony of that word which we profess."[50] Knox also used this argument in letter number VIII: ". . . the manifold and general assaults of the Devil raging against you and troubling your rest . . . doth certify unto me your very election, which the Devil envies in all the chosen of God."[51]

Mrs. Bowes also struggled with the concept of a sovereign God when she read the Scripture where God says, "it repenteth me that I made Saul king." This Scripture both perplexed and distressed her. She asked Knox for an explanation: Could Saul enjoy the blessings of God as one of his chosen and then subsequently be cut off? What assurance did she have that this could not happen to her? Knox's explanation of the biblical language resembled John Calvin's principle of God using accommodated language to communicate with us. "He means not, that Saul at any time was a member of Christ's body . . . ."[52] When God says repent, Knox declared "we must understand him to speak after the manner of men, [addressing] himself to our understanding . . . for understanding . . . you shall consider, that the Spirit of God must . . . submit himself oftentimes to our weakness, and speak unto us who, by corruption, are made ignorant and

---

50. *Works*, 3:356.

51. Ibid., 3:364–65.

52. Ibid., 3:358.

rude . . . ." This is done in order "that we may understand what he works by his incomprehensible wisdom and inscrutable providence." [53]

Mrs. Bowes questioned how she could possibly be a child of God when she faced constant trouble and tribulation. Knox assured her the attacks by Satan were all part of God's plan. These attacks come "not without permission of our heavenly Father, to further mortification of this wicked flesh. Every son [or daughter] whom the Father loveth, he chasteneth." [54] Sometimes, according to Knox, God "does turn away his face apparently even from the elect, and then they are in anguish . . . but mercifully returns he unto them, and gives gladness and consolation." [55]

On one occasion Mrs. Bowes told Knox she was terrified because she had committed the sin unto death. Knox believed she didn't know what that meant! He explained the sin unto death involved blasphemy of the word of life. "I am most surely persuaded in the Lord Jesus, that your heart shall never do [such a thing.]" Again, Knox explained that her security rested in Christ "You are engrafted in the body, and by Him you shall be defended." [56] As a result Knox could reassure Mrs. Bowes: "I am even equally certified of your election in Christ, as I . . . preach Christ to be the only savior. I have more signs of your election that presently I can commit to write." [57]

While Knox extended great patience with Mrs. Bowes, he made it clear she should not be so self-absorbed. She was not the only one with troubles. Hostile critics and people with health problems constantly bothered Knox. When he met with Sir Robert Bowes—the family patriarch—to request the hand of Elizabeth's daughter Marjory in marriage, Bowes emphatically rejected any such possibility. According to Knox, Sir Robert Bowes' words were disdainful: "yea, despiteful words have so pierced my heart, that life is bitter unto me. I bear a good countenance with a sore troubled heart." In such sorrow Knox demonstrated his trust in Christ. "Afflictions trouble me at this present, but yet I doubt not to overcome, by Him who will not leave me comfortless." [58]

53. Ibid.
54. Ibid., 3:355.
55. Ibid., 3:356.
56. Ibid., 3:369.
57. Ibid.
58. Ibid., 3:378.

PAPERS FOUND BY LORIMER

In 1875 Peter Lorimer—Professor of Theology at English Presbyterian College—published a book titled *John Knox and the Church of England*. This volume is based in large part upon documents never before published and thus not included in the collected *Works* of Knox, edited by David Laing in mid century. Lorimer found the papers in the Morrice Collection of manuscripts in the library of dissenter, Dr. Williams in London.[59] Remarkably, several distinguished historians had used these papers in their research—including Daniel Neal (1678–1743), best known for his *History of the Puritans* published in 1844. Neal and company apparently assumed these four documents, written between late 1549 and late 1552, were already in print and thus paid them no particular attention.

Lorimer deemed the documents significant enough to write a new book on the role of Knox in the early history of the Church of England and in the development of the *Book of Common Prayer*. Furthermore, he argued that the papers secured Knox a place in the "Knoxian" or Puritan wing of the church. The first two address the issue of kneeling while receiving the elements of Communion. The third paper is merely an annotated outline of what Knox used while serving the Lord's Supper in Berwick. Lorimer found a fourth document—written to John Knox by an unknown author and by a separatist church member—reacting to Knox's advice regarding worship and the marks of the true church of Christ. Knox and the writer of Puritan sympathies share much in common. He assured Knox they "would not go back again to the wafer-cake and kneeling, and to other knackles of Popery."[60] The Puritan sympathizer, however, resented some of Knox's advice. This cryptic letter illustrates the divisive nature of Protestant worship and foreshadowed the challenges Knox would soon face at the exile congregation in Frankfurt.

EPISTLE TO THE CONREGATION OF BERWICK

Knox began his epistle by encouraging his former congregation to walk worthy of their calling. He reminded them how "odious and detestable

59. Peter Lorimer, *John Knox and the Church of England: His Work in Her Pulpit and His Influence Upon Her Liturgy, Articles and Parties* (London: Henry S. King & Co., 1875, reprint edition, Kessinger Publishing), v and 245f.

60. Ibid., 300.

sin is in the sight of our heavenly Father."[61] His account of the passion of Christ in payment for our sins could not help but inspire his readers to live holy lives. He offered a biblically balanced view of justification by grace through faith alone and an anathema against those who denied the enduring quest for sanctification. Knox writes, "if any deny good works to be profitable or not necessary to a true Christian profession, let the ... maintainers of such a doctrine be accursed ...."[62]

One can safely interpret Knox as already moving beyond the Lutheran law/gospel hermeneutic with a strong emphasis on sanctification. In so many words, Knox is saying the covenant of works has never been abrogated. Knox also reminded his readers that God severely punishes sin, even the sin of the elect. God is eternal and unchanging and the sins he punished in one age, he will punish in another.[63]

Knox assumed a prophetic role in his second reason for writing. He warned the congregation regarding the certainty of coming persecution. He no doubt calculated the calamity which could fall upon Protestants if the sickly King Edward died. It is clear he had the Roman Church in mind when he warned them not to be taken in "if even an angel from heaven shall teach you another gospel."[64] Such cursed teaching included those who denied justification by faith alone or taught people to pray to someone other than God alone. The same pathos he demonstrated towards the spiritual crises of Mrs. Bowes is used now towards his beloved former congregation at Berwick. With tears he prayed for the church in Berwick.[65]

Despite Knox's genuine sincerity, the real purpose for writing was to explain what appeared to be an about face on the practice of kneeling during the Lord's Supper. While in Berwick, Knox preached with great vehemence: the proper posture during Communion was sitting not kneeling. He now goes on to explain why kneeling is an acceptable practice. Previously, Knox the puritan called kneeling during Communion "idolatry." The new "moderate" Knox now writes, "but as for ceremonies or rites, things of smaller weight" we can accept out of deference to our fathers

61. Ibid., 252.
62. Ibid., 259.
63. Ibid., 253.
64. Ibid., 257.
65. Ibid., 260.

and brothers, and so as not to trouble the "common order."[66] He makes it clear he much prefers sitting to kneeling, but he no longer uses the vehement language of idolatry to describe the practice. Knox also wrote this epistle to rebut the hint that the promotion to the King's court had not turned him into a hypocrite. His enemies apparently used his change of heart as a weapon to bludgeon him. He explained that he made the case in London, but the authorities prevented him from going further.

Archbishop Cranmer responded to Knox's requirement for an explicit command from Scripture for kneeling by labeling Knox an "Anabaptist!" Cranmer told Knox: "this . . . is the chief foundation of the error of the Anabaptists, and of diverse other sects. This saying is a subversion of all order as well in religion as in common policy."[67] Knox thus concluded such an issue was not worthy of generating the wrath of church officials. More important, they all agreed in principle. Kneeling did not constitute veneration of the elements, nor did such a practice promote superstition. With this understanding, Knox used his influence among his readers to encourage the practice of kneeling to avoid a "breach of charity." As Knox explained, it was "only for uniform order to be kept, and that for a time, in this Church of England."[68]

MEMORIAL TO THE PRIVY COUNCIL

In late October the Privy Council submitted the Articles of Religion (numbering 45) to the six royal chaplains for their "learned judgments." Specifically, they scrutinized the thirty-eighth article (later number 35), which directed the posture of kneeling while taking Communion. The author (no doubt Knox) stated his objections to kneeling in three points. He quotes the apostle Paul who wrote, "flee idolatry." Even if idolatry were not the intent of the one kneeling, it would unwittingly promote such an interpretation. Knox argued that it edifies no one and offends many. God told Moses to "destroy the altars, cut down their groves and beat to powder their images . . . lest they pluck your hearts from serving the Lord."[69] Early in his reign, young King Edward VI earned the title "King Josiah" for emulat-

---

66. Ibid, 261.

67. Diarmaid MacCulloch, *Thomas Cranmer* (New Haven: Yale University Press, 1996), 526.

68. *Works*, 3:261.

69. Lorimer, *John Knox and the Church of England*, 268.

ing the reforming efforts of the boy King. Like Josiah, Edward wanted to pull down the pagan altars and bring the nation back to a pure worship of God.[70] For Knox, the practice of kneeling constituted a reversal of form, and a huge, dangerous step back to Romanism. He believed the nation risked judgment and destruction if they offended God on this point.

Secondly, Knox argued that kneeling would offend the weaker brothers. If converts are told to follow the example of Christ, they would find it odd to engage in a practice Christ himself did not promote. Thirdly, the requirement of kneeling would constitute aid and comfort of those inclined toward idolatry. Paul tells us to abstain from the appearance of evil. Even for indifferent practices, we should be on the safe side and abstain from kneeling.

Knox then gave the positive arguments on why sitting is preferable to kneeling. Kneeling is the posture for beggars. We, however, are not beggars, but in fact by the grace of God we are rich in Christ. "We are the children of God, priests and kings united in by Christ's blood."[71]

With the exception of the addition of his commentary on the celebration of Passover, Knox's arguments here are not new. Perhaps influenced by the published work of Polish reformer John à Lasco—who served the exile community in London in the so-called "Stranger Church"[72]—Knox argued for the continuity of the remembrance of Passover, the annual commemoration of God's deliverance of his people from Egypt and the Lord's Supper. Joshua continued the commemoration by preparing the elect for their entrance into the land of Canaan. This work prefigured the work of the second Joshua, namely, Jesus. Christ Jesus, the perfect lamb of God, satisfied the demands of God and dissolved the old practice of standing to take the Passover meal. From this point the commemoration of Christ's sacrifice was to be joined to Christ at the Lord's Table. Like Joshua who would lead his people to the promised land, Jesus was the only mediator to God the Father who atoned for the sins of his people and prepared the way to the eternal promised land.

70. Christopher Bradshaw, "David or Josiah? Old Testament Kings as Exemplars in Edwardian Religious Polemic," in Bruce Gordon, ed., *Protestant History and Identity in Sixteenth-Century Europe,* 2 vols., (Brookfield, VT: Scholar Press, 1996), 2:77–90.

71. Lorimer, *John Knox and the Church of England,* 272; James Simpson, *Burning to Read: English Fundamentalism and its Reformation Opponents* (Cambridge, MA: Harvard University Press, 2007), 15–17.

72. Ibid., 284–89. See Lorimer's discussion regarding John à Lasco.

The council refused to accept the whole of Knox's objection, but the solution—the so-called "black rubric"—called for an inserted patch into the prayer book, mandating kneeling but explaining no adoration or superstition of the elements was intended.

4

The Exile Years:
The Education of a Reformer (1554–1556)

JOHN KNOX CONTRIBUTED TO the advance of the reform movement not only in England and Scotland, but also in Germany, France, and Geneva. Within months of Mary Tudor's accession to the throne, life for a convinced Protestant like Knox became untenable in England. Knox thus left England in January 1554 with uncertainty and deep sorrow. He feared the Church in England would experience a complete reversal of the reforms he and others had vigorously promoted during the previous four years.

With her Spanish entourage firmly in place, Mary sought to punish the Protestant heresy. Some modern scholarship seeks to divert blame from Mary. These scholars merely make her a pawn of ruthless fanatics—who pushed her to order the barbaric murders of nearly 300 men and women in the flames of Smithfield. Professor T.M. Parker also takes a rather benign position regarding Mary's guilt. "It was the tragedy of Mary Tudor to be a logical woman in an illogical and confused situation."[1]

It was not confusion, however, but the clarity of Mary's intent to restore Catholicism in England that led to the exile of over 800 Protestants to the Continent. They came to live in places such as Strasbourg, Zurich, Emden, Wesel, Frankfurt, and Geneva. Professor W. Stanford Reid warns against extending any pity for the exiled John Knox. He notes that colonies of Scottish merchants lived in the French ports of Bordeaux, LaRochelle, Lehavre, Rouen, and Dieppe—places where Knox could easily find fellow Scots and co-religionists.[2] The exile years actually provided an invalu-

1. T. M. Parker, *The English Reformation to 1558* (Oxford: Oxford University Press, 1966), 126.
2. W. Stanford Reid, *Trumpeter of God* (New York: Charles Scribner's Sons, 1974),

able experience for Knox. In Europe he rubbed shoulders with leaders of the Reformation and discussed strategies for reforming his native land. Eustace Percy says the exile made a European out of a provincial Scot.[3]

Knox traveled first to Geneva where he conferred with John Calvin about the ethics of female sovereignty and began developing his theory of resistance against tyrannical rulers. While in Geneva, he received an urgent request for his pastoral leadership in Frankfurt. Knox enjoyed his surroundings in Geneva and did not wish to leave this stimulating environment, but on the urging of Calvin, Knox reluctantly accepted the call of the English exiles in Frankfurt.

Knox's leadership came under serious assault in Frankfurt. The English exiles in Frankfurt, numbering about 200, called Knox and fellow exile Thomas Lever as their pastors. Troubles over the correct form of worship quickly led to Knox's expulsion. A majority of the congregation favored the second Edwardian prayer book, while Knox insisted on using an English translation of a Geneva liturgy.[4] Knox faced formidable opposition in one Dr. Richard Cox—chancellor of Oxford University, Dean of Westminster, and veteran of prayer book committees. Knox objected to the second prayer book because he could not find biblical support for some of its contents.[5] On liturgical practices, Knox differed somewhat from Calvin. In a letter to Knox, Calvin urged rejection of the Mass and superstitious practices, but toleration of some liturgical traditions which lacked precise biblical proof.[6]

As a result of some behind the scenes lobbying by the Cox party, the Frankfurt city council ordered Knox to stop preaching, an order Knox found impossible to obey. Following his expulsion from Frankfurt in March, Knox returned to Geneva where he would labor periodically as

---

105–6. See also, Thomas M'Crie, *The Life of John Knox*, (1812) abridged reprint ed., (Glasgow: Free Presbyterian Publications, 1976), 69. M'Crie portrays Dieppe as Knox's home away from home. By contrast see, H. Y. Reyburn, "Calvin and Scotland," *Records of the Scottish Church History Society* 1 no. 4 (1926): 209.

3. Lord Eustace Percy, *John Knox* (Richmond, VA: John Knox Press, 1966), 71.

4. N.M. Sutherland, "The English Refugees at Geneva, 1555–1559," *History Today* 27 (December 1977): 780–81.

5. A. G. Dickens, *The English Reformation* (New York: Schocken Books, 1969), 290–91.

6. Sutherland, "English Refugees," 780–81. See also Reyburn, "Calvin and Scotland," 209–16, and John Calvin, *Letters of John Calvin*, 4 vols., Jules Bonnet, ed., Marcus Robert Gilchrist, translator, (1858; reprint ed., New York: Burt Franklin, 1972), 4:184. This letter touches on the Mass and other practices that the reformers found repugnant.

the co-pastor of a church until his move to Scotland in the spring of 1559. While Geneva attracted an impressive assembly of theologians, scholars, and churchmen, John Calvin became Knox's most revered mentor. Five years before they met, Knox began reading Calvin's writings. In 1550, while a pastor in Berwick, Knox cited Calvin's sermons on Jeremiah and may have completed reading Calvin's *Institutes* at the same time.[7] In these exile years, Knox the busy pastor, husband, and father penned some of his most influential and his most notorious writings.

EPISTLE ON THE SIXTH PSALM

The thirty letters Knox wrote to Mrs. Bowes represent only part of his counseling efforts on her behalf. He also wrote a forty plus page treatise titled *An Exposition Upon the 6th Psalm of David* for the express purpose of offering hope to this sister who found herself in deep despair. He wrote it during the first half of January 1554 while in England, and then finished it the last day of February from the port city of Dieppe, France.[8]

In his effort to bring peace of mind to the very troubled soul of Mrs. Bowes, Knox used numerous examples from the Old Testament. Perhaps Mrs. Bowes could find a spiritual soul mate in David who "was sorely tormented . . . drinking some large portion of the cup of God's wrath."[9] The similarity of vexation between David and Mrs. Bowes is striking. She echoes David when he wrote, "O Lord, I feel what is the weight and strength of thy displeasure. I have experienced how intolerable is the heaviness of thy hand."[10] Knox insisted Mrs. Bowes learn well Job and David's lesson

7. W. Stanford Reid, "John Knox and His Interpreters," *Renaissance and Reformation* 10 (1974): 19. See also, Richard G. Kyle, *The Mind of John Knox* (Lawrence, KS: Coronado Press, 1984), 103.

8. Reid, *Trumpeter of God*, 118, 143. See also, Jasper Ridley, *John Knox* (Oxford: Oxford University Press, 1968), 164–66.

9. John Knox, Kevin Reed, ed., *Selected Writings of John Knox: Public Epistles, Treatises, and Expositions to the Year 1559* (Dallas: Presbyterian Heritage Publications, 1995), 105. Hereafter cited as *Selected Writings*. Reed has modernized the spelling and provides occasional explanations for archaic words. Reed also provides chapter and verse references in the margins, an improvement from David Laing, Knox's nineteenth-century editor of the collected *Works* who only provides the chapter references. The first English Bible to include both chapter and verse references was the *Geneva Bible* of 1560. Knox was the first to quote the *Geneva Bible* in print in his treatise on predestination against the Anabaptists.

10. *Selected Writings*, 105.

about the sovereignty of God. Both "prosperity and adversity" are gifts of God.[11] They are not the result of chance or fate. The question we all want answered is "why"? Why do the elect feel the anger and displeasure of God? Knox offered Mrs. Bowes three answers to these questions.

First of all, when we understand that sin is a root cause of our torment, it naturally guides us to a profound hatred of sin.[12] Such understanding leads to repentance and repentance to mercy. Again, from David's sin we see a model of God's mercy and forgiveness. The torment experienced by David led him "daily to fear, and earnestly to pray. It made him lowly, although he was a king; it made him merciful when he might have been rigorous."[13]

The second reason God ordains the elect sometimes to "taste the bitter cup" is to drive them to the central truth that our only hope is in Jesus Christ. We are so distracted by the cares of the world we forget it is God and God alone who gives us our daily bread.

Knox's third explanation for our troubles came from a lesson learned from Moses in Deuteronomy 7:22. The verse explained that the Lord would defeat Israel's enemies, "little by little . . . not . . . all at once." In this strategic delay of Israel's enemies, the Lord wanted to teach Israel trust and patience. If God suddenly slew all of the enemies of Israel, the wild beasts feeding on the corpses would multiply and pose a serious threat to God's covenant people. The Scots reformer applied this lesson to the wild beasts threatening God's people including "arrogance, oblivion and forgetfulness of the estate from which God had delivered us."[14] Knox explained to Mrs. Bowes: these sins "are the wild beasts that . . . devour no small number of men."[15] While we grow impatient in our suffering, it is in fact the vile tasting medicine God sends to heal us. Ironically, suffering is actually the medium for the healing power of Christ in our lives.

Psalm Six and Biblical Counseling

Part two of Knox's treatise to Mrs. Bowes focused on the first seven verses of Psalm chapter six. David made four requests of the Lord. He asked the

11. Ibid., 106.
12. Ibid., 109–10.
13. Ibid., 112.
14. Ibid., 115.
15. Ibid.

Lord to not punish him, to have mercy upon him, to heal him, and lastly to save his soul. Knox believed people (perhaps including Mrs. Bowes) had bought the lie of Satan, which said God is angry at us and does not want to hear us ask for help. This situation becomes a debilitating standoff because God is our only source of hope. Yet, we are tricked into ignoring God for fear his hot anger is aimed at us. We would rather ignore God, because of our fear of retribution, than humble ourselves and find certain relief in the mercy of God.

In his encouragement of Mrs. Bowes, Knox found three "grounds" or "foundations" why we should patiently place our trust in God for deliverance.[16] First, David knew that in the economy of God, sin has consequences. David was guilty of grievous sin and knew God's justice demanded punishment. At the same time, David confidently believed God to be both just and merciful. The same God who judges and punishes David will also forgive and extend mercy. Those who repent of their sins and cry out to God are always assured God will hear them and heal their soul.

The second ground of our confidence resides in the infinite goodness of God. Knox assured Mrs. Bowes "only the goodness of God remains, in all storms, the sure foundation to the afflicted, against which the Devil is never able to prevail."[17] Finally, Knox argued David's assurance was "the glory and praise of God's name to be shown and uttered in this life."[18] Fearing God might take his life, David raised this question: how can I praise God if I am slain? According to David, it was not possible short of a miracle to declare the goodness and praise of God from the grave. David made this promise: if God spared his life, he would use his breath to praise the wondrous works of God. Mrs. Bowes had a lesson to learn, namely, to trust in the goodness of God and praise him even under the most difficult circumstances of life

A GODLY ADMONITION OR WARNING

Knox began the so-called *Godly Letter* before his exile and finished it in Dieppe, France. He addressed the treatise to his former congregations in Berwick and Newcastle, who under duress, ignorance or cowardice felt pressured to attend the Catholic Mass. Knox argued from both Scripture

16. Ibid., 129.
17. Ibid., 133.
18. Ibid., 137.

and history to make two simple points: attendance at the Mass was idolatry and God would judge the sin of idolatry unmercifully. He also offered a "simple" solution to circumvent God's certain judgment: "Avoid and flee as well in body as in spirit, all fellowship and society with idolaters."[19] Most of the historical allusions link England with Old Testament Judah. He suggested the sweating sickness, which killed many in Newcastle and Berwick, illustrated God's judgment on those who trifled with his law. The sermon was a passionate, sometimes repetitive message to believers to stand firm against the attack of Satan and his Catholic minions. The title page contains the text of Matthew 10:22b: "he that continues to the end shall be saved."[20] This treatise admonished his former congregations to persevere.

Knox as Jeremiah

Perhaps the most striking feature of this admonition against participation in the idolatrous Mass is Knox's use of the prophet Jeremiah. In this letter Knox paraphrased or quoted Jeremiah over 60 times. His use of Jeremiah in the *Godly Letter* and elsewhere has led to the observation that Jeremiah was Knox's favorite Old Testament source.[21] Throughout the letter, Knox cited Jeremiah and then followed with a direct application to England. Sometimes Knox followed the interpretive principle of identifying an Old Testament "type" and its corresponding "anti-type" or fulfillment found in the New Testament. In Knox's innovative model, however, Jeremiah and his pronouncements provided the type while Knox passed over the New Testament and found the fulfillment in sixteenth-century England. He saw an unrestricted continuity between the Old Testament and his own day. His interpretive model thus takes on a "presentist" quality that electrifies his message with tremendous power.

Knox's citations of Jeremiah contain more than mere historical, moral, and edifying instruction. They inspire Knox to prophecy toward England, which has become the sixteenth-century anti-type of Judah. The immanence of God looms large through the letters and sermons of

19. Ibid., 148.

20. John Knox, *The Works of John Knox* 6 Vols. ed. David Laing (Edinburgh: Printed for the Bannatyne Club, 1846–1864), 3:163.

21. Richard G. Kyle, "John Knox: A Man of the Old Testament," *Westminster Theological Journal* 54 (1992): 70 footnote 25, and 73, footnote 39. See also, Roger Mason ed., *John Knox on Rebellion* (Cambridge: Cambridge University Press, 1994), ix.

Knox—the sixteenth-century Jeremiah. In this model, Jeremiah and Knox became "partners" in the cosmic drama of redemption. Jeremiah used a model of warning and the certainty of judgment, followed by the promise of God's mercy and blessing on the basis of repentance. This two-fold message of "woe and promise" by Jeremiah is commonly called a "jeremiad." This sermonic technique has two identifying models: a preacher warns of declension from God's law and makes frequent references to Jeremiah utilizing the twofold message of woe and promise.

Knox believed England deserved God's judgment because it committed the same sins that plagued ancient Israel. He likened the Catholic Mass—defended by Stephen Gardiner the Bishop of Winchester—to the "doctrine of the Devil," indistinguishable from Baal worship. Knox asked from Jeremiah 11:15a and 17b: "What has my beloved to do in my house seeing that multitude commits abominable idolatry in it. They have provoked me to anger by burning incense unto Baal."[22] Whereas Jeremiah predicted the destruction of Jerusalem, Knox predicted "the city of London would be made a desert" if Jezebel (Queen Mary Tudor) required attendance at the Mass.[23]

England Equated to Judah

The Godly Letter evidenced another striking feature. Knox argued that the prophetic warnings given by the prophet Jeremiah were applicable to sixteenth-century England. Knox gave a three point historical summary of similarities between the two, and then concluded with five arguments that England deserved judgment more than Old Testament Judah. He contrasted the two nations with England emerging the "loser."

1. In Jerusalem, many people responded to God's prophets and fled, leaving their possessions in order to escape God's judgment. In England, however, God's prophets threatened and warned, but too many of God's people remain in order to protect their property.

2. In Jerusalem, when Jeremiah was falsely accused by "pestilent priests," princes and nobles defended him. But in England, few nobility speak in defense of God's messengers.

---

22. *Selected Writings*, 164.
23. Ibid., 167.

3. In Jerusalem, God's prophet enjoyed the liberty to speak and defend his doctrine. But in England, no such freedoms exist.

4. In Jerusalem, Ebed-melech defended Jeremiah against false charges of the priests, and saved the prophet's life. In England, however, no one defends God's people from the "blood-thirsty lions and their prey."

5. Jeremiah's captors fed him well in prison despite food short-ages throughout the city. But in London, where food is plentiful, God's servants go hungry and are treated worse than thieves and murderers.[24]

Knox knew his conclusion regarding England would anger some people. "It may offend you that I call England worse than unthankful Judah."[25] His point was clear. If Judah could not escape judgment, how could England ever expect to evade God's wrath?

The "Godly Letter" as a "Jeremiad"

Like the prophet Jeremiah, Knox tempered the certainty of God's judg-ment with his forgiveness and mercy. This sermon, like the later Puritan jeremiads, contains both woe and promise. Idolatry without repentance so angered God: the destruction of the offender is certain. If, however, we obey God, he demonstrates his mercy, his fatherly love, and affection.[26] Near the end of the Godly Letter, Knox gave clear summaries of the peril of unbelief and the blessings of obedience, a further example of the woe and promise. The person who refuses to practice idolatry may be forced to leave the country. The one guilty of idolatry, however, will spend eter-nity in hell. Refusing idolatry may result in the loss of earthly possessions. The idolater will by contrast lose his or her heavenly riches![27]

The power behind Knox's jeremiads stemmed from his belief in the immutability of God. This confidence in God's unchanging nature led Knox to predict God's impending judgment against England. Even a cursory reading of the Godly Letter reveals Knox's identification between biblical times and his own. Knox delivered his warnings with certainty based on

24. Ibid., 168–71.
25. Ibid., 169–70.
26. Ibid., 175.
27. Ibid., 190–91.

the "immutable justice" of God, an idea used repeatedly in the sermon.[28] The Scots reformer spoke of the "covenant of the Lord" to illustrate God's immutability, but covenant keeping demanded complete separation from idolatry. Knox found himself in something of a theological conundrum. He warned England they would lose the covenant—a position his theology did not in fact support.[29] Knox spoke of it as conditional and reciprocal based upon human obedience. It appears that politics—where he emphasized the conditional nature of the covenant—rather than theology drove Knox's initial writing on this subject.

Such language is consistent with the Rhineland reformers like Huldrych Zwingli and Heinrich Bullinger. John Calvin, however, later argued that Christ's offer of the covenant obligated him to fulfill it. The incarnation, death, and resurrection of Christ fulfilled the covenant promises. The sacraments attest to the finished work of Christ. Infant baptism signifies and seals the covenant.[30] Thus Knox should not be seen as a double dealer speaking out of both sides of his mouth. His own views on the covenant matured over time. In the *Godly Letter* Knox emphasized the human obligations as they relate to the covenant. In his later writing on infant baptism, Knox emphasized the permanence of God's covenant to his people.[31]

ANSWER TO SOME QUESTIONS ON OBEDIENCE TO MAGISTRATES

In a letter dated May 10, 1554 written from Dieppe, Knox explained his whereabouts since he left, or more properly, fled England. He writes, "since the 28th of January, I have traveled all through the congregations of Helvetia (Switzerland) and have reasoned with all the pastors and many other excellently learned men."[32] By March of 1554, Knox had made his way to Geneva in order to pose questions to John Calvin. The untimely

28. References in the *Godly Letter* to the immutability of God are found in *Works*, 3: 169, 171, 191–93, 196 and 201.

29. Richard Greaves, "John Knox and the Covenant Tradition," *Journal of Ecclesiastical History* 24 (January 1973): 24.

30. Leonard J. Trinterud, "The Origins of Puritanism," *Church History* 20 (March 1951): 44–45.

31. Greaves, "John Knox and the Covenant," notes at least three ways Knox used the word covenant, 26–27.

32. *Works*, 3:220.

death of the reform minded Edward VI, and the ascension of the Catholic regime of Mary Tudor, drove Knox out of England and into a safer exile on the Continent. Here he pondered the very real issues of a Christian's responsibility to an idolatrous ruler. Knox's questions—regarding civil disobedience and the ethics and duties of a Protestant to a Catholic monarch—were thus not merely theoretical questions. As noted above, Knox considered attendance at the Catholic Mass a blasphemous practice akin to worshipping idols.

While Knox was in Geneva, Calvin wrote a letter introducing him to Heinrich Bullinger (1504–1575), the successor to Zwingli in Zurich. Knox conferred with Bullinger. And in a letter dated March 26, 1554, Bullinger sent Calvin the answers that he gave to Knox, "the Scotsman whom you commended to me."[33]

Central Questions Regarding the Church, State and Citizenship

Knox posed four, somewhat loaded questions to Bullinger. Knox appeared to be seeking justification for promoting an active disobedience against the idolatrous policies of Queen Mary Tudor. While partially agreeing with Knox, in his response Bullinger urged caution and patience more than he recommended active or armed resistance. In most cases both the questions and answers below are simplified translations of the originals.

Q. Should a minor son who is in line to inherit the throne from his father be obeyed? Should he be regarded as a lawful magistrate?

A. Bullinger's short answer is "yes." While Knox did not mention Edward VI by name, Bullinger took the hint. Yes, Edward was the duly appointed king, and legitimately he held all the rights of a sovereign king despite his tender age. Bullinger went on to say young Edward (at least as it related to religious reform) proved to be a more godly king than his three immediate predecessors in England.

Q. Can a female preside over and rule a kingdom by divine right, and so transfer the right of sovereignty to her husband?

A. Both the Old and New Testaments teach that women are to be subject to men and not in a position to rule over them. Bullinger then adds an important modifier. If a woman is acknowledged by

33. Ibid., 3:219.

the people as the Queen and acts in compliance to the laws of the land, "it is a hazardous thing for godly persons to set themselves in opposition" [to her]. Bullinger noted according to Scripture, Philip the eunuch did not remove Candace from the kingdom of Ethiopia. If the Queen in question is not godly like Deborah but ungodly and tyrannical, God will in his own time and own way restore justice as needed. He cited Jerubbaal, the Maccabees, and Jehoiada as historical examples supporting his case that God's justice was certain.

The other question Knox raised concerned transferring the right of sovereignty from a queen to her husband. This issue stemmed from the real fear for England's religious future when Queen Mary announced her wedding plans to Philip II of Spain. Opposition to the Spanish marriage (July 24, 1554) contributed to the uprising in England known as Wyatt's Rebellion. Bullinger dodged this issue when he said that someone better acquainted with the specific laws and customs of England should answer this question. While the Spanish match did bring an entourage of Catholic advisors to England, the prenuptial contract gave little of substance to the Spanish. In the event of Mary's death, Philip would not become the king of England.

> Q. Must subjects of the Queen obey her if she "enforces idolatry and condemns true religion?" May subjects defend themselves and the towns and fortresses under their jurisdiction against ungodly violence?

> A. Citing illustrations—from Daniel, Christ's command in Matthew's gospel, and the example of the apostles in Acts chapters 4 and 5—Bullinger assured Knox we must obey God rather than human beings. Furthermore, "the holy scripture not only permits, but even enjoins . . . a just and necessary defense." Bullinger then went on to counsel caution because the situations are often complex. It is best to err on the side of caution. In the New Testament, Paul sometimes used Roman soldiers for his own defense but under very similar circumstances, "he is recorded to have used only the arms of patience."

> Q. To which party must godly persons attach themselves, in the case of a religious nobility resisting an idolatrous sovereign?

A. Again, Bullinger refused to answer citing his lack of specific knowledge. Those who provided answers should follow the Word of God, obey the Law of God, and listen to the guidance of the Holy Spirit. He left Knox with a twin note of caution and encouragement. [God] "is our only true deliverer . . . Let us lift our eyes to Him, waiting for his deliverance, abstaining in the meantime from all superstition and idolatry, and doing what he reveals in his word."[34]

Knox was not finished with these topics. They would occupy his attention for the rest of his life. While Knox did later advocate the overthrow of Queen Mary, he did not follow a one size fits all strategy. As Professor Jane Dawson has noted, there are "two John Knoxes" in that he gave different counsel to Christians under similar circumstances in England and Scotland.[35]

TWO COMFORTABLE EPISTLES
TO HIS AFFLICTED BRETHREN

After his sojourn in France and Switzerland, Knox returned to Dieppe where he received news about the sad state of religious affairs in England. Just as he provided pastoral counsel to Mrs. Bowes, Knox now extended his counseling office to all of the congregations and churches he had served in England through two letters dated May 10 and May 31, 1554. In order to comfort and encourage his fellow believers in England—who were trying to live lives as faithful Christians under the hostile atmosphere imposed by Queen Mary and her Catholic advisors—Knox wrote these two letters in which he explained biblical parallels to their own plight.

An Epistle to His Afflicted Brethren in England

Just as the Church suffered bewilderment and despair after Christ's crucifixion, so too did the true church in England face trials and tribulations.

---

34. Ibid. 3:222–26.

35. Jane Dawson, "The Two John Knoxes: England, Scotland and the 1558 Tracts," *Journal of Ecclesiastical History* 42 (October 1991): 555–76. See also a rejoinder to Dawson, Scott Dolfe, "The Two John Knoxes and the Justification of Non-revolution: A Response to Dawson's Argument from Covenant," *Journal of Ecclesiastical History* 55 (January 2004): 58–75. For an analysis of the Knox-Bullinger talks see, Richard Greaves, *Theology and Revolution in the Scottish Reformation* (Grand Rapids: Christian University Press, 1980), 128f.

Between the death of Christ and his resurrection, the church was scattered, terrified, and despondent. The faith of believers in the early church was so weak even the appearance of angels and Christ himself failed to remove the doubt in the hearts of many Christians. Peace, assurance, and joy did arrive, however, and it transformed the countenance of the true believers. Knox then drew the biblical precedent to encourage the afflicted brethren in England through the story of Christ's resurrection. Knox sincerely hoped Christ, who was crucified in England through Romanist theology, would soon rise over the enemies of the gospel. He hoped the weak and troubled followers of Christ would soon hear the comforting words of Christ: "Peace be unto you. It is I, fear not."[36]

Knox presented a twofold message: namely, hope in Christ and assurance that oppressive and tyrannical enemies will face certain punishment both in this life and the next. The same God, who protected his fledgling church in the first century, was present with the believers in England. Knox assured his readers: "God knows...so can I not but rejoice, knowing that God's most merciful providence is no less careful this day over his weak and feeble servants, than he was that day over his dispersed and sorely oppressed flock."[37]

A portion of the comfort Knox offered his readers was the coming judgment of their oppressors. He focused on the tyrants discomfort in order to bring comfort to the oppressed. Knox did not promote vengeance or the spirit of vengeance, but the certainty of divine justice. Speaking of ironhanded rulers, Knox wrote, "besides their perpetual condemnation in Hell, they shall also be plagued in this present life, except they repent."[38] In painting such a vivid portrait of divine punishment, Knox confessed some sorrow for them. "These tyrants are more to be pitied and lamented than either feared or hated."[39]

He concludes his letter of comfort not by bludgeoning his enemies but with the deft literary touch of a poet. Christ our Savior, he assured his readers, "will visit us again by the brightness of his word to our sure

---

36. *Selected Writings,* 202.

37. Ibid., 201.

38. Ibid., 204.

39. Ibid., 205.

comfort and consolation, when all our enemies shall tremble, fear and be confounded."[40]

A Comfortable Epistle Sent to the Afflicted Church of Christ, Exhorting Them to Bear His Cross with Patience

Knox's second letter dated May 31, 1554 from Dieppe largely echoed his earlier epistle. There are, however, some subtle differences as the second letter is several pages longer. Returning to biblical history, Knox notes that the first century church—despite (or perhaps because of) persecution and dispersion—increased and multiplied. This illustrated the wonderful providence of God. The early church could echo the words of Joseph in Genesis: what they intended for evil, God meant for good. The present troubles believers faced in England were God's refining fire. God burnt away the wood, hay, and stubble in order to purify the persecuted church and make it more fruitful.

He told them to avoid both vengeance and hate. "Presume not to be revengers of your own cause, but that you resign over vengeance unto him who only is able to requite them, according to their malicious minds."[41] He gave a similar counsel of restraint against the temptation to hate their oppressors. "Hate not with a carnal hatred . . . but that you learn of Christ to pray for your persecutors."

Knox offered both words of comfort as well as practical suggestions against tyrannical oppressors. He believed God sometimes used the tyrants to accomplish his own purpose. God rebuked sinners and then brought them to repentance. Thirdly, it caused the reprobate to admit their impenitence. Finally, the intensity of God's wrath poured out on sinners demonstrated the power of God and his hatred of sin.

Knox found biblical precedence for this order of rebuke and repentance. God used this very order in his judgment against Pharaoh, Saul, Herod, and others. Furthermore, he believed the first three were already employed in England. Thus it was just a matter of time before this divinely ordained strategy would take its desired effect against the "pestilent Papists" in England. "Assuredly," Knox writes, "shall we see God's extreme plagues poured forth upon them, even in this . . . life; that some of us may

40. Ibid, 205.
41. Ibid, 212.

witness to the next generation . . . the wondrous works that the Lord has wrought, and will work this in our age."[42]

Knox fearlessly (at least from a distance) named specific papists whom he believed God would single out for punishment. They included Cuthbert Tunstall (1474–1559), whom he called the "false bishop of Durham," and Stephen Gardiner (1483–1555), the Bishop of Winchester and a key advisor to Queen Mary. Knox wrote with the assurance of a prophet of God that their fate was sealed. "A kingdom begun with tyranny and blood, can neither be stable nor permanent, but that the glory, the riches, and maintainers of the same shall be as straw in the flame of fire."[43]

A FAITHFUL ADMONITION TO THE PROFESSORS OF GOD'S TRUTH IN ENGLAND

After sending his two "comfortable epistles," Knox received additional information each day about the declining state of the reformed church in England and the plight of Protestants. According to Knox, Queen Mary began her reign with assurances: she would not alter the religious affairs in the realm nor force anyone to worship in a way contrary to their conscience. Within a few months, however, Mary revoked this good faith pledge. Protestant leaders in Edward's church were removed from office, replaced by Catholic bishops, and placed under house arrest. The authorities now required subjects of the Queen in England to attend and partake of the Mass.[44]

Knox's tone turned more serious and the language more strident in this 70 page treatise because the stakes in England bore eternal consequences. The change in his thinking, in the six weeks between the "comfortable epistles" and the *Admonition,* is striking. Knox learned that many believers in England failed to follow his earlier counsel in the "comfortable epistles" about the serious dangers of practicing idolatry.

The argument of this treatise is threefold. First, Knox encourages his fellow believers to stand firm in the face of persecution; secondly, he rebukes believers for forsaking the gospel; and thirdly, he delivers powerful imprecatory prayers calling for God's vengeance against Queen Mary and

42. Ibid., 215.
43. Ibid., 216.
44. *Works*, 3:254.

her spiritual advisors. It is not clear if Knox's vehement rhetoric inflamed the passions of Queen Mary on her heresy hunt against Protestants. In a letter to John Calvin, Knox's critics—in the chaotic exile church in Frankfurt—blamed him for inciting the burnings at Smithfield that began in early 1555.[45]

Calm in the Time of Storm

Why, Knox wonders, is the elect church in England experiencing hostility, opposition, and persecution? He blames himself and other preachers in England for their lack of fervency and courage in promoting the gospel and denouncing sin. Speaking for the preachers, Knox confessed they failed to consider whether the Scriptures apply to us here and now, not merely to God's people long ago. The preachers failed to be the preserving salt in England. Without this savoring salt, the realm began to rot spiritually and God removed himself from their presence.

Knox used the example of the disciples at sea as a metaphor for the present troubles believers faced in England. "This great tempest that now blows against the poor disciples of Christ . . . comes from the great mercy of our heavenly Father, to provoke us to unfeigned repentance."[46] Knox found the story of the disciples at sea in Matthew chapter eight to be an illustrative text for their temporary troubles. The disciples followed Jesus into a boat where Jesus soon fell asleep. They found themselves in the midst of a raging storm and feared for their very lives. Terrified, the disciples awakened Jesus who spoke to the winds and miraculously calmed the sea.

This storm-tossed boat, Knox argues, is a figure of Christ's Church. The blowing tempest is the devil. Knox described Satan's tools: "When the light of the gospel is taken away, the devil reigns by idolatry, superstition, and tyranny."[47] He also noted that in Matthew chapter 14, the disciples found themselves buffeted by the wind, yet they did not give up and return to shore. They continued to labor faithfully when they could have easily succumbed. Jesus rescued them from certain death, but not until the "fourth watch" of the night. Believers in England should take heed. Jesus hears your cry. He will come and calm your storm, but he will do so

45. Ibid., 3:255–56.
46. *Selected Writings*, 230.
47. Ibid., 241.

when the time is right. Knox used the metaphor of the tempest tossed sea to make his point that the Lord would not allow his church to suffer indefinitely. If the faithful rowed against the vehement wind of persecution and did not turn back to the shores of idolatry, the Lord would provide a safe harbor of refuge.[48] "Take heart, the Lord will come to you in the hour of your trouble; and thereafter, be not afraid; this storm shall cease, and you shall be delivered."[49]

The Dangers of Nicodemism

The second major purpose of Knox's treatise was the rebuke of believers in England, who under the pressure of persecution, submitted to attendance at the Roman Mass. When Knox learned about the duplicity of some believers in England, he admonished them not only for their participation in idolatry but also the hypocrisy of defending their actions. Some of the believers in England complied outwardly by going to Mass and going through the motions of an outward piety. Inwardly, however, they did not believe the Pope was the Vicar of Christ nor accept the centerpiece of Catholic theology: the transubstantiation of Christ in the Lord's Supper. Some believers attended Mass as it were, with their fingers crossed, merely to satisfy the demands of the Catholic Queen.

Knox found such double dealing an outrageous betrayal of Christ. Knox does not charge them specifically with Nicodemism, but clearly he had this on his mind. Luther and Calvin both wrote treatises condemning those cowardly Christians, who in the face of opposition or persecution, hid their true faith under a bushel. Like Nicodemus in John chapter 3—who came to Jesus under the cover of darkness for fear of being seen—some believers in England failed to demonstrate an unfeigned faith by thinking merely in temporal terms, not in terms of eternity. They did not ask, "what must I do to be saved." They instead asked themselves, what must I do to save myself from Mary's clutches?

Knox used a sermon he delivered in the town of Buckinghamshire as the basis for his exhortation to those believers flirting with idolatry. He turned from the gospel lessons of comfort and encouragement to the stern warnings of the Hebrew prophet. He again employed Jeremiah, his favorite Hebrew prophet. We can see the familiar "jeremiad" of woe and promise.

48. Ibid., 244.
49. Ibid., 261.

The reformer aimed the message both at the individual who was turning from God, as well as to the consequences for the entire realm of England if idolatry prevailed. "O England, these plagues are poured out upon you . . . . But will you yet obey the voice of your God . . . you will find mercy and the state of your commonwealth shall be preserved. But, O England, if you obstinately will return to Egypt: [through] marriage, confederacy, . . . so shall England taste what the Lord has threatened by his prophets before."[50]

Knox ended his sermon with hope. The woe and warning could be null and void if God's people came to their senses, repented of their sin, and abandoned idolatry. "God grant us," Knox writes, "true and unfeigned repentance of our former offences."[51]

The Scots reformer offered a final encouragement to the elect who had "returned to their abominations." As he reminded them, hope still existed for the apostate because we learn from Scripture that all of Christ's apostles abandoned him and denied him publicly or in their hearts. He assured them the root of faith remained in the elect. "Neither danger . . . doubting, nor backsliding, may utterly destroy and quench the faith of God's elect."[52] In order to "test" whether their faith was genuine, Knox posed seven questions. If they could answer "yes" to all these questions, then they had assurance they were not altogether destitute of faith and the Lord would stretch forth his mighty hand and deliver them.

Death to Tyrants!

Knox also wrote the *Admonition* to expose the sins and hypocrisy of England's tyrannical rulers. Earlier he made it clear the tools the devil used to buffet the church included, "idolatry, superstition and tyranny"—all of which were evident in England.[53] Having confessed and repented of his own cowardice as a preacher in England to rebuke iniquity, he now aimed squarely at Queen Mary and her bishops. In the tradition of Jeremiah, Knox wrote, "I ought to have said to the wicked man expressly by his name, thou shall die the death. For [this] I find Jeremiah the prophet to

---

50. Ibid., 266.

51. Ibid., 267.

52. Ibid., 288.

53. Ibid., 241.

have done to Pashur the high priest, and the Zedekiah the king."[54] Knox now assumed the mantle of Jeremiah and delivered this same message to England's Zedekiah, that is, Queen Mary Tudor.

He wished Queen Mary was already in hell because it would have spared England untold anguish. Knox wondered how a woman could demonstrate such cruelty and bloodlust toward innocent people. He compared Mary to Jezebel who murdered the prophets of God and Naboth for his vineyard. The reformer regarded Mary worse than Jezebel because she erected more gallows than Jezebel. Mary was a liar and a fraud who promised never to marry a foreigner. Knox feared Mary promoted treason because he believed the Spanish marriage with Philip would transfer the English crown to a foreign nation.

Mary's counselors were as bad or worse than the Queen, a "monstrous mistress." Knox's alliteration of the "pestilent papists" provides a tragically colorful summary. "Now the devil rages in his obedient servants, wily Winchester, dreaming Durham, and bloody Bonner, with the rest of their bloody butchery brood."[55] Stephen A. Gardiner—the bishop of Winchester and Queen Mary's cousin—had earlier written a book titled *True Obedience* in which he labeled Rome a false church and rejected papal supremacy. After Gardiner's dramatic reversal of affections, Knox called him a "dissembling hypocrite, and a double-faced wretch." He was the "son of Satan . . . brother to Cain, and fellow to Judas the traitor."[56] The Queen and her bishops were guilty not only of promoting idolatry, but they required people to participate in the Mass.

Forcing people against their wishes to commit sacrilege was more than Knox could bear. This is the context for his imprecatory prayers against Mary and her advisors who mandated idolatry and false religion. Drawing from the Psalms, Knox offered prayers of confession and entreated the Lord for justice against England's tyrants. "Repress the pride of those bloodthirsty tyrants; consume them in thy anger . . . pour forth thy vengeance, O Lord! But let death devour them in haste; let the earth swallow them up, and let them go down quick to the hells."[57]

54. Ibid., 227–28.
55. Ibid., 243.
56. Ibid., 256.
57. Ibid., 286.

If Knox considered Mary worse than Jezebel, he also wished for the Lord to send a modern day Jehu against the Queen of England. "God himself shall rise to your defense . . . He shall send Jehu to execute his just judgments against idolaters, and against such as obstinately defend them. Jezebel herself shall not escape the vengeance and plagues that are prepared for their portion."[58]

Some months earlier, Knox traveled around Switzerland where he conferred with the Swiss reformers regarding the ethics of dealing with idolatrous magistrates. In the *Admonition,* Knox began to develop his own views, which we see here only in seed form. As conditions worsened in England, Knox's counsel became increasingly radical. At this point he was content to use the spiritual weapons of prayer, exhortation, and admonition. Later Knox gained notoriety by his justification of the overthrow of idolatrous rulers. In his writings he advocated the duty of believers in England to play the role of Jehu to execute God's justice. [59]

A BRIEF HISTORY OF THE TROUBLES AT FRANKFURT

While Knox was in Geneva conferring with Calvin and others about female sovereignty and a biblical theory of resistance against tyrannical rulers, he received an urgent request for his pastoral leadership in Frankfurt. At the urging of Calvin, Knox reluctantly accepted the call to serve the English refugee church in Frankfurt. The exiles numbering around 200 called Knox and Thomas Lever as their pastors. Troubles over the form of liturgy quickly exploded into a "worship war" and soon led to Knox's expulsion. A majority of the congregation favored the second Edwardian prayer book of 1552, while Knox preferred an English translation of a Genevan liturgy. Knox faced formidable opposition in Frankfurt from Dr. Richard Cox—chancellor of Oxford University, Dean of Westminster, and veteran of prayer book committees.

Knox objected to the second prayer book for the same reason he rejected the Mass. The prayer book promoted practices not explicitly supported in Scripture. These were mere inventions from the mind of human beings that may be rooted in piety, but not in Scripture. Such inventions

58. Ibid., 286–87.

59. Patrick Collinson, "The Authorship of a Brief Discourse of the Troubles Begun at Frankfort," *Journal of Ecclesiastical History* 9 (October 1958): 188–208. See also, Martin A. Simpson, in Duncan Shaw, ed., *Reformation and Revolution* (Edinburgh: St. Andrew Press, 1967), 17–33.

included kneeling at the Communion, the use of surplices, use of the cross in baptism, and the ring in marriage. Calvin was invited by the principle parties to take a stand on the "worship wars" in Frankfurt. He sided with Knox or at least Knox's version of the issues. The Knox party also included John Foxe and William Whittingham. In a letter dated May 1555, Calvin defended Knox and lamented the unchristian treatment he received at the hands of the Cox party. On liturgical practices, Calvin in fact differed somewhat from Knox. In a letter to Knox, Calvin urged rejection of the Mass and superstitious practices, but advocated toleration of some liturgical practices, which lacked strict biblical proof.

Using excerpts from some of Knox's belligerent comments about Holy Roman Emperor Charles V, the Cox party convinced the Frankfurt city officials to silence Knox. He ignored the city council's order against preaching and was expelled from Frankfurt. Book Four of Knox's collected *Works* contains considerable material related to the debacle, including letters from several of the chief participants. English historian Patrick Collinson has proved convincingly that Thomas Wood, and not William Whittingham, is the likely author of one version titled "*A Narrative of the Troubles at Frankfurt,*" first published in 1575.

Knox's short version of the *Troubles* is titled *A Narrative by Knox of the Proceedings of the English Congregation at Frankfurt in March 1554.* This version reveals Knox's exasperation with Thomas Lever and Richard Cox for their duplicity and their resolve to structure a church with an "English face." Andrew Lang, the rather hostile biographer of Knox, is probably correct when he argued that this quarrel in Frankfurt "marks the beginning of rupture between the fathers of the Church of England and the fathers of Puritanism, Scottish Presbyterianism, and Dissent."[60]

LETTER TO THE QUEEN DOWAGER

Alexander Cunningham and William Keith urged Knox to write a letter to Mary of Guise, the Queen Regent, in an attempt to move her to evangelical sympathies, or at least persuade her to grant religious toleration. They wanted her to read something "that might move her to hear the word of God."[61] Knox timed the letter prudently because Mary, for

---

60. Andrew Lang, *John Knox and the Reformation* (London: Longmans, Green, and Co., 1905), 53.

61. John Knox, *History of the Reformation in Scotland*, trans. William C. Dickinson 2

political reasons, was promoting a mildly pro-Protestant policy. Knox infers in his letter that she had protected him from an earlier heresy charge leveled against him. The Earl of Glencairn personally delivered the letter to the Queen Regent, who the next day passed it to James Beaton, Bishop of Glasgow. She treated it as a joke, inviting Bishop Beaton to read this lampoon.[62] Knox was very respectful towards Mary, but his mood and serious content of the letter was anything but jocular.

Lessons from History

Knox offered the Queen a sweeping narrative of biblical history. He cited Pharaoh, Nebuchchadnezzar, and Cyrus as examples of kings through whom God worked his perfect will and delivered his elect people, namely, the "afflicted flock." He followed with a natural question: "Your Grace perchance doeth wonder to what purpose these things be recited."[63] Knox explained to the Queen: if she continued her moderation and clemency towards those her Catholic advisers called heretics, she could expect a place of honor and blessing with those in Scripture who assisted God's covenant people. He had reason to thank her for not listening to those who called Knox a "heretic," a "false teacher, and seducer of the people."[64] This was God's doing. "God the Father . . . by the dew of his heavenly grace . . . quenched the fire of displeasure" in the Queen's heart.[65] The result of her policies, the Scots reformer explained, frustrated Satan and his plans in Scotland. If the Queen had the good sense to continue this policy, he promised her present government would be praised and her posterity blessed.

Speaking Truth to Power

After having praised and thanked the Queen for her moderation, he took a stern tone recognizing the irony of a man of his "base estate" presuming to lecture the Queen. He explained that the Queen should beware because she was surrounded by a company of flatterers, who would not dare to tell her the truth. Again, assuming the mantle of the biblical prophets, Knox believed he was compelled to tell her the truth without pulling

vols., (New York: Philosophical Library, 1950), 1:22, hereafter cited as *History*.

62. Ibid., 1:23.
63. *Works*, 4:77.
64. Ibid., 4:78.
65. Ibid., 4:77.

any punches. If she followed the popular pattern of princes persecuting Protestants, she could expect "torment and pain everlasting."[66]

He explained though this was strong medicine, he could no more fail to warn her than he could fail to stop her from drinking poison. She must abandon religion that is defended by sword and fire. She must discard superstition and any religious practices stemming from humankind's own invention. Don't be fooled, he warned, by the opinion that the Roman Church is infallible, or bishops cannot err. Instead, she must "lay the book of God before [her] eyes and let it be a judge."[67]

Knox reiterated his chief point: "Your Grace must dissent from the multitude of rulers, or else you can possess no portion with Christ Jesus in his Kingdom and Glory."[68] If the Queen took up the cause for Christ, she could expect "double benediction," including "riches, glory, honor and long life."[69] Sadly, the Queen did not follow Knox's prophetic counsel. She died four years later, on the eve of the Scottish Reformation, resolute in her Catholic faith.

A LETTER OF WHOLESOME COUNSEL ADDRESSED TO HIS BRETHREN IN SCOTLAND

After his expulsion from Frankfurt in 1555, Knox and his party made their way to Geneva. They found a greeting from John Calvin, who had also welcomed exiles from France, Italy, Germany, Spain, and Poland. Between 1549–1560 the census data—from the Geneva edition of the *Livre des Habitants*—records 5,000 immigrants entering the city, boosting the total population to over 21,000.[70] These religious refugees brought a variety of skills, trades, and professional training that contributed greatly to the Genevan economy. Perhaps most notable were the printers, including Jean Crespin, whose presses enhanced the Genevan reputation as one of the most significant printing and publishing centers in Europe.

66. Ibid., 4:78.

67. Ibid., 4:84.

68. Ibid., 4:81.

69. Ibid., 4:84.

70. Alister E. McGrath, *A Life of John Calvin: A Study in the Shaping of Western Culture* (Oxford: Blackwell Publishers Inc., 1990), 121–22. See also E. William Monter, *Calvin's Geneva* (New York: John Wiley and Sons, Inc.,1967), 2, 165–66 and W. Fred Graham, *The Constructive Revolutionary: John Calvin and His Socio-Economic Impact* (Lansing, MI: Michigan State University Press, 1987), 30f.

W. Stanford Reid calls the five years, which Knox spent in Geneva, "perhaps the most formative of his life."[71] Life in Geneva provided Knox the opportunity to study Scripture and the biblical languages and confer with experienced continental reformers and theologians. After six months in Geneva, however, Knox's studies were interrupted when he received a request from believers in Scotland, inviting him to return after an eight year absence. They hoped his preaching and leadership could inspire the faith of the believers in the underground church. Knox obeyed the summons and traveled the eleven day journey from Geneva to Dieppe, where he awaited for a ship for Scotland.[72]

He was apparently amazed at the receptivity he found in Scotland.[73] He then spent nearly a year in Scotland as an itinerant preacher—hosted by lairds, burgesses, and some nobility—finally returning to Geneva in September of 1556. His preaching and administering the Sacrament did aid the fledgling Protestant church movement in Scotland. But the Catholic Queen Regent, Mary of Guise—backed by the French military, political, and spiritual advisers—made a complete reformation of the church in Scotland impossible at that time. David Laing, the nineteenth-century editor of Knox's *Works,* said the positive influence exerted by Knox toward the cause of the Reformation in Scotland is nearly incalculable.[74]

With Calvin's help, William Whittingham, Anthony Gilby, and others established a church in Geneva for the English refugees. With an initial membership of about 50 in November 1555, the church grew to nearly 220.[75] They modeled an informal worship style from Valerand Poullain's *Liturgia Sacra* titled *The Form of Prayer and Ministration of the Sacrament.* Many in the congregation were with Knox in Frankfurt and still considered him their duly constituted pastor. In Knox's temporary absence, the congregation elected Christopher Goodman and Anthony Gilby to serve as their pastors.[76]

71. Reid, *Trumpeter of God*, 130.

72. *Works*, 3:253.

73. Mason, *John Knox on Rebellion*, xiii.

74. *Works*, 4:71.

75. M.M. Knappen, *Tudor Puritanism* (Chicago: The University of Chicago Press, 1939), 118–33; and Reid, *Trumpeter of God*, 133.

76. Mason, *John Knox and the British Reformations*, 132. A Genevan law required the annual election of two pastors for each congregation. See P. Hume Brown, *John Knox: A Biography* 2 vols., (London: Jonathan Cade, 1929; reprint ed., Port Washington, NY:

Several months later the congregation wrote to their pastor in exile and requested that he return from Scotland to serve the refugee congregation in Geneva. Knox returned, but not as a single man. He brought his new wife Marjory, his mother-in-law Elizabeth Bowes, a servant, and a pupil with him to Geneva. The *Letter of Wholesome Counsel* contains Knox's advice and encouragement to the scattered clusters of believers in Scotland with whom he had labored for nearly a year.

The Centrality of the Word of God

Knox expressed with both power and eloquence the matchless majesty of God's Word as the source of spiritual health. God's Word would provide them sustenance in a bleak and spiritually hostile landscape. It was their lamp in a dark world. Knox reminded them of the *Shema,* found in Deuteronomy six, and the proper reverence for God's law. Instead of Moses' command, "Hear O Israel," Knox is saying in effect, Hear O Scotland! Knox believed the triumph of the Reformed faith in Scotland would come through the faithfulness of the parents and their determination to pass biblical truth on to their children. Perhaps Knox unconsciously echoed Martin Luther's admonition: unless we educate, this thing called the Reformation will not last.

Like Moses, Knox charged the parents to teach the children the Word of God "in thy house, and as thou walkest by the way, and when thou liest down, and when thou risest up."[77] Knox further implored them, "you must make them partakers in reading, exhorting and in making common prayer . . . in every house once a day at least." He also anticipated this objection: a daily diet of the Word might become as tiresome as the manna the children of Israel came to despise. Knox answered that such an objection is a reflection of a person's spiritual health—or lack thereof! Everyday, we eat bread, we drink wine, and we enjoy the beauty of the sun. If these material blessings do not become tiresome, how much more should we find joy, sustenance, and fulfillment in the bread of life—the eternal Word of God!

Instructions for Worship

For good reason, Knox placed great emphasis on family worship. Given the realities of the spiritual climate in Scotland and the hostility to the

Kennikat Press, 1972), 1:193.

77. *Selected Writings*, 328.

Reformed faith, the family setting was the only safe place to worship. At the same time, Knox reminded them that they were part of the larger body of Christ. Worship and fellowship with other believers were essential. Knox wrote, "because we are called the body of Christ, I think it necessary for the [consultation] of scriptures, assemblies of brethren be had." In the 1540s believers in Scotland would form a loose network of underground churches and worship secretly in lay led conventicles. By the late 1550s—under the leadership of itinerant Protestant preachers—the conventicles and Protestantism gained strength and organized into so-called "privy kirks."[78]

Using the Apostle Paul's instructions, Knox offered the essential elements of worship. They included weekly worship beginning with a confession of sin, an invocation asking for the Spirit's help, followed by the reading of Scripture. The Scriptures were then discussed, questions raised and answered, and an exhortation given. Knox also offered caution against individuals who liked to hear themselves talk and tried to dominate the conversation. If these informal assemblies raised a question about a text they could not answer, they should record it and pose the question to a learned Bible scholar. Each assembly should conclude with prayers of thanksgiving and prayers for "princes, rulers, and magistrates."[79]

Knox also reminded them to pray for persecuted believers in places where he had first-hand knowledge, especially those in France and England. Knox concludes with a nostalgic fondness for his co-laborers in Scotland. He wished to be back with them studying the Scriptures. "Of myself . . . I will more gladly spend fifteen hours in communicating my judgment with you in explaining . . . any place of scripture, than half an hour in any other matter beside."[80] While Knox is no doubt using hyperbole to make his point, he resembles the person he warned against: the one who wants to dominate the conversation.

FORMS OF PRAYER

When Knox responded to the call to return to Geneva in order to take up his pastoral duties, he found both a church and a liturgy formed in his

---

78. James Kirk, *Patterns of Reform: Continuity and Change in the Reformation Kirk* (Edinburgh: T and T Clark, 1989), 1–15.

79. *Selected Writings*, 333.

80. Ibid., 332–33.

absence. The so-called *Forms of Prayers and Ministrations of Sacraments* used by the refugee congregation in Geneva was not an English creation. Its roots go back to Calvin's Catechism for use in Geneva in 1536. In addition the Reformed churches in several parts of Europe, including Helvetia and France, used it as a model.[81] When pastor Valerand Poullain led the French Reformed congregation from Strasbourg to a temporary haven in England in 1551, he brought the Genevan liturgy with him, translated it into Latin (*Liturgia Sacra*), and used it with his congregation of Walloon weavers in Glastonbury.

Poullain subsequently used the Genevan liturgy as a model in worship in Frankfurt when the death of King Edward VI of England once again forced the French Reformed congregation into exile. When English exiles looked for a place of refuge, city officials in Frankfurt allowed them to share a church with the French Reformed congregation. They could only do so, however, with the proviso that they must use similar liturgies. Thus the earliest English arrivals in Frankfurt adopted the Genevan inspired *Liturgia Sacra*.[82]

As later exiles from England joined the congregation in Frankfurt, trouble soon erupted. Would they use the (well-traveled) Genevan model of worship or the model found in the English *Second Book of Common Prayer* (1554)? The expulsion of the co-pastor John Knox from Frankfurt to Geneva meant the original Catechism of John Calvin had traveled full circle back to Geneva. Knox later brought it to Scotland, where in 1562 the General Assembly charged the ministers to "dispense the sacraments and to celebrate marriage 'according to the book of Geneva.'"[83] In 1564 the Assembly required every "minister, exhorter and reader" to use the order of the so-called "Knox's liturgy."[84]

81. *Works*, 4:143–44.

82. Ibid., 4:144–47.

83. Reyburn, "Calvin and Scotland," 213. See also, Sutherland, "The English Refugees," 780–86.

84. Reyburn, "Calvin and Scotland," 213.

5

The Outburst Against Idolatrous Rulers (1556–1559)

AFTER SPENDING A YEAR in Scotland, Knox sailed for Dieppe in July 1556. He stayed for a few weeks and then with his family made his way to Geneva. Why he left Scotland is not entirely clear. While he faced some danger in Scotland, the threat was no greater than before. In fact, affairs in Scotland were improved. The answer probably lies in the fact that his congregation of English refugees in Geneva called him. Still, that "little flock" did not lack preachers, and their needs did not compare to reforming the entire nation of Scotland. The call of this congregation, however, was important and Knox did enjoy the peaceful years in Geneva.

During the last leg of his exile years (1556-59), Knox produced some of his most contentious political writings plus a major attack on the Anabaptists in which he defended predestination. Some of these works were penned in Geneva and some in Dieppe. What prompted these writings? Knox's outburst against political rulers had been a long time coming, but the explosion came in the late 1550s. During these years, Mary Tudor's persecution of Protestants in England intensified. Elsewhere in Europe, the Catholic forces were on the march and the survival of Protestantism hung by a thread.

The English refugees in Geneva, including Knox, were in close touch with these events. Such developments pushed Knox over the edge. He abandoned the time honored duty to obey the secular rulers and at worst to engage in passive resistance to idolatrous commands. Instead, Knox advocated rebellion against idolatrous (Catholic) rulers. What prompted his outburst against the Anabaptists and his defense of predestination is more debatable and will be encountered in a later chapter.

WRITINGS FROM DIEPPE

Knox arrived in Geneva in September of 1556 and spent the winter there. In May 1557 he received letters from Scottish lords urging him to return because the situation, as they described it, seemed conducive to Protestantism. Knox reluctantly left Geneva and reached Dieppe in October intending to take the first ship to Scotland. But here a letter informed him that the Protestant nobility had reconsidered their invitation, and urged him to wait in Dieppe for a final decision on the matter. The Queen Regent's negotiations for the marriage of Mary Queen of Scots to the Dauphin had reached a critical stage, and the nobility believed Knox's preaching would impair a successful bargain.

The sudden change in plans had a radical effect on Knox's thinking. He now had to face two questions. Could one depend on the Scottish nobility to reform religion? Were the common people responsible to bring about "true religion"? The nobles now attempted to bring about some kind of compromise with Mary of Guise because they felt they could not effect a reformation of religion by force. On the other hand, Knox believed no compromise was possible. Why? In his eyes, the Queen Regent was a Guise dedicated to the maintenance of French and Catholic power in Scotland.[1]

First Letter

While Knox indignantly waited in Dieppe during the closing months of 1557, he wrote three letters that revealed his state of mind just prior to his vigorous pamphleteering of 1558. In the first letter, dated October 27, Knox set forth a bold conception of the nobles' constitutional and religious functions in society. Previously, he said magistrates must establish "true religion." Apparently, he now considered the nobility as magistrates and included them in that task. The nobles were entitled to be called "princes of the people" by reason of their office and duties and not because of their bloodline.

The nobles' responsibilities were twofold: They must protect their citizens and establish true religion. And they must carry out these functions even in the face of royal opposition. Here Knox advocated a course of action that ran counter to the doctrine of Christian obedience. He

---

1. W. Stanford Reid, *Trumpeter of God* (New York: Charles Scribner's, 1974), 142–43; Alec Ryrie, *The Origins of the Scottish Reformation* (Manchester, UK: Manchester University Press, 2006), 148–49.

stated that the nobility were duty bound to compel the kings to introduce a reformation. But he did not specify the means—whether physical or moral—by which this compulsion should be applied.[2]

While waiting at Dieppe, Knox's worst fears were confirmed. He received news that the lords were using the Protestant movement for purely a selfish end. The role of Chaterlherault especially aroused his mistrust. Knox feared Chaterlherault—"who in the beginning of his authority and government began to profess Christ's truth, but suddenly sliding back, became one cruel persecutor of Christ's members"—would use the Congregation to further the dynastic ambitions of the House of Hamilton.[3] Four years earlier, Bullinger had warned Knox that the nobles might rebel against the monarch under the guise of religion, although their motives were worldly.

Third Letter

Knox's second letter (December 1) addressed *To the Professors of Truth in Scotland*, said little in regard to political theory. But in the third letter (December 17), he attempted to clarify his thinking on the subject of rebellion for righteousness sake. He cautioned the Protestants not to "disobey or displease the established authority in things lawful." Yet at the same time, they must openly confess their faith and seek government support in furthering Protestantism or, at least, its toleration.

If the government, however, failed to reform religion, Protestants should take several steps. They must make a public protestation of their obedience to the crown "in all things not plainly repugning to God." Following that, they must demand the free preaching of the gospel and the proper administration of the sacraments. Knox also instructed the nobles—even in the face of royal opposition—to defend their Protestant subjects from persecution at all costs. He concluded by warning the Protestants against cooperating with those seeking their own profit.[4]

In these letters to the Protestants, Knox specifically appealed to the nobility and not to the magistrates. Why? Knox probably considered the

2. John Knox, *The Works of John Knox* 6 Vols., ed. David Laing (Edinburgh: Printed for the Bannatyne Club, 1846–1864), 1:272. The first of the three letters to the nobility is found in Knox's *History* while the last two are found in *Works*, 4:262–86. See footnote 27 of this chapter, which cites a quotation in the body.

3. *Works*, 4:285.

4. Ibid., 4:284–85.

nobility to be magistrates with the authority to suppress an idolatrous monarch. These letters show Knox continuing down the road to rebellion, but with reservations. Even in late 1557, he had emphasized obedience at least as much as resistance, and he did not completely trust the aristocracy to bring about the Reformation.[5]

An Apology

The tensions in Knox's mind were evident even in his additions and preface to *An Apology* for Protestants imprisoned in Paris (December 1557). In the preface he referred to the problem dominating his thought—the duty of obedience and resistance to rulers. Knox denied that Protestantism was seditious. Rather Protestants, as he claimed, had always upheld the honor of rulers. Indeed they that affirmed every individual, "be he Pope or Cardinal," must obey emperors, kings, and rulers.

In *An Apology,* Knox was more reticent about the right of subjects to resist idolatrous rulers than he had been in *A Faithful Admonition* (1554), probably because the circumstances had changed. Knox now desired to impress the authorities that Protestants were not traitors. He had no interest, nevertheless, in merely replacing a corrupt pope with an equally corrupt prince. Rather, Knox desired a religious reformation and he would not approve of any prince or king who failed to further this cause. He urged "that either Princes be reformed, and be compelled also to reform their wicked laws, or else that good men depart from their service." By this statement he meant that Protestants should resign from the service of Catholic kings.[6]

It is understandable that Knox had doubts as he formulated his religious doctrine to justify revolution. Though precedents to armed resistance existed both in fact and theory, Tyndale's doctrine still held sway. Knox must have been under great pressure from not only the leaders of the Church of England in exile but also from Calvin, whom he greatly admired.

Such caution also had a complex political background in the negotiations between the Lords of the Congregation and the Queen Regent. It

---

5. J. H. Burns, "The Political Ideas of the Scottish Reformation." *Aberdeen University Review* 36 (1955–1956): 258; Richard L. Greaves, "John Knox, The Reformed Tradition, and Resistance Theory," *The Journal of Modern History* 58 (September 1976): 19; Reid, *Trumpeter of God*, 143, 145. In a later letter to Cecil, Knox also seemed to consider the nobility as magistrates with the authority to suppress idolatry. *Works*, 6:32.

6. *Works*, 4:297–309; 324–25, 327.

is just possible, however, that the magnitude of what Knox contemplated caused him to hesitate. He wrote four revolutionary, political pamphlets in 1558, and one of them created a greater uproar than anything that had been published in Europe since Luther's three great treatises.[7]

Circumstances, however, propelled Knox past any hesitancy he might have had. Politically, the rapid progress of the negotiations for the French marriage of Mary Queen of Scots alarmed Knox. In religion, the continuing persecution in England right up until Mary Tudor's death added fuel to the flames. Personally, there was the rudeness with which Mary of Guise received his courteous letter of 1556, and of his being burnt in effigy by clerical authorities after his departure from Scotland. Moreover, he had experienced four years of exilic turmoil. Besides, at this time, chances for a successful revolution in Scotland were improving.

THE FIRST BLAST OF THE TRUMPET

Yet Knox's hesitation was more apparent than real. By December of 1557 he had already begun work in Dieppe on *The First Blast of the Trumpet Against the Monstrous Regiment of Women*, published secretly in Geneva in the spring of 1558. As Knox looked at the situation in Scotland and England, he saw the malevolent work of the female sex. Women had usurped the natural authority of men and were now causing problems for "true believers." This situation particularly applied to England. Here Mary Tudor had actually handed the kingdom over to her husband Philip of Spain, thus placing it in bondage to the most militantly Catholic power in Europe.[8]

Central Thesis

The central thesis of *The First Blast* said that it violated the law of God, as well as of nature, for a woman to rule a kingdom. Moreover, a woman ruler could not even turn over the power of government to her husband, particularly if he were a foreign monarch: "To promote a Woman to bear rule, superiority, dominion, or empire above any Realm, Nation, or city, is repugnant to Nature; contumely to God, a thing most contrary to his

7. Jasper Ridley, *John Knox* (New York: Oxford University Press, 1962), 225, 264; J. H. Burns, "John Knox and Revolution." *History Today* 8 (August 1958): 569–70.

8. Knox's *History* provided a background for that period of time. *Works*, 1:248–312; Burns, "John Knox and Revolution," 571; David McRoberts, ed. *Essays on the Scottish Reformation 1513–1625* (Glasgow: John S. Burns and Sons, 1962), 15–16.

revealed will and approved ordinance; and finally, it is the subversion of good Order, of all equity and justice."[9]

The First Blast gained for Knox a reputation among his contemporaries of being a revolutionary, and among later generations of being a woman hater. Knox's misogynist image, however, is not accurate because—outside of *The First Blast*—his writings contained few denunciations of the female sex. On the contrary, out of Knox's surviving letters, more than half were written to women and many of them showed a high regard for the female sex.[10]

In fact, Knox's attack on female sovereigns was by no means original. Similiar views were expressed for antagonism to a woman ruler ran high in the sixteenth century. Despite the fact that there had been several female sovereigns in Europe at that time, or perhaps because of it, many feared the consequences of a woman ruler.[11] The inferiority and subjection of women to men were accepted both in theory and in practice in all ranks of society. Paradoxically, society considered women ineligible for any public office except that of head of state. In *The First Blast*, Knox exposed the illogical nature of this system, which was to continue for another three hundred and fifty years. In doing so, he attacked the special position of the crown. Some theologians taught —though women must obey men in all areas of life—men must obey a queen as they would a male sovereign. In teaching this idea, they believed the divinely ordained power of the monarchy was strong enough to prevail over the divinely ordained power of men over women. Because *The First Blast* directly challenged this notion, many considered it to be seditious.[12]

---

9. *Works*, 4:373, 413.

10. It would seem that Knox preferred the company and friendship of women to that of men. He married twice and was on cordial terms with several others (e.g., Mrs. Bowes, Mrs. Locke, Mrs. Hickmkan, and Janet Adamson). On the other hand, Christopher Goodman appeared to be the only man for whom Knox felt a personal affection. *Works*, 3:155–58, 338–97;5:227–34;6:4–97; Ridley, *John Knox*, 267; Richard L. Greaves, "John Knox and the Ladies, or the Controversy over Gynecocracy," *Red River Valley Historial Journal* 2 (Spring 1977), 8–9.

11. The sixteenth century saw Mary Tudor as queen of England, Margaret of Austria and Mary of Hungary as regents in the Netherlands, Mary of Guise as regent in Scotland, and Catherine de'Medici as regent in France. Elizabeth Tudor and Mary Stewart became queens in England and Scotland respectively after Knox wrote *The First Blast*. See Greaves, "Controversy over Gynecocracy," 8–9.

12. Ridley, *John Knox*, 269–70.

Intellectual Sources

In the preface of *The First Blast*, Knox criticized the "Watchmen of England" for their negligence in not warning the people about the sin of establishing a woman ruler.[13] Then he assumed the role of watchman, believing himself to be called of God to this function. In supporting the proposition that a woman is not fit to rule, Knox used three sources: the Word of God, the ancient writers, and the ordinance of nature.

Though Knox used Scripture at large, he especially employed Pauline passages to support his contention "that woman in her greatest perfection was made to serve and obey man, not to rule and command him." Understandably, he stressed the doctrine of original sin in asserting that woman's subordinate position came by the sentence of God: "Thy will shall be subject to thy husband, and he shall bear dominion over thee."[14] If, as Knox wondered, Scripture forbade female rule in the home and church, how could women have authority over an entire nation? Knox, along with many medieval thinkers, resorted to the writings of such church fathers as Tertullian, Augustine, Ambrose, and Chrysostom in order to place the female sex in a subordinate position.[15]

In addition, Knox made much more in *The First Blast* than in any of his earlier works concerning the concepts of nature and natural law. Female government, he alleged, is "repugnant to Nature" and an absurdity. If man were to submit himself to the rule of a woman, then he would do what no other species had done, for no male was prepared to be governed by his female: "For nature has in all beasts printed a certain mark of dominion in the male, and a certain subjection in the female, which they keep inviolate. For no man ever saw the lion make obedience, and stoop before the lioness . . . ." And yet man—who has been appointed by God to have dominion over women—has to his own shame and in violation of God's appointed order "stoop[ed] under obedience of woman . . . ."[16]

Knox's premise, that female rule had subverted both the divine and natural order, did not seem so startling. What alarmed Europe was his conclusion: The faithful, if afflicted by a female sovereign, "ought to re-

---

13. *Works*, 4:365–71.

14. Ibid., 4:377–78. Some Pauline passages employed by Knox were: 1 Corinthians 11 and 14; 1 Timothy 2.

15. Ibid., 4:381–86.

16. Ibid., 4:393.

move from honor and authority that monster in nature," and if any support her they ought to "execute against them the sentence of death."[17] Using Old Testament prototypes, Knox cited the case of Athaliah to spur the nobility into action. Jehoiada, the high priest (Knox) had called upon the captains and chief rulers of the people to depose Athaliah (Mary Tudor) and place Joash on the throne. Knox pointed out to the nobility that the faithful Jews had executed both Athaliah and the high priest of Baal (Stephen Gardner).

Implications

At this point Knox introduced a major departure in his teaching. The duty of removing a woman sovereign falls not only upon the nobility as estates, but also upon the people—especially the lairds and burgesses who favor Protestantism. His general argument said that "God by his own word has appointed an order" in the body politic. And if female rule perverts that order, the community acting either for themselves or through their authorized leaders must restore it. Moreover, not only must Mary be removed, but all those supporting her must be executed.

In this idea, a principle emerged that Knox would make more of in *The Appellation*—he no longer considered tyrannicide as the exclusive mission of divinely inspired individuals, but the vocation of every saint who would assume it. Previously, Knox had established the principle that it was sin to even tolerate sin. He now applied this precept to a female ruler. *Not* to revolt against an idolatrous ruler was "plain rebellion against God."[18]

To incite the nobility and common people to revolt against and even execute an idolatrous female sovereign was a revolutionary idea. Even more radical were the implications of such a principle if it were more broadly applied. In *The First Blast*, however, Knox tempered these principles by allowing for exceptions. He advocated no rebellion against either a male sovereign or even a Protestant queen. He brushed the counterexample of the biblical Deborah aside with the argument that an exceptional case did not establish a general rule. Still, he acknowledged that God, at times, exempted women from their subordinate status. Knox wrote *The First Blast*

17. Ibid., 4:415–16.

18. *Works*, 4:415–16. See also Greaves, "John Knox and Resistance Theory," 19–20; Burns, "The Political Ideas of the Scottish Reformation," 260; Michael Walzer, *The Revolution of the Saints* (New York: Atheneum, 1973), 108.

before Elizabeth's accession, and Deborah was not then the favorite figure of Protestant writers. In any case, Knox minimized her importance at this time.[19] In subsequent writings, however, he amplified his view of Deborah as an exception, even as he extended the principle of active resistance to male sovereigns.

Reaction

Christendom was appalled at *The First Blast*. Though some of Knox's contemporaries agreed with his attack on female rule, many disagreed with his radical solutions.[20] Catholics, of course, very much opposed the views expressed, for they struck at both Mary Tudor and Mary Stewart. Yet this resistance surprised no one. More important to Knox was the criticism raised by Protestants of all shades. The remnants of the English congregation in Frankfurt were quite upset and attempted to excuse Knox. Calvin refused to take any responsibility for the Scottish reformer's views. As he explained to Cecil in 1559, he had not read the book until over a year after its publication and earlier had cautioned Knox against taking too radical a position in regard to female rule.

The stir caused from *The First Blast* came as much from its timing as from the argument itself. Knox directed *The First Blast* against Mary Tudor—despite the generality of the title—and she died a few months after its publication. Elizabeth was naturally indignant at *The First Blast*. In view of the weakness of her position, Knox embarrassed her by calling into question the basis of her rule. Despite some tactless efforts by Knox to make amends for his blunder, Elizabeth never forgave him.[21]

---

19. *Works*, 4:403–4, 406–8. Knox contended that Deborah did not usurp the magistrate's authority, but rather she judged Israel and rebuked idolatry by the Word of God and not by temporal authority.

20. *Works*, 4:351–62; Burns, "John Knox and Revolution," 571. On this subject, Knox's colleagues Goodman, Whittingham, and Gilby were certainly in accord with him. Furthermore, Bishop Ponet insisted that women should not rule.

21. *Works*, 6:15–21. Quite appropriate was the comment by John Aylmer, one of the Anglican exiles. He insisted that *The First Blast* would have been acceptable if limited to the person of Mary Tudor, but since it was not, "The Blast was blown out of season." *Works*, 4:355–56. In a letter to Cecil, Knox acknowledged that he had become odious to Elizabeth. *Works*, 6:31; 4:357f; Ridley, *John Knox*, 381; Reid, *Trumpeter of God*, 148. Normally Calvin rejected female rule, but he was more flexible than Knox in regard to exceptions to this situation. See D. E. Holwerda, ed. *Exploring the Heritage of Calvin*, (Grand Rapids: Baker Books, 1976), 236 f.

From 1559 to his death in 1572, Knox seldom mentioned the subject. Knox retained his views on gynecocracy, however, until the end of his life—even defending the thesis of *The First Blast* in 1568 and 1571. In 1571, he responded to those in the General Assembly who had accused him of contradicting the views he had enunciated in *The First Blast.* That treatise, he said, was "grounded upon good reason, upon God's plain truth, and upon most plain and just laws . . . ."

Though Knox defended his views on female rule to the end, the real object of his dislike was not merely female sovereigns per se—nor women in general—but Catholic monarchs, especially female Catholics. In the context of the time, and in the first of several outbursts in 1558 that would gradually refine his views, Knox understandably failed to make clear the ultimate object of his dislike. After all, the female rulers with whom he had experience were all Catholics—namely, Mary Tudor, Mary of Guise, Mary Stewart, and Catherine de Medici. He had not yet encountered any sixteenth-century Deborahs.[22]

LETTER TO THE REGENT OF SCOTLAND

Knox did not feel the repercussions of *The First Blast* for several months because it took time for the book to circulate and for readers to discover the identity of the anonymous author. Meanwhile Knox's pen was busy. By the summer of 1558, he had published three tracts in Geneva that put forward his views on revolution even more clearly. He wrote one to Mary of Guise, one to the nobility, and the third to the common people of Scotland. Moreover, he appended the abortive *Second Blast* to the last tract.

In these works, Knox condemned Tyndale's doctrine of Christian obedience to rulers as sinful. Most sixteenth-century theologians urged the people to obey the monarch—not from fear of earthly punishment—but from fear of God. Knox now instructed the opposite. If the people obeyed the unjust commandments of evil rulers, they would receive a far more terrible punishment from God than any sovereign could inflict upon them. In earlier works, Knox implied the right of resistance. He now imposed upon the nobility, estates, and common people the duty of armed resistance to a Catholic sovereign.

22. *Works*, 6:594, 558–59; Greaves, "Controversy over Gynecocracy," 15–16; Greaves, *Theology and Revolution*, 157–68; Robert Healey, "John Knox's History: A Complete Sermon on Christian Piety," *Church History* 61, no. 3 (1992): 319–33.

While in Scotland in 1556, Knox had originally written a letter to the Queen Regent. But she ridiculed it. He now broadcast it again with additions that drove home his point more forcefully. The nature of the two letters was entirely different because of the harsh additions in the second. Knox's theme stated that the Queen Regent should cooperate in reforming the Scottish church because Romanism had corrupted it. If, however, she failed to perform this duty, God's judgment would befall her.

In this letter, Knox once again asserted the concept of corporate responsibility for consenting to sin. Divine judgment would fall on those maintaining tyranny "or that do consent to their beastly cruelty." Then he attacked what he considered to be a Satanic lie: The civil magistrate cannot reform religion because such matters are referred to the church. To support this position, Knox maintained that God has established the secular power to reform religion and check the transgressions of the church. Yet what if the state merely supports the idolatrous practices of the church? Then the people must resist. Even lowly individuals—if they speak as God's ambassadors—have the authority to rebuke princes for their transgressions. The vocation of the prophet (which Knox believed himself to be) is to condemn idolatrous rulers. This second letter to the regent, because of its personal nature, did not intend to incite rebellion. But it did, for the first time, present revolt as a general religious proposition. *The First Blast* had been even more specific in its objective. Knox now repeated his assertion that the real treason was not to oppose an idolatrous monarch to the death.[23]

THE APPELLATION

Having little hope of receiving a favorable hearing from Mary of Guise, Knox next turned his attention to the nobles. What he had said to the Queen Regent, he now put more clearly in *The Appellation*. *The Appellation* hammered at two points. One, the nobility were obligated to actively oppose and punish idolatrous rulers. Two, all subjects were duty bound to actively oppose and punish idolatrous rulers. This pamphlet took the form of an appeal from the sentence of Scottish bishops—who had tried Knox in *absentia* and burned him in effigy—to the nobles and Estates of

23. *Works*, 4:435–36, 441, 445, 452, 458–59.

Scotland. In theory, at least, Knox did not appeal to the nobility as a class to take arbitrary action, but to an established constitutional body.[24]

Civil Authority

Knox went to considerable lengths to sustain his charge that the establishment of "true religion" pertained not only to the ecclesiastical estate, but to the civil authority as well. In this context, he referred to the nobility as the civil power. In the "Commonwealth of Israel," the magistrate was superior to the priest. In all matters, Moses the magistrate prevailed over Aaron the priest. Knox went on to cite many godly kings of Judah and Israel as illustrations of temporal authorities interpreting God's law and reforming religion.[25]

With these numerous Old Testament precedents, Knox found it inconceivable for anyone to question the right of the magistrate—or more specifically of the nobility—to reform religion. And Knox was greatly concerned that the nobility fulfill these duties. He told the nobles to prevent bishops from persecuting Protestants, to ensure the "right" instruction in religion, and to depose and execute those defrauding the people of God's Word.[26] God honored the nobles by placing them above other people for the purpose of promoting his religion and not just to honor them. As Knox put it: "God . . . has appointed you to be his lieutenants, and by his own seal has marked you to be Magistrates, and to rule above your brethren, to whom nature . . . has made you like in all points." Thus it would be horrible ingratitude if "you should be found unfaithful to him [who] has honored you."[27]

If Knox had found a monarch to reform religion, he would not have turned to the nobility. But he found no such sovereign. He therefore emphasized that when a ruler fails to maintain true religion, the task falls to the nobility. The nobles are duty bound to perform this charge even if it means rebellion against their sovereign. In this notion Knox espoused a doctrine similar to what Beza and Viret had previously embraced. To the nobles Knox said, "Now if your King be a man ignorant of God, enemy to his true religion, . . . and a persecutor of Christ's members; shall you be

24. Ibid., 4:469–70.
25. Ibid., 4:485–87.
26. Ibid., 4:481–82.
27. Ibid., 4:481.

excused, if with silence you pass over his iniquity?" Certainly not, retorted Knox. God did not place the nobility in authority to "flatter your king in his folly or blind rage." Rather they must assist the sovereign in areas honoring God but "correct and repress" him in matters "repugning God's Word."[28]

In *The Appellation,* Knox denounced the orthodox doctrine of Christian obedience as sinful. He declared blind compliance to a wicked command to be sin. God has not required obedience to rulers when they decree impiety. To say that God does is no less blasphemy than to make God the author of sin. Moreover, if the nobles and people comply with their sovereign in manifest wickedness, they will be punished along with him.[29]

In *The Appellation,* Knox also laid the foundation for the theme of his *Letter to the Commonalty,* which declared, "None provoking the people to idolatry ought to be exempted from the punishment of death." The personal status of such an individual was of no consequence, be they monarch or commoner. Moreover, the punishment of idolatry and blasphemy does not pertain only to kings and rulers. Rather, it relates to all persons according to their Christian vocation and the opportunity afforded to them by God to administer vengeance. Citing Deuteronomy 13, Knox issued the call for revolution—he directed Moses' commandment to slay idolaters to all people, not just to the nobles.[30]

Yet Knox never called for indiscriminate slaughter. He distinguished between the treatment to be accorded idolaters, who had never known "true religion," and those who had known it but had forsaken it. The apostles did not put non-Christians to death because they had never known God's Word. It was different, nevertheless, for England. This nation had established Protestantism under Edward VI and then had backslidden into idolatry. All English subjects—nobility and commoners alike—should have revolted against Mary and executed her along with her priests and assistants. Knox did not advocate the slaying of all Catholics in Catholic states, but for an application of the death penalty by a Protestant government against Catholic counterrevolutionaries.[31]

---

28. Ibid., 4:495–96. Knox also opened the door to revolt in the case of a tyrant's oppressing the people.

29. Ibid., 4:495, 497–98.

30. Ibid., 4:499–501.

31. *Works,* 4:500, 507; Ridley, *John Knox,* 276.

Covenant Obligations

Knox's concept of disobedience—particularly his extension of active resistance to the people—occurred in a covenant context. In his *Godly Letter,* Knox spoke of a covenant between God and the elect. The *Faithful Admonition* implied the existence of a league between the king and the people. In *The Appellation,* Knox now gave the covenant new political implications. Previously the covenant obligation only demanded separation from idolatry. But now the godly (nobles and people) must punish idolatry.

The covenant provided an important theological argument for Knox. It enabled him to overcome the idea that only the lesser magistrates can revolt, thus leading him to advocate popular rebellion as a means for removing idolatry and tyranny. Knox insisted that not only the magistrates, but the people are also bound by the covenant to uphold the rule of godliness and to revenge any injustices done to God's majesty or laws. The covenant binds not only the chief rulers but the whole people to punish idolatry and tyranny.

The Appellation witnessed three types of the covenant, all designed to promote true worship. A covenant existed between the sovereign and the people of Scotland, and Knox included the nobility in this covenant. Along with the monarch, they have obligations to the people to support "true religion." Furthermore, Knox saw a covenant between God and the nobles and magistrates to reform religion. Lastly, he still maintained the notion of a covenant between God and the people. This covenant provided the basis for his *Letter to the Commonalty.*[32]

LETTER TO THE COMMONALTY

Did Knox depend solely on the nobility? No! Because he felt the nobility had let him down before, he refused to leave the reformation of religion solely in their hands. He therefore penned A *Letter to the Commonalty.* He did not address this pamphlet to the lower classes—whom he designated elsewhere as a "rascal multitude"—but more to the middle class, that is,

---

32. *Works,* 4:488–89, 500–6; Greaves, "John Knox and Resistance Theory," 16, 18, 22; Richard L. Greaves, "John Knox and the Covenant Tradition," *Journal of Ecclesiastical History* 24 (January 1973): 27–28.

the lairds and burgesses. Though the nobility were powerful, the middle class played a major role in bringing about the Reformation.[33]

The Letter to the Commonalty accompanied *The Appellation* and contained a similar theme: "What I have required of the Queen Regent, Estates, and Nobility, I cannot cease to require of you . . . which be the Commonalty of the same."[34] Knox began by establishing the spiritual equality of the commonality. When he mentioned equality in his writings, he did so in a spiritual, not political context. Knox acknowledged a divinely ordained distinction between rulers and common people in civil policies. In regard to salvation, however, all are equal and share equal responsibility for promoting the faith.[35]

Knox then proceeded to lay down the duties of the commonalty in matters of religion. Subjects may legally require from their civil rulers the provision of "true" preachers and expel false prophets (i.e. Catholics). If the temporal powers refuse, then the people may provide for their own ministers and defend them against persecution. Moreover, the Protestants could withhold their tithes from the Catholic Church. Knox informed the people that they could not use their lowly status as an excuse for not establishing "true religion." Failure to reform religion would bring divine vengeance. God indeed punishes not only the chief offenders, but all who consent to iniquity.

Knox based his arguments here—as he did elsewhere—on the thesis that people who yield to the rule of idolaters commit idolatry themselves.[36] He required the commonalty to work with Parliament and the nobles in repressing tyranny, rather than against them. Yet, Knox did not desire anarchy or democracy, but rather reform in accord with God's law and the covenant obligation. Anarchy is obviously contrary to divine law and not conducive to the reform Knox had in mind. Moreover, in the social and political context of sixteenth-century Scotland, no one even considered social or political democracy as options.[37]

---

33. W. Stanford Reid, "The Middle Class Factor in the Scottish Reformation," *Church History* 16 (1947): 150.

34. *Works*, 4:523.

35. *Works*, 4:527–28. See also Richard Greaves, "Calvinism, Democracy, and the Political Thought of John Knox," *Occasional Papers of the American Society for Reformation Research*, 1 (1978): 86–87.

36. *Works*, 4:533–35.

37. Greaves, "John Knox and Resistance Theory," 22, 23; Greaves, "Democracy and

THE SECOND BLAST

Knox attached the abortive *Second Blast*, which he never completed, to his letters to the nobility and commonalty. Apparently, *The Second Blast* would have been more radical than *The First Blast*. Why? Here he applied revolutionary principles to cases other than female rule. *The Second Blast* acknowledged Knox's authorship to *The First Blast*, and then proceeded to set forth further propositions.

First, a king does not rule over a Christian people by birth only, "but in his election must the ordinance of which God has established in the election of inferior judges be observed." Next, no manifest idolater should be given public office in a kingdom that has once acknowledged Jesus Christ and the gospel. Third, no oath can bind people to obey and maintain tyrants against God and his known truth. Finally, if people have elected a ruler who then turns out to be an idolater, the people may depose and punish such a sovereign.[38]

The first proposition of *The Second Blast* declared that the basis of political authority depends on the ordinance of God. This statement may contain the climax of Knox's political thought. Still, *The Second Blast* also implied the covenant idea or social compact between the people and their rulers. Though Knox acknowledged that rulers receive their authority from God, he seemed to say that God bestows this authority through the people and estates.

Actually, at this point Knox attempted to answer a question that perplexed many sixteenth-century religious leaders: How are evil or tyrannical magistrates sometimes set in authority over people? Martin Bucer and Peter Martyr still insisted—as a just punishment for sins—that such a situation must be due to the ordinance of God. Knox gave a different answer. He did not mention how rulers are chosen. He indicated, however, that if a people discover they have an idolatrous or tyrannical ruler, this situation can only mean that they made a mistake in selecting such a person. They failed to read the signs God had provided in order for people to recognize a godly ruler.[39]

John Knox" 83.

38. *Works*, 4:539–40.

39. *Works*, 4:539–40; Burns, "The Political Ideas of the Scottish Reformation," 260; Greaves, "John Knox and Resistance Theory," 23; Quentin Skinner, *The Foundations of Modern Political Thought*, 2 vols. (Cambridge: Cambridge University Press, 1978), 2:229–30.

Four pamphlets published prior to August 1558 spelled out Knox's ideas regarding government and religion—namely, the rights of subjects against idolatrous and oppressive rulers. He introduced his ideas in *The First Blast*, but detailed his position in three subsequent pamphlets. Knox first asked the Queen Regent, Mary of Guise, to reform the church. She ignored him. So he then requested the nobles to force such reforms and called upon the lairds and burgesses to pressure the rulers toward the same objective. The Scottish reformer made his position unambiguously clear: Nobles have the right to depose an unrepentant monarch and, if the rulers fail to act, the common people can set up their own "reformed church." After the radical ideas of these four pamphlets, Knox more or less amplified or modified similar themes for the remainder of his career.

A BRIEF EXHORTATION TO ENGLAND

But Knox was not completely through with political ideas. He once again turned his thoughts to England. Mary Tudor had died in November 1558, but the English refugees on the Continent were not certain whether Elizabeth would make England Protestant once again. Accordingly, Knox penned *A Brief Exhortation to England*. This work—completed in January 1559—urged Elizabeth's subjects to accept in religion only what Scripture expressly commands.

Repeatedly, Knox insisted that England had broken the covenant obligations by submitting to idolatry during Mary Tudor's reign, or at least in not resisting her. Knox presented many testimonies from the Old Testament as a mirror for England. These illustrations all had one theme: Failure to resist idolatry incurs corporate guilt and will be punished collectively.[40]

England could only purge this corporate guilt by re-establishing Protestantism and by putting the Catholic leaders to death. In removing Catholicism and restoring Protestantism nothing must be a snare. It mattered little whether king or Parliament approved because only God's Word set the standard in matters of religion. God's commandments must be so established that no ruler would attempt to change them. If they did, they would become unfit to govern and be sentenced to death as God commanded.[41]

---

40. *Works*, 5:507, 510, 512–13, 517.
41. Ibid., 5:515–16.

Knox's indebtedness to Hebrew ideas was clearly manifested in his insistence that subjects are responsible for the religious policies of their sovereigns. Such a concept indeed completely eliminated any notion of religious toleration for Knox: Neither "power nor liberty" may "be permitted to any to live without the yoke of discipline by God's Word . . . or to change, to disannul . . . one jot in religion." Knox made it a religious duty for Protestants to oppose a Catholic monarch—but if Catholics should resist, they would be rebelling against God.[42]

In *A Brief Exhortation to England*, Knox went beyond destroying Romanism and establishing Protestantism. Shades of the Christian commonwealth envisioned in the *Book of Discipline* could be seen. Not only must the civil government install Protestantism, but the ruling authorities must also take definite steps to preserve such a religion. All papists must be removed from civil offices for no Catholic can rule over a Protestant nation. Next, ministers must be maintained in most cities and towns. Furthermore, the church and state must work closely in discipline, with the state bringing its laws into harmony with Scripture. Lastly, schools ought to be set up and run by Protestant magistrates and educators.

In this exhortation, Knox saw the state supporting the church in maintaining the Christian commonwealth. But at the same time, he exhorted ministers not to become entangled in civil affairs. Knox, of course, would insist in later writings that the ministers could critically evaluate the practices of government in the light of Scripture.[43]

LETTER TO CECIL

In April 1559—shortly before Knox returned to Scotland—he wrote a letter to William Cecil, Elizabeth's secretary of state. In addition to condemning Cecil for his collaboration with idolatry during Queen Mary's reign, Knox proposed a bargain with the English government. Elizabeth should concede that female rule as a general principle was unlawful. In turn, he would then proclaim her to be a Deborah and an exception to the rule. Knox was willing to take a more generous view of Deborah than he did in *The First Blast*, that is, she was exempt from the probation against female rule. He would not, however, admit that such an exception nullified the general principle. Nor was the tone of the reformer's letter apologetic.

42. *Works*, 5:516; Greaves, "John Knox and Resistance Theory", 24.

43. *Works*, 5:515–16.

Knox and Elizabeth agreed on two things: In general women should be subject to men, and Elizabeth herself was an exception. Elizabeth believed that she ought to be exempt because she was a queen. Conversely, Knox regarded her as an exception because God had appointed her to be queen. Elizabeth, of course, accepted Protestantism. But she believed her subjects should obey her even if she were a Catholic. On the other hand, Knox contended they should obey her only so long as she remained a Protestant. This incongruity presented a deep disagreement and one not easily reconciled.[44]

It is difficult to measure the impact of Knox's writings on Scotland before his return brought the force of his personality into play. The pamphlets written in the spring and summer of 1558 could hardly have circulated widely before autumn. By then—as the Edinburgh riot on St. Giles Day (September 1) demonstrated—Protestant strength and indignation together with social unrest had already created an explosive situation. Though ideologies in themselves usually do not make revolutions, a movement of this kind needs an ideology. And there can be no doubt that Knox's writings and preaching did much to provide such ideas.

44. *Works*, 6:15–21; 2:16–22; Ridley, *John Knox*, 312.

6

Confronting the Anabaptists and Defending Predestination (1557–1560)

DURING HIS EXILE YEARS, Knox had more things on his mind than formulating a theory of resistance to Catholic rulers. Along with the other Protestant Reformers, John Knox waged a war against two fronts—the Catholic establishment and the left wing radicals. While his great enemy was the Catholic Church, recognized by law and backed by the power of the state, he was not about to be outflanked on the left. So he vehemently opposed these radicals, whom he loosely identified as Anabaptists. His attack on these radicals, however, came largely in the realm of ideas for little is known about his actual dealings with them. In the process of answering the Anabaptists, the reformer also elaborated upon his doctrine of predestination. By no means can Knox's writings regarding the Anabaptists and predestination be seen as the centerpiece of his career, but they did occupy about one sixth of his writings and thus cannot be ignored.

Knox and most of the Protestant reformers tended to tar all radicals with the same brush. In doing so, they often failed to distinguish between peaceful or violent radicals or between orthodox or heretical dissenters. In fact, for Knox and many reformers the derisive term Anabaptist was a generic label for all kinds of nonconformity—a term virtually synonymous with fanaticism or heresy. Thus they frequently linked the term with the Pelagians (freewillers), Novationists, Arians, Manichaeans, Antinomonians, Familists, and other groups that had no relationship with historic Anabaptism.[1]

1. Irving B. Horst, "England," *Mennonite Encyclopedia* (Scottdale, PA: Mennonite Publishing House) 2:218; Harry Loewen, *Luther and the Radicals* (Waterloo, ON: Wilfred Laurier University Press, 1974), 21; William Balke, *Calvin and the Anabaptist Radicals* (Grand Rapids: Eerdmans, 1981), 11, 21–22, 41, 116; John Oyer, *Lutheran Reformers*

Along with the other Protestant reformers, Knox generally opposed the Anabaptists on two grounds—a volatile mixture of civil instability and false doctrine. Theologically they tended to part company with the Anabaptists over such issues as baptism, human nature, predestination, sacraments, civil government, the use of force, the nature of the church, and perfectionism in the Christian life. With some radicals, even the Trinity and the authority of Scripture became contentious issues. More important than doctrine, however, was the threat Anabaptists seemed to pose to the civic order and social stability. Several violent incidents—especially the Peasants' War associated with Thomas Müntzer and the violent overthrow of the city of Münster—had sent chills through both Protestant and Catholic ranks.[2] In general, they lumped the Anabaptist radicals all together and identified them as anarchists, blasphemers, heretics, and the enemies of God.

References to the Anabaptists are sprinkled throughout the six volumes of Knox's complete works. While these statements are brief, they do reveal his differences with the Anabaptists over specific issues. But two of his treatises contain more than passing references. They are entitled *To His Brethren in Scotland* and *An Answer to a Great Number of*

Against Anabaptists (The Hague, Netherlands: Martinus Nihoff, 1964), 8–40; Galen Johnson, " The Development of Calvin's Doctrine of Infant Baptism in Reaction to the Anabaptists," *Mennonite Quarterly Review* 73 (October 1999): 807–8. To some extent, Bucer was an exception to the above generalizations. While he attempted to counter the Anabaptists, he was more conciliatory toward them. See John S. Oyer, "Bucer Opposes the Anabaptists," *Mennonite Quarterly Review* 68 (January 1944): 24, 36. Krahn sees Bucer as having a more hostile attitude toward the Anabaptists than does Oyer. See Henry G. Krahn. "Martin Bucer's Strategy Against Sectarian Dissent in Strasbourg," *Mennonite Quarterly Review* 50 (July 1976): 163–80.

2. Johnson, "Calvin and Infant Baptism," 803–8; Balke, *Calvin and the Radicals*, 41; Oyer, *Lutheran Reformers Against Anabaptists*, 127, 157; George Huntston Williams, *The Radical Reformation* 3rd ed. (Kirksville, MO: Sixteenth Century Journal Publishers, 1992), 912–42; Hans-Jürgen Goertz, "Thomas Müntzer: Revolutionary Between the Middle Ages and Modernity," *Mennonite Quarterly Review* 64 (January 1990): 23–31; Hans J. Hillerbrand, "The Propaganda of the Münster Anabaptists," *Mennonite Quarterly Review* 52 (October 1988): 507–11; Richard Bailey, "The Sixteenth Century Apocalyptic Heritage and Thomas Müntzer," *Mennonite Quarterly Review* 52 (January 1983): 27–44; James M. Stayer, *Anabaptists and the Sword* (Lawrence, KS: Coronado Press, 1976); Hans-Jürgen Goertz, "The Mystic and the Hammer: Thomas Müntzer's Theological Basis for Revolution," *Mennonite Quarterly Review* 50 (April 1976): 83–113; Abraham Friesen, *Thomas Muentzer, a Destroyer of the Godless* (Berkeley, CA: University of California Press, 1990); James M. Stayer and Werner O. Packull, *The Anabaptists and Thomas Müntzer* (Dubuque, IA: Kendall/Hunt, 1980).

Blasphemous Cavillations Written by an Anabaptist and Adultery to God's Eternal Predestination. Still, little is known about Knox's actual dealings with the radical groups. So any analysis of Knox's relationship with the Anabaptists must focus on his writings against them. In fact, Knox's bark was worse than his bite. Despite the fact that he had the opportunity to harm the radicals, there is no record of him actually doing so.[3]

LETTER TO HIS BRETHREN

As noted in a previous chapter, when Knox was in Geneva he received a letter from the Scottish lords urging him to return to Scotland to promote the Protestant cause. He made the trip to Dieppe with the intention of getting a ship for Scotland. Here a letter informed him that the lords had reconsidered their invitation and requested that he wait in Dieppe for a final decision on the matter. While waiting, he penned three letters to his brethren. The first and third letters concerned political matters and do not speak to the subject at hand.

But the second letter, dated December 1 and addressed *To His Brethren in Scotland.* warned them to avoid the pernicious influences of radical groups. Knox never used the word "Anabaptist" in this letter—indeed, Anabaptism in any strict use of the word did not reach Scotland until well after Knox's death.[4] The radicals were clearly on his mind, however. And in the 1557 letter, he promised to write more against them—a task he accomplished in a later, extensive treatise on predestination and the Anabaptist errors that appeared in 1560.[5]

Knox's thinking on the subject had been conditioned by his earlier contacts with the Anabaptists near London. The radical move-

---

3. Several works devote a substantial number of pages to Knox and the Anabaptists. See Richard Kyle, "John Knox Confronts the Anabaptists: The Intellectual Aspects of His Encounter," *Mennonite Quarterly Review* 75 (October 2001): 493–515; Irvin Buckwalter Horst, *The Radical Brethren: Anabaptism and the English Reformation to 1558* (Nieuwkoop, Netherlands: De Graff, 1972); Jasper Ridley, *John Knox* (New York: Oxford University Press, 1966); M.T. Pearse, *Between Known Men and Visible Saints: A Study in Sixteenth-Century English Dissent* (Cranbury, NJ: Associated University Presses, 1994), 130–41. One unpublished and somewhat polemical manuscript contains a chapter on Knox and the Anabaptists: Kevin Reed, *John Knox: The Forgotten Reformer* (Dallas: Presbyterian Heritage Publications, 1997). This work is available on CD-ROM.

4. Ridley, *John Knox,* 298.

5. John Knox, *The Works of John Knox* 6 Vols. ed. David Laing (Edinburgh: Printed for the Bannatyne Club, 1846–1864), 4:271; Pearse, *Between Men and Saints,* 132.

ments in England had been marked by a considerable overlapping of anti-Trinitarianism, Anabaptism of the Melchiorite strain, Libertinism, Freewillers, and Spiritualism.[6] So in his letter of 1557, Knox warned his brethren in Scotland against radical or Anabaptist tendencies rather than a clear discernable movement. In doing so he railed against three sectarian inclinations: a Christological heresy, which he called Arianism; the denial of predestination; and most important, a bent toward perfectionism.[7]

Nature of the Church

At the time of this letter, Protestantism had not yet been established by law in Scotland. Accordingly, Protestants existed in "privy kirks"—that is, house churches in which they studied the Bible and administered the sacraments. The Protestant movement had been growing largely because of immorality within the Catholic Church. It seemed the tables were now being turned against them on precisely this issue. According to the radicals, the sinful lives of the Protestant nobles had discredited the whole movement. And people were now separating from the "privy kirks" in search of a more holy life. Such perfectionists became the object of Knox's attack.[8]

Knox began the letter *To His Brethren in Scotland* by castigating the Catholics for both their diabolical doctrine and their corrupt lives. But he quickly turned to the primary focus of the letter—an argument against

6. Not until later in the sixteenth century, did Anabaptism become clearly distinguishable from English Calvinist separatism. See Williams, *Radical Reformation*, 1196–1201; Horst, "England," 215–18; C. Norman Kraus, "Anabaptist Influence on English Separatism as Seen in Robert Browne," *Mennonite Quarterly Review* 34 (January 1960): 5–19; O. T. Hargrave, "The Freewillers in the English Reformation," *Church History* 37:3 (1968): 271–80; Andrew D. Penny, "The Freewill Movement in the Southeast of England, 1550–1558," (Ph.D diss. University of Guelph, 1980), 9–12, 46–47, 176–88; Peter Pauls, "A Pestiferous Sect: The Anabaptists in England from 1530–1660," *Journal of Mennonite Studies* 3 (1985): 63–65; Duncan B. Heriot, "Anabaptistsm in England During the 16th and 17th Centuries," *Transactions Congregational Historical Society* 12:7 (1936): 252, 257; Horst, *Radical Brethren*, 31–36; Pearse, *Between Men and Saints*, 24, 141; C. J. Clement *Religious Radicalism in England 1535–1565* (Edinburgh: Rutherford House, 1997), 6, 28, 30–31, 106; Merc Pearse, *The Great Restoration: The Religious Radicals of the 16th and 17th Centuries* (Carlisle, UK: Paternoster Press, 1998), 119–20.

7. *Works*, 4:270; Pearse, *Between Men and Saints*, 131.

8. *Works*, 4:261–75; Richard Greaves, *Theology and Revolution in the Scottish Reformation* (Grand Rapids: Christian University Press, 1980), 49–50; Ridley, *John Knox*, 256; W. Stanford Reid, *Trumpeter of God* (New York: Scribner's, 1974), 143; James Kirk, *Patterns of Reform* (Edinburgh: T and T Clark, 1989), 1–15; Pearse, *Between Men and Saints*, 131.

the perfectionist sectarians who were to be "no less lamented" than the Catholics. Despite some invective language, Knox's tone in this letter was generally conciliatory. In fact, he states that he had no malice toward the sectaries but desired to communicate with them the light of God's Word.[9]

These radicals, claimed Knox, had not only separated from the "privy kirks" but had also displayed contempt for the church sacraments. In doing so, they made two mistakes. First, they judged a church's doctrine by the lives of its members. Second, they required an unrealistic level of purity and justice from the church—greater "than was ever found in any congregation since the beginning." According to Knox such reasoning was absurd. Many Turks live a stricter moral life than is required by Scripture, while sin has abounded in the household of God. For prime examples, he cited David and the "congregations of Corinth, Galatia, and Thessalonica" in which grievous transgressions were committed: "fornication, adultery, incest, strife, debate, contention, and envy."[10]

Despite these transgressions, Knox still affirmed these congregations as "true kirks of Christ Jesus." Righteousness, he insisted, was required of all Christians but it was not the ultimate test of the "true church." If so, the old Catholic Church could just be reformed. Rather, the marks of a true church were the preaching of God's Word and the correct administration of the sacraments: "Where Christ Jesus is affirmed, preached and . . . where his sacraments are truly ministered . . . there is the true kirk of Christ Jesus." From such a church "ought no man to separate himself . . . ."[11]

Knox further contended that people should not separate from the "true church" just because some individual members led immoral lives—which is exactly the same argument used by reputable Catholic leaders to prevent an exodus from their church to Protestantism. Knox insisted Protestants had left the Roman Church for reasons other than the evil lives led by Catholics: namely, their doctrines blasphemed Christ and his sacraments were "polluted and profaned by the vain inventions of men." To be sure, some Protestants were not living exemplary lives. But the privy kirks were not guilty of false doctrine and corrupting the sacraments. And

9. *Works*, 4:263.

10. Ibid., 4:263–64, 266.

11. *Works*, 4:266–67; Reid, *Trumpeter of God*, 143; Richard Kyle, "The Nature of the Church in the Thought of John Knox," *Scottish Journal of Theology* 37:4 (1984): 489–91. *The Scots Confession* notes three marks of the church—the two noted plus church discipline.

unless the sectaries could prove such a charge, they were not justified in leaving the Protestant church.[12]

Ancient Heresies

Knox next took another line of attack. He linked the radicals in Scotland with the ancient heresies of Pelagianism and Arianism. In so doing, he implied that they were Anabaptists because he accused them of the same errors that he later elaborated in his 1560 treatise against the Anabaptists. These heresies included an assertion of free will, justification by works and not by faith, and a rejection of election and reprobation. Like Arius, some of these radicals even denied the doctrines of Christ's divinity and the Trinity.[13]

Knox regarded these Anabaptist-like radicals as a group to be feared more than the Papists. To him they were "more covert, and therefore more dangerous . . . for under the color and cloak of mortification of the flesh, of godly life, and of Christian justice, they become private blasphemers of Christ Jesus." Their major mistake is their elevation of rationalism over faith. "The fountain of this their damnable error" is that "they acknowledge no justice except that which their foolish brain is able to comprehend . . . ."[14]

Accordingly, Knox urged the Scottish Protestants to be on guard against such teachers and professors. They are to "try the spirits" and "suffer no man without trial and examination to take upon him the office of preacher, neither to travel amongst the simple sheep of Christ Jesus, assembling them in private conversations." Knox was determined to guard the flock against these radicals. In particular, no Protestant preacher outside the developing Reformed Church was to formulate a "privy kirk."[15]

AN ANSWER TO THE ANABAPTIST

Knox probably wrote his second treatise against the Anabaptists—*An Answer to a Great Number of Blasphemous Cavillations Written by an Anabaptist, and Adultery to God's Eternal Predestination*—in late 1558 and early 1559 and it was published in 1560. *An Answer* is Knox's longest

12. *Works*, 4:267–68; Ridley, *John Knox*, 256–57; Greaves, *Theology and Revolution*, 51–52.

13. *Works*, 4:269–70; Ridley, *John Knox*, 257.

14. Ibid., 4:270–71.

15. *Ibid.*, 4:271–72.

work, extending to some 170,000 words, excluding the lengthy quotations from the work he was refuting.[16]

Apparently he had two main purposes in writing this volume: he intended to defend the doctrine of predestination and he wanted to attack all the opinions and sects labeled as Anabaptist. Consequently, he usually addressed his Anabaptist opponent concerning salvation, predestination, free will, and other related issues—e.g. the nature of God and humanity. The work seldom mentions other critical differences between Knox and the Anabaptists—such as the nature of the church, infant baptism or the use of the sword.

Not all scholars, however, accept this assessment. Richard Greaves disputes the notion that *An Answer* was written to refute the challenge of an anonymous Anabaptist. Knox wrote his treatise on predestination shortly after the publication of *The First Blast*—a work that not only displeased Calvin but upset some English Protestants. Greaves contends that Knox wrote *An Answer* largely as a pedantic exercise to maintain his working relationship with Calvin and his disciples, and as a message to the English Protestants to remain loyal to Reformed doctrine.[17] This interesting theory has merit. *The First Blast* had indeed upset Calvin, and Knox may now have desired to please the Swiss Reformers. Nevertheless, no solid evidence exists to reject Knox's own stated purpose for writing his treatise—i.e to reply to an Anabaptist and thus counter what he regarded as a radical threat against the Reformed Church.[18]

The Anabaptist Threat

What Anabaptist threat did Knox perceive? Anabaptism arrived in England—largely as an influx of persecuted refugees from the Netherlands—during the 1530s just when Henry VIII's break from Catholicism created an environment in which religious nonconformity could flourish. The Dutch-Flemish brand of Anabaptism found fertile

16. The volume is 468 pages (Laing's edition). See Knox, *Works*, 5 and Ridley, *John Knox*, 290.

17. Greaves, *Theology and Revolution*, 28–29; Richard Greaves, "The Knoxian Paradox: Ecumenism and Nationalism in the Scottish Reformation," *Records of Scottish Church History Society* (Summer 1973): 91–92.

18. Richard Kyle, "The Concept of Predestination in the Thought of John Knox," *Westminster Theological Journal* 46:1 (1984): 55, 56; Richard Kyle, *The Mind of John Knox* (Lawrence, KS: Coronado Press, 1984), 104–5.

soil in England, where Lollardy had long been active. And indeed, the two movements were often confused with each other. At the same time, Anabaptism quickly blended in with a number of heretical and noncon-formist groups—both past and present—and became a term by which opponents could label anyone suspected of being a latter day Manichaean, Pelagian, Catharist, Donatist, or Arian.[19]

Moreover, since people tended to equate the belief in free will with Anabaptism, virtually all English dissenters who embraced anti-predestinarian ideas or similar beliefs were linked with Anabaptism. Besides, with or without Anabaptist influences, the gathered church as an organization was gaining steam in England—especially among the Freewillers. Although continental Anabaptism clearly had some impact, seldom did English radicalism embrace the practice of believers baptism—the hallmark of genuine Anabaptism. Thus, the people designated as English Anabaptists might be better seen as fellow travelers with continental Anabaptism and identified by the more general term "radical".[20] Nonetheless, since Knox labeled his radical opponents as Anabaptists, this study will utilize that term.

During the reign of Edward VI, Knox was forced to deal with this growing radical, or Anabaptist movement. In the winter of 1552–1553 while Knox was in London, he had an encounter with a free-thinking extremist who was categorized as an Anabaptist by both Protestants and Catholics. According to Knox's description of the meeting six years later in *An Answer*, this person had come to him requesting a private meeting. Because of the weighty matters to be discussed—"of such importance, as since the days of the apostles"—Knox promised not to reveal their conversation to anyone. The Anabaptist presented Knox with a book, which he claimed to be as much written by God as any of the canonical Scriptures, and asked for Knox's opinion of its content. After reading the first proposition—in which the author declared that the devil, not God,

19. Horst, *Radical Brethren*, 35–36; Horst, "England," 216; Pauls, "A Pestiferous Sect," 60–63; Kraus, "Anabaptist Influence," 5–7; Heriot, "Anabaptism in England," 37, 312–13; Hargrave, "Freewillers in the English Reformation," 271–73, 278; Alan Kreider, ed. "An English Episcopal Draft Article Against the Anabaptists, 1536," *Mennonite Quarterly Review* 59 (Jan. 1975): 38; Penny, "Freewill Movement in England," 45–48, 176–88, 220–22; Clement, *Religious Radicalism in England*, 6, 28, 31, 106.

20. Pearse, *Great Restoration*, 119–20, 138; Pearse, *Between Men and Saints*, 23–25, 61, 141; Clement, *Religious Radicalism in England*, 3, 6, 25, 28, 30–31, 106, 337, 342–43.

had created the world and the wicked creatures in it—[21]Knox saw evidence of the ancient Manichaean heresy.

He nevertheless gave a gentle reply, questioning how any reasonable person could "believe things directly fighting against God's true and plain Word revealed?" When the Anabaptist insisted that he could prove his doctrine with as good a word as written Scriptures, Knox's rejection of this claim to extra-biblical revelation took on a much harsher tone: "Ye deserve death as a blasphemous person and denier of God, if you prefer any word to that which the Holy Ghost has uttered in his plain Scriptures." At this reply, the Anabaptist snatched the book from Knox's hand and departed, insisting that he would have his book confirmed by men more learned than Knox. Looking back six years later, Knox regretted that he had not kept the book and reported the Anabaptist to a magistrate. Though it probably spared the Anabaptist's life, this failure to reveal the Anabaptist could have created serious problems for Knox. Yet even six years later, Knox would not mention the Anabaptist's name, which still could have led to his arrest and death in Elizabethan England.[22]

Thus *An Answer* was Knox's reply to an Anabaptist whose identity is also still unknown. It does seem clear that Knox knew him personally. He was a radical who supported religious toleration and opposed predestination. Moreover, the author was obviously knowledgeable and well educated—apparently drawing materials from radicals and Catholics alike such as Sebastian Castellio, Michael Servetus, Albert Pighi, and Jacopo Sadeleto.

The book itself, *The Confutation of the Errors of the Careless by Necessity*, exists only in manuscript form without attribution. Several sources have suggested the name of Robert Cooche, and in many ways he matched the general profile. We know that Cooche represented liberal Protestantism during the reign of Edward VI and embraced many Anabaptist views, including some described by Knox. In addition, Cooche was a talented man with a good education who held several minor appointments at the court of Edward VI. Still, we can only say that Cooche's authorship of the *Confutation* remains an educated guess.[23]

21. *Works*, 5:420–21, Ridley, *John Knox*, 126.

22. *Works*, 5:421; Ridley, *John Knox*, 127.

23. *Works*, 5:23–25; Horst, *Radical Brethren*, 117–20; Horst, "England," 217; Michael T. Pearse, "Robert Cooche and Anabaptist Ideas in Sixteenth-Century England," *Mennonite Quarterly Review* 58 (July 1993): 337, 339, 343, 347, 350; Reid, *Trumpeter of God*, 151; Williams, *Radical Reformation*, 1119; Pearse, *Great Restoration*, 128; Clement, *Religious*

The Anabaptist Makes His Case

The struggle between Knox and the Anabaptist took place in a broader context of theological controversies and debate centered on the doctrines of paedobaptism, predestination, and the Trinity. In 1553 Michael Servetus had been burned at the stake for rejecting the doctrines of infant baptism and the Trinity. Knox supported this execution.[24] But the event evoked considerable protest from people like Sebastian Castellio—a professor of Greek at Basel who argued that the beliefs in "the Trinity, predestination, and free justification are non-essentials to be debated at pleasure"—and Jerome Bolsec, an ex-Carmelite who attacked Calvin's views on predestination.[25]

For the radicals, opposition to predestination was more than an intellectual exercise. In their eyes, predestination in official Reformed theology drew people into an inclusive church—thus producing moral laxity—and it led inevitably to the religious coercion of the Reformation state churches. In fact, for many of them anti-predestinarianism took precedence over the separation of church and state.[26] *The Confutation of the Errors of the Careless by Necessity* appeared in this context. Its attack on predestination, its defense of the freedom of the will, and its advocacy of religious toleration—[27]all drawing on the controversial doctrines being espoused by Castellio and Bolsec—placed the treatise squarely within some of the most heated debates of the time.

The argument of *The Confutation* appealed to biblical exegesis, theology, philosophy, logic, and even the experience of personal abuse. At

---

Radicalism in England, 237–60; Pearse, *Between Men and Saints*, 116–30. Penny ("Freewill Movement in England," 251–60) offers John Champneys as a possible alternative to Cooche. Cooche himself did not participate in believers baptism, so in this sense he may not have been a genuine Anabaptist.

24. *Works*, 5:221–22, 224, 226–31. Servetus had been condemned by Protestants and Catholics alike.

25. Sabastian Castellio, *Concerning Heretics*, ed. Roland Bainton (New York: Columbia University Press, 1935), 110 (quote); Greaves, *Theology and Revolution*, 26–27; Kyle, "Predestination in the Thought of Knox," 58.

26. Pearse, *Between Men and Saints*, 130, 136, 139–40; Pearse, *Great Restoration*, 139.

27. Horst, *Radical Brethren*, 117–18; Ridley, *John Knox*, 291–92. No copy of the *Confutation* has ever been located. However, a version of it can be found in Knox's reply to the Anabaptist. During the sixteenth century, controversialists commonly cited part of an opponents' work. But Knox's lengthy reply went beyond the common practice and he may have quoted the entire book.

critical points the author reinforced his exegesis with the judgments of religious authorities. But the main theme of the text was a rejection of predestination and support of free will by appealing to Scriptural references. For example, in one place the Anabaptist confronted Knox with a passage from Ezekiel: "I will not the death of a sinner, but rather he convert and live."[28]

In general, the Anabaptist followed two lines of attack. God loved all humankind and God had not created anyone with the intent of inflicting them with misery: "And think you that God ordained his just and innocent creatures to condemnation?" This would be tyranny and unrighteousness, "for even the most wicked man in the world, yes, the Devil himself do, then to condemn the innocent and just man."[29]

The chief difficulty with the doctrine of predestination arose in regard to its negative side—reprobation. Therefore, the Anabaptist centered his attack on reprobation, which he called "this horrible doctrine."[30] He constantly asked Knox to produce biblical evidence for reprobation: "I pray you, show me any testimony of the Scripture which so manifestly proves that God has reprobated any before the foundations of the world. God has no respect of persons."[31] The Anabaptist also applied logic to the use of Scripture. To Knox's claim that God reprobated and ordained individuals to damnation, the Anabaptist replied that "in creation God made all men after his own image good and righteous . . . ." If Knox's opinion is correct—said the Anabaptist—then God's decree to elect did not conform with his ordinance in creation. If God created human beings in his own image unto life, why did he reprobate some before creation to be cast away?[32]

The author also made much of the issue of lifestyle. If people were irrevocably elected to eternal life, he argued, then they had no incentive to live a moral life. In fact, the title of his book contained the phrase "careless by necessity." By this he meant that those who believed in predestination felt they would be necessarily saved regardless of how they lived. Furthermore, the Anabaptist called the adherents of predestination "care-

28. *Works*, 5:408–9. The text is from Ezekiel 18 in the *Geneva Bible*.

29. Ibid., 5:90.

30. Ibid., 5:89.

31. Ibid., 5:93.

32. Ibid., 5:106.

less libertines," meaning that they lived a dissolute life.[33] "With the congregation of Thyatira . . . you have the spirit of the prophetess Jezebel, teaching a careless and libertine life." Indeed, he declared the "careless by necessity" to be "more injurious to God then atheists" and even blasphemers.[34]

Knox Lashes Out Against the Anabaptists

Knox responded to these arguments with a twofold approach. On one hand, he launched a frontal attack on any radical opinion that could loosely be called Anabaptist. On the other, he countered the Anabaptist's specific arguments against predestination with his own ideas on the subject. Because he was first and foremost a preacher, not a writer, the reformer made no attempt to systematize his theology. This nonsystematic, pragmatic style was evident in *An Answer*.[35]

Though *An Answer* is a lengthy treatise, it is far from being a systematic one. Instead of developing an orderly argument, Knox assailed the Anabaptist's book, chapter by chapter. The result was repetition, and repetition that was not always consistent with itself. In his haphazard approach to predestination, Knox clearly leaves the impression that he was not truly at home in the subject.[36]

An Answer fumed against most aspects of the Radical Reformation, from Thomas Müntzer to the controversy surrounding the execution of Michael Servetus. Nearly every libertine or nonconformist idea or group became fair game—including the opponents of dogma, the supporters of religious toleration, Freewillers who opposed predestination, Müntzer and the peasants' uprising, and the rationalists who rejected the Trinity. Knox linked all of these radical elements to past heresies—the Donatists, Cathars, Pelagians, and Manichaeans—and considered them to be all

---

33. *Works*, 5:208, 232, 267. Ridley, *John Knox*, 291, 294; Penny, "Freewill Movement in England," 232–51; Pearse, *Between Men and Saints*, 131.

34. *Works*, 5:88, 90.

35. See Kyle, *Mind of Knox*, 16–17, 105; Kyle, "Predestination in the Thought of Knox," 56.

36. James S. McEwen, *The Faith of John Knox* (Richmond: John Knox Press, 1961), 64; Greaves, *Theology and Revolution*, 29–30; Kyle, "Predestination in the Thought of Knox," 56; Kyle, *Mind of Knox*, 105; O. T. Hargrave, "The Predestinarian Offensive of the Marian Exiles at Geneva," *Historical Magazine of the Protestant Episcopal Church* 42 (1973): 118. Pearse (*Between Men and Saints*, 135) contends that Knox was comfortable with the subject of predestination, although this view does not consider the totality of Knox's writings.

part of the same camp.[37] In an invective typical of the age, he denounced the Anabaptists as "venomous liars, persons defamed, and blasphemers of God" and frequently labeled them as "libertines" and "blasphemers." In at least one instance, Knox even spoke of the Anabaptists as having a devil: "I have to do not only with a blasphemer, but even (as it were) with a Devil incarnate . . . ."[38]

More specifically, Knox linked the Anabaptists with other advocates of free will, both past and present. Since, for example, Castellio had attacked Calvin's doctrine of predestination, Knox repeatedly referred to Castellio as the Anabaptist master, captain, champion, and great angel.[39] Knox also connected the Anabaptists with other advocates of free will—the Pelagians and contemporary Catholics such as Albert Pighi and Jacob Sadoleto.[40]

While *An Answer* focused on Knox's disagreement with the Anabaptists over free will and predestination, he also mentioned other areas of contention. To claim that a human being could reject election was to deny God's omnipotent power, said Knox. This made the Anabaptists guilty—like the Manichaeans—of acknowledging a power greater than God.[41] In response to the Anabaptist condemnation of the execution of Servetus, Knox dismissed the Anabaptists as both blasphemous and heretical. "Servetus was an abominable blasphemer against God; and you are justifiers of Servetus," he thundered, "therefore you are blasphemers before God, like abominable as he was." Knox also linked them with a number of Servetus' other heretical views. "Your great prophet" denied the Trinity and the divinity of Christ.[42]

In other places, Knox condemned the notion of the celestial flesh doctrine set forth by Melchoir Hofmann and Menno Simons—that Christ had a heavenly flesh, not that of a man.[43] Knox further soundly

37. *Works*, 5:13, 64, 121, 153, 167, 416–19, 423–35; Horst, *Radical Brethren*, 119; Ridley, *John Knox*, 291.

38. *Works*, 5:54, 115, 167, 172, 175–76, 178, 216, 224, 228, 267, 352, 392, 405.

39. Ibid., 5:16, 37–38, 111, 126, 147, 184, 222, 227, 295, 348, 355, 359, 395–98.

40. Ibid., 5:13, 24, 121, 153, 163, 171, 416, 419.

41. Ibid., 5:64, 421.

42. *Works*, 5:221–28; Ridley, *John Knox*, 196; Horst, *Radical Brethren*, 119; Pearse, *Between Men and Saints*, 139; Pearse, *Great Restoration*, 126, 138.

43. *Works*, 5:228, 455; Williams, *Radical Reformation*, 597; C. Arnold Snyder, *Anabaptist History and Theology* (Kitchner, ON: Pandora Press, 1995), 359–61, 365–66; J. A. Oosterbaan, "The Theology of Menno Simons," *Mennonite Quarterly Review* 35 (July 1961): 92–93; Clement, *Religious Radicalism in England*, 108, 220.

condemned the Anabaptists for denying the power of the civil magistrate, for holding all goods in community, and even for maintaining a plurality of wives.[44] In depicting the Anabaptists as promoters of civic unrest, Knox listed the evils perpetrated by the "pestilent sect" in the Peasant War of 1525 and the Münster debacle of 1535. In doing so, he borrowed substantial portions from John Sleidan's *A Famous Chronicle of Our Time*. This story, of course, portrayed the Anabaptists as wrecking horrible deeds, and Knox recorded them in detail with the intent of discrediting the radical movement. "If that I list to note particular examples, I might show in your sect, and among you, to have been so horrible enormities, as more horrible were never from the beginning."[45]

In Defense of Predestination

In *An Answer* Knox did more than hurl insults at the Anabaptist and lash out against the Radical Reformation. He countered the Anabaptist's arguments theologically, giving particular attention to the doctrine of predestination. From the very beginning of his lengthy reflections on the topic, Knox insisted that he was in full agreement with the judgment of John Calvin.[46] For Knox, the doctrine of predestination was not just a theoretical matter but had great practical importance, revealing a mainspring of his thinking and action.[47]

In *An Answer* Knox went to great lengths to emphasize the practical necessity of predestination in his view of salvation.[48] Without the doctrine of predestination, faith could not be taught nor established. True faith springs from election and not the reverse, for "if you understand that

---

44. *Works*, 5:211, 463. See Penny, "Freewill Movement in England," 102–3.

45. *Works*, 5:423–61 (quote on 461); Pearse, *Between Men and Saints*, 141.

46. *Works*, 5:30. See also James Kirk, "The Influence of Calvinism on the Scottish Reformation," *Records of the Scottish Church History Society* 18 (1974): 158 and V. E. D'Assonville, *John Knox and the Institutes of Calvin: A Few Points of Contact in Their Theology* (Durban, South Africa: Drakensberg, 1960), 33–34, 43. Given Knox's frequent references to Calvin and the content of this work, such a statement seems essentially correct. However, the predestinarian thought of the two reformers exhibited secondary differences due to the methodology and circumstances, and possibly even one variance on a substantial issue. But such nuances lie beyond the scope of this study. See Kyle, "Predestination in the Thought of Knox," 69–71; Kyle, *Mind of Knox*, 117–19; Greaves, *Theology and Revolution*, 38–43; McEwen, *Faith of Knox*, 70.

47. Reid, *Trumpeter of God*, 152.

48. *Works*, 5:25.

election has no promise without faith, I answer, that God's free election in Jesus Christ needs neither promise nor faith . . . but (only) his good pleasure in Christ."[49] Redemption, from start to finish, depended on God's free election, and without it no salvation was possible."[50] In fact, Knox implied that predestination and the gospel were nearly synonymous.[51]

Though Knox accentuated predestination more in the context of soteriology, he certainly integrated it into other areas of dogmatics—such as God and providence, the church, human nature, and good works. Salvation depends on election, but Knox grounded predestination in his concept of God. Of course, for Knox God is immutable and absolutely sovereign. Consequently, predestination is an immutable and sovereign decree.[52] God can never repent of election, neither can the elect refuse election nor finally perish despite their sin. Conversely, Knox regarded reprobation as equally immutable and divinely determined.[53] Just as Calvin had done in the 1530 edition of the *Institutes* and Zwingli even earlier, Knox connected divine predestination and providence: predestination was but a decree within the larger context of providence.[54]

Though never developed systematically, Knox's ecclesiology rested squarely on predestination. The church consists of the elect of God; and if there is no election there is no church.[55] Actually, only the small flock and the invisible church experienced predestination, for the notion of an elected church opposes the national concept of the church. In fact, Knox dedicated his predestination treatise to the church for its instruction: "But yet I say, that the doctrine of God's eternal Predestination is so necessary to the Church of God, that, without the same, can faith neither be

49. Ibid., 5:279–80.

50. Ibid., 5:26–28, 63, 273–81.

51. Ibid., 5:28.

52. *Works*, 5:27, 63–67, 70, 73, 280–81. See also Pierre Janton, *Concept et Sentiment de l'Eglise Chex John Knox; le réformateur ecossaise* (Paris: Presses Universitaries de France, 1972), 91–109; Richard Kyle, "The Divine Attributes in John Knox's Concepts of God," *Westminster Theological Journal* 48:1 (1988): 161–72.

53. *Works*, 5:405–6.

54. *Works*, 5:31–32; D'Assonville, *Knox and the Institutes*, 43, 44; Gottfried W. Locher, *Zwingli's Thought: New Perspectives* (Leiden: E. J. Brill, 1981), 124. See also Richard Kyle, "John Knox's Concept of Divine Providence and Its Influence on His Thought," *Albion* 18:3 (1986): 359–410.

55. Janton, *Concept et Sentiment*, 94–95. See also Kyle, "Nature of the Church in the Thought of John Knox," 485–501.

taught, neither surely established."[56] Predestination not only establishes and multiplies the church but also preserves it. Thus Knox largely related predestination to his ecclesiology in times of stress (e.g. while exiled from 1553 to 1559, when fearful of the Counter-Reformation in 1565). This preservation theme confirmed predestination as a doctrine for the elect more so than for the damned.[57]

Knox also rested his notions of sanctification and good works on his doctrine of predestination. The reformer's sequence was election, true faith and salvation, and then good works. Without the doctrine of predestination human beings could not have a humble knowledge of themselves. True humility comes when the elect become aware that God has illumined their eyes and elected them to salvation, while leaving others in darkness and perdition. The humility that comes through the knowledge of election is the parent of all virtue and the root of all goodness. Thus Knox contended in *An Answer* that the doctrine of predestination established good works. No other doctrine could make one thankful to God and cause one to obey him according to his commandments.[58]

Predestination for Knox included both election and reprobation, which covered all of humanity in God's decree. In the eternal counsel of God, a difference existed in humankind even before creation.[59] Knox did not speculate about the number elected to life or reprobated to death. Rather, he simply stood on what he believed to be clearly revealed—the fact of individual election and reprobation.[60] In response to the accusation that he used logic more than Scripture to support the doctrine of double predestination, Knox insisted the position was biblical, and logical arguments were only handmaidens of Scripture.[61] Still, it must be noted that Knox placed more emphasis on the positive election of sinners to salvation, than on the reprobative aspect of predestination.[62]

---

56. *Works*, 5:25.

57. *Works*, 5:293, 299; 6:249–51; Janton, *Concept et Sentiment*, 97, 102.

58. Ibid., 5:25–30.

59. Ibid., 5:36, 73.

60. Ibid., 5:394.

61. *Works*, 5:61. According to D'Assonville, Knox emphasized philosophic determinism as a cause of reprobation. See *Knox and the Institutes*, 95.

62. *Works*, 5:61–62. Janton notes that, except for *An Answer*, reprobation received little development in Knox's thought from 1554 to 1566. See *Concept et Sentiment*, 95.

Knox acknowledged a corporate side to predestination in that the invisible church consisted of those individuals elected to eternal salvation. Nevertheless, he categorically rejected the Anabaptist's argument for a general election of all humanity, rather than the election of individuals.[63] He not only insisted on only one election—of individuals to eternal life—but in *An Answer* he denied that God loved all human beings. In Knox's words: "You [the Anabaptist] make the love of God common to all men; and that we constantly deny."[64]

Freedom, both human and divine, played a major role in Knox's concept of predestination. In *An Answer* he insisted no activity—regardless of its apparent unimportance—took place without God's ordaining it to come to pass. Yet this absolute providence does not destroy human responsibility nor make God the author of sin. Predestination is so closely related with providence that it must be associated with the same conclusions. Thus, on one hand, Knox insisted on outright predestination. But on the other, he placed great stress on human responsibility and the fact that God did not predestinate humans to sin: "Although I say that so he ordained the fall of man I utterly deny him to be the author of sin."[65]

God's freedom—more so than human freedom—was important to Knox, and he never tired of emphasizing the fact of God's free election. God freely chose whom he would save without considering any foreknown works or faith on the part of a human being. God knew in advance who would believe and who would not, and he elected or rejected accordingly. The Anabaptists and other adherents of freewill emphasized prescience which based divine election on God's foreknowledge of events and endeavored to achieve a synergism—a kind of cooperation between God and humankind in election. But in *An Answer,* Knox faithfully followed Calvin on this matter and bitterly opposed the traditional doctrine of foreknowledge.[66] Knox acknowledged the existence of prescience but he gave it a different definition: "But we say that all things be so present before God that he does contemplate and behold them in their truth and perfection."[67] Knox adamantly refused to separate divine foreknowledge

63. *Works*, 5:72–73, 97.

64. Ibid., 5:56–60, 235.

65. Ibid., 5;169–70.

66. D'Assonville, *Knox and the Institutes*, 48–49.

67. *Works*, 5:36. According to D'Assonville, Knox took his definition almost literally from the *Institutes*. See *Knox and the Institutes*, 49.

from divine will. When God foresees something, it comes to pass because his power is omnipotent.[68]

Reprobation

For the defender of predestination, more problems arise in respect to its negative aspect—reprobation. Consequently, the Anabaptist opponent focused his assault on this doctrine. So Knox, in *An Answer*, found himself defending a subject not developed in his writings, and one with which he was uncomfortable.[69] In his attempt to expound Calvin's view in regard to double predestination, Knox apparently deviated from Calvin at two points—confusion between double and single predestination and a different emphasis on the cause of reprobation. These variations arose partly because Knox, being bound by his opponent's argumentation and terminology, constantly gave the appearance of escaping from a tight corner. Of course, this situation led to confusion, shifts of thought, and even outright contradictions.[70]

According to its usual representation in Reformed theology, the decree of reprobation comprises two elements: preterition, or the determination to pass by some people; and condemnation, or the determination to punish those who are passed by for their sins. That Knox held to double predestination is not a matter of debate, for he clearly referred to both election and reprobation.[71] But whether his concept of predestination contained both the elements of preterition (passing by) and condemnation (dishonor and wrath) or just that of preterition (which resembles only single predestination) is a difficult matter. Both elements were present in Knox's thought. But, for the most part, he spoke of reprobation either so generally that the components were not discernible, or as if this decree were primarily an act of preterition—with condemnation coming as a natural result of God bypassing some individuals.

The aspect of condemnation can be found in *An Answer*. Like Calvin, Knox specifically placed reprobation and punishment in a cause-and-effect relationship: "And from that same eternity he has reprobated others,

---

68. *Works*, 5:133–34.

69. Janton, *Concept et Sentiment*, 95; Greaves, *Theology and Revolution*, 37.

70. See Kyle, "Predestination in the Thought of Knox," 69; Kyle, *Mind of Knox*, 117.

71. *Works*, 5:41, 61–62, 65, 73, 171, 394 and others.

whom . . . he shall adjudge to torments and fire inextinguishable."[72] More numerous and explicit, however, were the passages presenting reprobation as a decree of preterition, as Augustine had presented it. Knox referred to reprobates as those whom God "leaves to themselves to languish in their corruption . . . until that they come to perdition."[73] Representative of Knox's teaching on passive reprobation was the following: "what God in his counsel . . . has of one mass chosen vessels of honor . . . and of the same mass he has left others in that corruption in which they were to fall, and so were they prepared to destruction."[74] Why Knox accentuated the element of preterition can be attributed to several factors,[75] but only one is relevant to the issue at hand: an emphasis on preterition presented fewer difficulties in his debate with the Anabaptist.

Knox insisted on two causes for reprobation—the hidden will of God and the sin of humanity. According to V.E. D'Assonville, in arguing that the hidden will of God was the primary source of all things, including reprobation,[76] Knox ran counter to Calvin at this point and created difficulties for himself in his debate with the Anabaptist. Calvin emphatically stated that people should concern themselves with the secondary cause of reprobation—human sin—rather than with the primary source, God's hidden will. The Geneva reformer guarded against meaningless speculation about the hidden cause while stressing the reason indicated by Scripture—human transgressions.

But now Knox did just the opposite. To him, any cause sought outside the will of God led to confusion. Thus Knox made God's will not only the primary source of reprobation but almost the exclusive cause: "But because that in his Word there is no cause assigned (God's good will only excepted) why he has chosen some and rejected others."[77] Due to the difficulties presented by his Anabaptist opponent, however, Knox at times

---

72. Ibid., 5:61.

73. Ibid., 5:125–26.

74. *Works*, 5:112–13. See also Dan G. Danner, "The Theology of the Geneva Bible: A Study in English Protestantism" (Ph.D. diss. University of Iowa, 1967), 164–67.

75. For the other factors see Kyle, "Predestination in the Thought of Knox," 71; Kyle, *Mind of Knox*, 119; McEwen, *Faith of Knox*, 70; Greaves, *Theology and Revolution*, 42–43.

76. *Works*, 5:39.

77. *Works*, 5:391. See also 5:408: "If you say, that death and damnation cometh not by God's will, but by sin and unbelief of man, you have relieved yourself nothing." See also D'Assonville, *Knox and the Institutes*, 60–61.

shifted his emphasis to the point of near contradiction. He grudgingly acknowledged a second but subordinate cause of reprobation—human sin. Though Knox stressed that God's ordinance was the primary basis for reprobation, he insisted that reprobation did not cause sin. "Man therefore falls (God's providence is ordaining), but yet he falls by his own fault."[78]

Authority

In a *Letter to His Brethren in Scotland* and *An Answer*, three subjects predominated—perfectionism in the church, predestination, and a general attack on the Radical Reformation. But Knox also briefly challenged the Anabaptists on two other issues—authority and baptism.

In respect to authority, the opinions of the radical reformers covered a wide spectrum. Apart from the strict biblicists, the Radical Reformation evidenced two extremes: the spiritualists and rationalists. The spiritualists tended to identify the scriptural Word with the inner voice, to the point of subjectivism. Conversely, the rationalists often imposed reason and conscience upon the Scriptures, turning church into a school of ethics and worship into study.[79] Knox, however, made few distinctions in this regard. Seldom did he mention the biblicists. And, when he did, he disagreed with their interpretation of Scripture—sometimes harshly, labeling them as blasphemers, and more gently on other occasions, simply elevating the view of a church father such as Augustine.[80]

Knox primarily targeted the Anabaptists' appeal to the inner voice, reason, and extra-biblical sources. Like Calvin and Luther, he savagely opposed those Anabaptists who, he believed, substituted an inner light for the written Scripture. Though the Bible needed the work of the Holy Spirit to become operative, Knox did not speak of God's Word as some subjective experience divorced from Scripture.

Similarly, Knox condemned the Anabaptists for subordinating the written Word to reason. In a *Letter to His Brethren in Scotland* he noted

---

78. *Works*, 5:71, 112, 168.

79. Williams, *Radical Reformation*, 1254–1255: Eric W. Gritsch, "Thomas Muentzer and the Origins of Protestant Spiritualism," *Mennonite Quarterly Review* 37 (July 1963): 172–94; Walter Klaassen, "Spiritualization in the Reformation," *Mennonite Quarterly Review* 37 (April 1963): 67–77; Jan J. Kiwiet, "The Theology of Hans Denck," *Mennonite Quarterly Review* 32 (January 1958): 3–27; Claus-Peter Clasen, *Anabaptism: A Social History*, 1525–1618 (Ithaca, NY: Cornell U. Press, 1972).

80. *Works*, 5:331–32.

that the wellspring of Anabaptist errors is that they limit divine activity and justice to what they can rationally comprehend.[81] In *An Answer* Knox repeatedly linked the Anabaptists with the rationalists Castello and Servetus.[82] In doing so, he accused the larger movement of their errors. Knox told the Anabaptists that the Protestant faithful must preach Christ not only to the Jews, Turks, and Catholics—"but also against you enraged Anabaptists, who can admit in God no justice which is not subject to the reach of your reason."[83]

Knox leveled his sharpest attack at those who added to the biblical canon. Following the Reformation tradition, Knox identified the canon as the Word of God, assuming it to include all the New Testament books plus the Old Testament writings found in the Hebrew Bible. His predestination tract explicitly warned the flock against anyone who made the non-canonical writings equal in authority to the books recommended by the Holy Spirit to the church and written by Moses, the prophets and evangelists, and apostles.[34]

Knox strongly maintained the canon had closed. Accordingly, and in contradistinction to the medieval canon, he gave no recognition to the apocryphal writings—i.e., the Old Testament books contained in the Septuagint but not in the Hebrew Bible. These books, he believed, were not of the Holy Spirit. The teachings contained therein were acceptable for edification—providing they did not contradict the canonical Scriptures—but Knox would not allow them to establish doctrine: "To your [the Anabaptist] scriptures which you allege from the book of Wisdom, and from Esdras (his fourth book), I will shortly answer, that although you will ten thousand times decore (decorate) them with the title of the Holy Ghost, I will not the more credit them . . . Let them serve, if so please you, to exhortation, but for confirmation of any doctrine shall they never serve unto me."[85] Apparently the Anabaptist had challenged Knox's doctrine of predestination by appealing to extra-biblical sources—i.e. dreams, revelations, and non-canonical books—in addition to the canonical scriptures. Therefore, Knox frequently

81. Ibid., 4:271.

82. Ibid., 5:16, 37–38, 126, 147, 184, 231, 222, 224, 226–27, 229, 295, 348, 355, 359, 395–98.

83. Ibid., 5:392.

84. *Works*, 5:420. See also Richard Greaves, "The Nature of Authority in the Writings of John Knox," *Fides et Historia* 10:2 (1978): 36–51; Kyle, *Mind of Knox*, 36–45.

85. *Works*, 5:102.

declared that "the plain Scripture confutes this your error . . . ." "We affirm nothing which God's Word does not plainly teach us . . . ."[86]

Baptism

Knox and the Anabaptists obviously had major differences over the subject of baptism. Most of his thought on baptism came in a 1556 treatise, *Answers to Some Questions Regarding Baptism*. But this is a subject for another chapter. In both the Catholic and Anabaptist doctrines of baptism, Knox found real threats to the fledging church he desired to establish. Essentially, he repudiated the Catholic baptism as an idolatrous practice. However, since Knox also rejected Anabaptist rebaptism as a disintegrating threat to both church and society, he said those baptized in infancy under the Catholic rite need not be baptized again.[87]

Like the magisterial reformers, the Anabaptists argued that baptism cannot save or purify. But they went further to emphasize the non-sacramental nature of baptism. They also rejected the idea that there was any continuity between circumcision under the Old Covenant and baptism under the New Covenant. By more radically implementing the doctrine of repentance and justification by faith, they insisted on baptism of the contritional, conscious believer in adult life. Because the Anabaptists related baptism to discipleship, they would not baptize for future faith—nor as a means to encourage faith or for the faith of the infant's sponsors. For believers, baptism symbolized their newness of life and their determination to follow Christ.[88]

Knox condemned the Anabaptist approach to baptism with both secular and theological arguments. Insofar as the Anabaptist sectaries presented a disruptive threat to both church and society, he would not consent to rebaptism under any circumstances. In *An Answer* Knox referred to the Anabaptist rejection of infant baptism in the context of

---

86. Ibid., 5:59 (quote), 310, 421.

87. Ibid., 4:119–28; Greaves, *Theology and Revolution*, 86.

88. Williams, *Radical Reformation*, 300–4; Gerhard J. Neumann, "The Anabaptist Position on Baptism and the Lord's Supper," *Mennonite Quarterly Review* 35 (April 1961): 140–41, 143; Vincent G. Harding, "Mennon Simons and the Role of Baptism in the Christian Life," *Mennonite Quarterly Review* 33 (October 1959): 329, 333–34; Myron S. Augsburger, "Conversion in Anabaptist Thought," *Mennonite Quarterly Review* 34 (July 1962): 244, 246–47, 250–54; William Estep, *The Anabaptist Story* (Grand Rapids: Eerdmans, 1975), 150–75.

their political and economic distinctives—i.e., their reluctance to use the civil courts, their refusal to take the oath, and their holding of property in common. In particular, he appeared to identify the entire Anabaptist movement—including adult baptism—with the debacle at Münster.[89]

The basic point of the entire dispute over infant baptism concerned the doctrine of the church. The Anabaptists aimed at a gathered church, with adult baptism as a testimony of faith, whereas the magisterial reformers defended the infant baptism because they viewed the church as a community in league with God containing those making an external profession.

Knox accorded an important place to the invisible church, which is known only to God and is synonymous with the elect.[90] Still, he spoke most often of the visible church which came in two forms: the small flock—normally a non-established church—and the national church (kirk), established by law and encompassing most of Scottish society. Though Knox regarded the small flock as the visible church most likely to contain the elect, even this church included the wicked.[91] The national church—to even a greater extent—was a variegated organization containing the godly and ungodly. Baptism, therefore, signified entrance into the visible church, which was a mixed body. Thus Knox insisted that doctrine and the correct administration of the sacraments—not morality—distinguished the "true" church from the "malignant" church.[92]

KNOX'S SOLUTION

To say Knox opposed the Anabaptists would be an understatement. Their unorthodox social and political views seriously threatened the stability of society, he believed. Worse yet, Knox regarded their doctrines as "most horrible and absurd," as "rotten heresies" and "damnable error." He considered the holders of such opinions as "blasphemers" and "vile slaves of

---

89. *Works*, 5:432–33, 437–38, 455–56, 459.

90. *Works*, 5:25; 2:108–9; Alex C. Cheyne, "The Scots Confession of 1560," *Theology Today* 17:3 (1966): 334.

91. John Knox, "Epistle to the Congregation of Berwick, 1552," in *John Knox and the Church of England*, comp. Peter Lorimer (London: Henry S. King, 1875), 225; Richard Kyle, "The Church-State Patterns in the Thought of John Knox," *Journal of Church and State* 30:1 (1998): 71–87; Kyle, "The Nature of the Church," 37.

92. *Works*, 4:262–67; Greaves, *Theology and Revolution*," 49–50; Kyle, "The Nature of the Church," 493–96.

Lucifer."[93] Even the collective works to which Knox contributed took a similar view of the Anabaptists as "enemies to the Christian religion." And the Confession of the English Congregation of Geneva had even harsher words for the Anabaptists, describing them as "limbs of the Antichrist."[94]

But Knox went beyond criticizing the Anabaptists and warning against their wayward ways. He also advanced some remedies in response to their threat. Since the root of the Anabaptist error rested in their false teachings, Knox offered as a corrective sound doctrine, beginning with a proper understanding of salvation. Such an understanding, of course, rested on the belief that a sovereign God predestined some to be saved and others to be lost.[95]

Still, even the elect had a life to live. For Knox, Anabaptist separatism was not an option. Rather, the faithful were to be in the church and avail themselves of the Word truly preached and the sacraments rightly administered. "No man is so regenerate, but that continually he has need of the means which Christ Jesus . . . has appointed to be used in his kirk . . . ."[96] To prevent Anabaptist tenets from taking root in the church itself, Knox insisted on a stringent examination for those who would labor in the vineyard—namely, the pastors and teachers.[97]

In the end, however, Knox acknowledged that correct doctrine and church order alone would not suffice. The Anabaptists put great emphasis on holy living and so must the faithful in Scotland. Godly living would silence both their Catholic and Anabaptist detractors. So, quoting Paul, Knox admonished the faithful to, "Let so your light shine before men that they may see your good works, and that they may glorify your Father which is in heaven."[98]

93. *Works*, 4:270–71; 5:315; 6:173.

94. *Works*, 2:334; Reed, *Forgotten Reformer*, 238,

95. *Works*, 5:391.

96. Ibid., 4:121.

97. Ibid., 4:271.

98. *Works*, 4:268–69; Reed, *Forgotten Reformer*, 239–42.

7

History Through the Eyes of John Knox
(1559–1571)

Upon returning to Scotland in 1559, Knox began writing his *History of the Reformation in Scotland*, a task that would last until 1571. This substantial work occupies the best part of two volumes in Knox's complete works. It consists of five books and chronicles the events of the Scottish Reformation from 1492 to 1567. This history tells us much that is known about Knox. Were it not for this book, the celebrated reformer would be a much less regarded figure to historians than he now is.

Yet authorities differ as to the factual reliability and impartiality of Knox's *History*. The attempt at unbiased history is an eighteenth and nineteenth-century development. Consequently, nearly all sources acknowledge that he was a biased historian, but they disagree over the degree and effect of his partiality. Andrew Lang sees Knox as a party pamphleteer who exceeded the limits of honest journalism. This criticism is directed to Book Two where Lang concludes that Knox deliberately concealed the truth on several points.[1] Conversely, while the reformer's admirers, Thomas M'Crie and Hume Brown, have praised his *History* almost without qualification, other historians—such as W. C. Dickinson, W. Stanford Reid, Maurice Lee, and David Murison—admit Knox's partiality but contend his *History* was basically reliable and constitutes a major contribution to an important epoch.[2]

---

1. Andrew Lang, "Knox as Historian," *The Scottish Historical Review,* 2 (January 1905): 130. In essential agreement with Lang's evaluation is an article by R.S. Raitt. See R. S. Raitt, "Scotland and John Knox," *The Fortnightly Review,* 78 (July-December 1905): 101, 103, 107.

2. P. Hume Brown, *John Knox,* 2 vols. (London: Adam and Charles Black, 1895), 2:217–21; John Knox, *John Knox's History of the Reformation in Scotland,* ed. William Croft Dickinson , 2 vols. (Edinburgh: Thomas Nelson and Sons, Ltd., 1949), 1:1xviii–xcv;

Yet for the purpose of investigating Knox's concept of history, his lack of objectivity presents less of a problem than it would for a history of events. The complete accuracy of Knox's *History* is not as important as the philosophy contained therein. The fact that his *History* is biased is, in some ways, an advantage to the intellectual historian. According to Maurice Lee, John Knox, like Karl Marx, used history to demonstrate his single-track philosophy. And his philosophy said, "The hearts of men, their thoughts, and their actions are but in the hands of God." Lee said Knox's *History* was a sermon without an audience, a preaching book, one long inflammatory speech in behalf of God's truth as the reformer saw it.[3]

FAITH SHAPES HISTORY

John Knox's concept of history represents a significant aspect of his religious faith. It pervaded most areas of his thought and served as an important source of motivation in his drive to establish Protestantism in Scotland. As a result, the primary purpose for studying Knox's view of history is for what it reveals about his religious ideas, rather than for any significant contributions that he might have made to the development of historical thought. Such a study opens another window to Knox's thinking and in some ways summarizes his religious thought.

As noted earlier, Knox was not a "speculative theologian" or a political thinker. Still, he produced theology and political thought. By extension, it can be said that he was not an historian in any strict sense. He wrote history to further the reformation in Scotland. In fact, Knox saw himself as a preaching—rather than a writing—prophet. According to Maurice Lee, Knox wrote only when he could not preach to the people whom he wished to address: "When he could preach to a live audience, he did not write: he only took to his pen when his voice was silent." Nevertheless, Knox wrote frequently, producing pamphlets, a *History of the Reformation*

David D. Murison, "Knox the Writer," in *John Knox: A Quatercentenary Reappraisal,* ed. Duncan Shaw (St. Andrew Press: Edinburgh, 1975), 42–43; Matthew Mahoney, "The Scottish Hierarchy, 1513–1565" in *Essays on the Scottish Reformation 1513–1565,* ed. David McRoberts (Glasgow: John S. Burns and Sons, 1962), 77; W. Stanford Reid, *Trumpeter of God* (New York: Scribner's Sons), 203. See also William Croft Dickinson, *Andrew Lang, John Knox and Scottish Presbyterianism* (Edinburgh: Thomas Nelson and Sons, Ltd., 1952).

3. Maurice Lee, "John Knox and His History," *Scottish Historical Review,* 14 (April 1966): 80, 87–88.

in Scotland, and numerous letters, which all told fill more than six volumes.[4] The reformer normally wrote in response to pastoral or practical problems and did not systematize his thinking. It is, therefore, no surprise that Knox did not deliberately formulate a philosophy of history, despite authoring a major work of history. In fact, his notion of history is derived from and largely dependent on his religious faith. Key beliefs include his concepts of God, providence, predestination, the covenant, Scripture, and the Christian commonwealth. Also important were his hermeneutical principles, his calling to be a prophet, and his apocalyptic thought.

This relationship between faith and history, however, does not imply that other sources (e.g. Martin Luther, John Calvin, and the English apocalyptic tradition) did not influence, directly or indirectly, Knox's sense of history. Rather, it is to say that Knox's concept of history must be reconstructed in piecemeal fashion—along with much of his other religious thought—not only from his *History* but also from his other writings.

Along with many sixteenth century Protestant figures, Knox believed history to be providential, dynamic, linear, apocalyptic, and containing a sense of mystery. These characteristics are not mutually exclusive and tend to support one another. Still, God's providential role in history and the sense of an apocalyptic struggle throughout the ages clearly dominated Knox's concept of history. Because the apocalyptic component has a predestinarian twist—a sense of God's determining a cosmic conflict between good and evil—the providential element logically took precedence over the apocalyptic factor in the reformer's view of history.

Knox's concept of history—particularly the providential and apocalyptic components—were largely an outgrowth of his religious faith. His personal faith and experiences powerfully molded his sense of history. In fact, David Murison contends that Knox's *History* is a volume of selective and frequently impressionistic memoirs, a trait not unknown among Scottish historians of the sixteenth century.[5]

---

4. Unfortunately, many of his letters were never recovered and thus his actual writings go well beyond six volumes.

5. Murison, "Knox the Writer," 33. For other Scots using this method see Jhone Leslie, *The History of Scotland,* ed. Rev. Father E.G. Cody, vols. 1,2 (Edinburgh: William Blackwood and sons, Ltd., 1837); Robert Lindesay, *The Historie and Cronicles of Scotland,* ed. A. J. G. Mackey, vols. 1–3 (Edinburgh: William Blackwood and Sons, Ltd., 1899).

The Prophetic Element

Knox's powerful sense of vocation helped to shape his notion of history. His initial call in 1547 left a lasting impression on him, directing his action and thinking for the remainder of his life. Knox saw himself as a preacher, a watchman, cast in the mold of the Hebrew prophets.[6] More than any of the major reformers, Knox most strongly identified himself with the prophetic tradition. In his own eyes, he was essentially a propagandist—God's mouthpiece, a trumpet—as he repeatedly called himself. And his concept of history reflected these feelings.[7] Consequently, his sense of history emphasized an omnipotent God directing each episode of the cosmic struggle between his servants and those of Satan.

Knox arrived at his belief in the importance of prophecy in history more from personal experiences than from reading or training. A number of factors intensified Knox's fear of Catholicism and prompted him to see all of history in terms of a life and death struggle. Included would be the persecution of Protestants in Scotland (especially the death of George Wishart, whom Knox admired as a prophet), Knox's enslavement in a French galley, England's violation of the covenant and Mary Tudor's subsequent oppression of the Protestants, and the trauma of being exiled from Scotland and then from England. Like the first Christians, Knox lived in a world where "martyr" and "apostate" were a grim polarity, even though it might be a gradual apostasy of little compromises.[8]

Scripture and History

Knox's methods of interpreting Scripture affected both the ways in which he wrote history and how he applied it to the situation in Scotland and England. The reformer employed a range of interpretative principles to

6. John Knox, *The Works of John Knox*, ed. David Laing, 6 vols. (Edinburgh: Printed for the Bannatyne Club, 1816–1864), 6: 229. Hereafter this reference will be cited as *Works* followed by the appropriate volume and page number.

7. *Works*, 3:173; 4:102, 366; 1:268; Richard Greaves, *Theology and Revolution in the Scottish Reformation* (Grand Rapids: Christian University Press, 1980), 56; Murison, "Knox the Writer," 43.

8. *Works*, 1:4–5, 119, 169–170, 212, 271, 467; 2:59; 3:165, 167, 170–71, 187; 4:103, 106, 433, 479; 5:413; 6:12, 21, 192, 251; W. Stanford Reid, "John Knox and His Interpreters," *Renaissance and Reformation*, 10 (1974): 15–19; Katharine R. Firth, *The Apocalyptic Tradition in Reformation Britain, 1530–1545* (Oxford: Oxford University Press, 1979), 114–15, 130; E. G. Rupp, "The Europe of John Knox," in *John Knox: A Quatercentenary Reappraisal*, 8.

Scripture, but his prophetic hermeneutic—that is, his method of applying the Old Testament burdens of Israel almost literally and unequivocally to the religious and political situation of his day—significantly influenced his perspective of history.

Scripture exhibits both a large degree of continuity and discontinuity between the Old and New Testaments. Knox experienced problems over these issues and failed to observe a discontinuity between the two testaments. He thus over-identified the Old with the New Testament, losing sight of the historic process in divine revelation. In addition, Knox emphasized the primacy of the literal sense of Scripture—which related the things done and said in the Bible—as ascertained by a straightforward, natural approach to the text.

The Scottish reformer interpreted Scripture so literally that the Bible often became a book of precedents, a handbook for the judgment of God upon nations and powers in the world. Biblical interpretation can stress the substantive content of Scripture or the literal form of the Bible, and Knox so emphasized the latter method that Scripture often became a set of regulations.[9] For example, in 1556 to some women in Edinburgh, Knox wrote, "In the religion of God, and that in everything that is done it must have the assurance of his Word . . . or else it is the religion of the Devil."[10]

Knox's failure to recognize the Bible's discontinuity, his habit of applying the Old Testament uncritically and often literally to his day, influenced his sense of history in several ways. First, he often transferred people and events from the Old and New Testaments so literally that historical repetition occurred. Knox frequently drew comparisons between Israel and Scotland and Israel and England—comparisons that often went beyond analogies or lessons and seem to become historical equations.[11]

---

9. *Works*, 1:197; 2:111, 135; 3:35–38, 280f., 516–17; James S. McEwen, *The Faith of John Knox* (Richmond: John Knox Press, 1961), 39–40; V. E. D'Assonville, *John Knox and the Institutes of Calvin: A Few Points of Contact in Their Theology* (Durban: Drakensberg Press Limited, 1968), 70–75; Richard Greaves, "The Nature of Authority in the Writings of John Knox," *Fides et Historia*, 10 no. 2 (Spring 1978): 30–51; Pierre Janton *Concept et Sentiment De L'Eglise Chez Jean Knox: le reformateur ecossaise* (Paris: Presses Universitaires De France, 1972), 174–76. For a discussion on Knox's methods of interpreting Scripture see Richard Kyle, "The Hermeneutical Patterns in John Knox's Use of Scripture," *Pacific Theological Review*, 17, no. 2 (1984): 19–32.

10. *Works*, 4:272. The spellings in all quotations from Knox's writings have been modernized.

11. *Works*, 3:280f; D'Assonville, *Knox and the Institutes*, 74–75; Kyle, "Hermeneutical

Second, Knox's tendency to employ the Old Testament instructions regarding worship so literally that they became legal precedents fostered a sense of an apocalyptic struggle in his historical thought. In religion, and when religion interacted with other aspects of society such as politics as it did so often in the sixteenth century, Knox saw no middle course. Consequently, he interpreted historical events in sharp categories: everything was either the work of God or the devil, or of their lieutenants, that is, the true or false church.[12]

God Is in Charge of History

Knox's concept of God, more than any other aspect of his faith, determined his philosophy of history. The reformer attributed many qualities to God, but divine sovereignty and immutability dominated his historical thought. As an aspect of sovereignty, the characteristic of divine immutability pervaded nearly every area of his thought. In fact, without divine immutability, the reformer's thought on history, and virtually everything else, had little basis. Indeed, as Knox often noted, the character and law of God never changes. Therefore, God must respond to sin in the same manner in England and Scotland as he did in the Old Testament or anywhere. The justice of God is infinite and immutable, and what he damned in one place and in one time cannot be excused in another.[13] For example, in 1554 Knox comforted the Protestants in England—who were being persecuted by Mary Tudor—by declaring that because God is immutable, he would stir up another Jehu against their idolatrous rulers.[14]

On occasions, Knox saw God as responding to a situation in the same way at all times, and consequently somewhat of a prisoner of his own nature. Thus the stress on divine immutability led Knox to demand that God's law be upheld in the Commonwealth of Scotland as if it were Old Testament Israel. Coupled with the reformer's method of interpreting Scripture, this emphasis on immutability inclined Knox to parallel events

Patterns," 31.

12. *Works*, 1:119, 197; 3:284–85; 4:272, 298, 303–4: 6:271.

13. *Works*, 3:171, 191; 4:399; 6:408. For a discussion on Knox's concept of God see Richard Kyle, "The Divine Attributes in John Knox's Concept of God," *Westminster Theological Journal* 48 (1986): 161–72.

14. *Works*, 3:247.

and people from the Old and New Testaments so literally that history seemed to be reenacted.[15]

Knox adamantly argued for God's sovereign and omnipotent control over all realms of history. The reformer noted these divine characteristics in his 1559 predestination tract, in which he declared that God demonstrated his omnipotence in the battle with Satan, whose purpose God constantly frustrates. What seems at times as a victory for Satan is only an appearance, "for God is omnipotent, and is compelled to suffer nothing which he has not appointed in his eternal counsel . . . ."[16]

Writing to the congregation at St. Andrews in 1548, Knox said that God uses the forces and circumstances destroying the just for his glorification and for the profit of his congregation. For example, when Joseph's brothers sold him into slavery, God thwarted the evil purpose of Satan by making Joseph second only to Pharoah.[17] Knox believed that all events are ordained by an omnipotent, immutable God whose eternal will and purpose cannot be frustrated by any creature, whether human or angelic. As a consequence, Knox insisted that God's sovereignty be established in a real sense in Scotland. In his 1561 confrontation with Mary Stewart, he said, "my travail is that both princes and subjects obey God."[18]

Knox's concept of history largely rested upon his understanding of God's nature and work in the universe because a providential view of history was the centerpiece of his historical thought. Utterly persuaded of the sovereignty of God over all history, the reformer thus believed all events from the largest to the smallest to be ordained by God for reasons known only to himself. Along with the vast majority of the religious figures of his time, Knox knew nothing of a "watchmaker" God—a God who set the universe into motion and then merely let it run.

The notion of providence concerns God's permanent and universal activity in the world. God not only created the world, but having once created it, he remains its absolute master, takes an interest in it, intervenes in it at any moment, and abandons none of his power to the play of natural

15. Ibid., 3:280f.

16. *Works*, 5:194. Knox said that God is omnipotent and when the Holy Ghost used phrases such as "God suffers" or "sorrows," God was simply subjecting himself to human languages in order to help human understanding. See also *Works*, 1:23; 3:5–84; 5:33, 133, 390; 6:415.

17. *Works*, 3:5–8.

18. *Works*, 2:283.

laws or chance. This definition describes the idea—common to Luther, Calvin, Zwingli, Bucer, and Knox—of a continuous action of God in the midst of his creation.[19]

Knox spoke most directly to the issue of divine providence in his 1559 treatise concerning predestination, where he defined God's providence as "that sovereign empire and supreme dominion, which God's providence always keeps in the government of all things in heaven and earth contained."[20] Knox, along with Calvin, eliminated all chance from the universe and rejected the notion that God's predestination and providence resembles the fatal necessity of pagan stoicism.

The Scottish reformer affirmed God as Lord, Moderator, and Governor of all things. He concluded that God's providence not only governs the heaven and earth and all insensible creatures, but all the wills and counsels of human beings, "so that they tend and are led to the scope and end which he has proposed."[21] Furthermore, Knox held that God's providence does not fail in its purpose—namely that all the universe, including the sun, moon, and stars obey God and that all creatures execute his commandments, and that nothing transpires contrary to the will of God.[22]

Knox firmly maintained a providential view of history that saw the hand of God intervening in all events. Still, he was no fool in this regard, for he also recognized that events had secondary causes (i.e. human agents), and he knew the importance of the worldly considerations to these weak instruments of the Lord. For example, in a note to England written in 1559 requesting money for the Congregation, he said that dire poverty had weakened the Scottish Protestants to the extent of making them susceptible to French overtures. "France seeks all means to make them friends, and to diminish our number."[23]

Yet the victory was always God's. Knox's philosophy of history had a single focus: the hearts of human beings, their ideas, and their actions were determined by God.[24] Nevertheless, this statement is not to imply that the Scottish reformer saw history as a meaningful clear process. The

19. Francois Wendel, *Calvin: The Origins and Development of His Religious Thought* (New York: Harper and Row, 1963), 177–78.

20. *Works*, 5:35.

21. Ibid., 5:32.

22. Ibid., 5:172.

23. *Works*, 6:80; Lee, "Knox and His History," 80–81.

24. Lee, "Knox and His History," 80–81.

reader of Knox's *History* can detect the sense of mystery that he held in the relationship of God to history, for after all, the reformer believed the ways of God to be inscrutable to human beings.

An Apocalyptic Perspective

The second major motif in Knox's concept of history was his apocalyptic thought. Knox's historical thought never separated the providential and apocalyptic elements. They were intertwined throughout his writings with the former the logical cause of the latter. Still, a strong providential view of history does not necessarily demand an equally significant interest in the apocalyptic tradition. For example, despite Calvin's emphasis on a sovereign God dynamically working his will in history, the reformer's thought did not contain many apocalyptic characteristics.[25]

The adjectives *apocalyptic* and *millennial* are not synonymous. Rather, *apocalyptic* denotes the generic term and *millennial* a species that postulates the expectancy of a future, collective, imminent transformation of life on earth through a supernatural agency. English apocalyptic thought in general contained three characteristics—a polarized view of the universe, a catastrophic explanation of the events, and a firm concern with prophecy and its fulfillment. These three traits combined to make apocalyptic thought a creed of action, which operated as a powerful rational and emotional weapon in ideological dispute.[26]

The first two traits loomed the largest in Knox's historical thought, though the third was not absent. Protestant interest in apocalyptic thought during the 1540s, when Knox came into contact with this tradition, was expressed in either of two ways. One, the prophecies served as a guide on moral or doctrinal grounds to the character and manifestation of the antichrist. Two, the prophecies assumed a chronological significance ranging

25. David E. Holwerda, "Eschatology and History: A Look at Calvin's Eschatological Vision," in *Exploring the Heritage of John Calvin*, ed. David E. Holwerda (Grand Rapids: Baker Book House, 1976), 110, 127–28, 131; H. Quistorp, *Calvin's Doctrine of the Last Things*, trans. Harold Knight (Richmond: John Knox Press), 158–62. For a discussion of Knox's apocalyptic thought in general see Richard Kyle, "John Knox and Apocalyptic Thought," *Sixteenth Century Journal*, 15, no. 4 (1984): 449–69.

26. Paul Christianson, *Reformers and Babylon: English Apocalyptic Visions from the Reformation to the Eve of the Civil War* (Toronto: University of Toronto Press), 5, 7.

through human history from the beginning to its consummation in the future.[27] The first expression clearly dominated Knox's historical thought.

During Knox's formative years, the mood of Europe was certainly conducive to the growth of an apocalyptic atmosphere. By 1545 papal reform was stirring, the military power of the Empire had experienced a resurgence, and Europe moved toward the terrible period of religious wars. Luther had been quoting from Daniel and Revelation, and in Knox's writings, as well as in the *Scots Confession,* there appeared an apocalyptic undertone, a new sense of collision between the true and false church and the appearance of the antichrist—something normally reserved for the radical sects. Apocalyptic thought seems to recur in those moments in history when things come to a head, and when the linear perspective of historical development of calmer days is replaced by a spiral view—that is, a circular but progressive movement. Certainly, the volcanic mood of Europe in the 1550s crept into Knox's writings.[28]

Knox wrote no commentaries on Scripture, thus his detailed thoughts on Daniel and Revelation are largely unknown. He preached from Daniel, but less from the Apocalypse. The reformer did not do as others had done, namely, write a history of the church with chronological periods drawn from Revelation. Yet he cast the present into the apocalyptic context of the final battle between two armies. In writing his predestination tract, Knox clearly noted his approval of Augustine's dichotomy of two cities. Knox apparently had absorbed John Bale's two images and further sharpened the division to accommodate his own militant understanding of both historical and contemporary events. In sum: the two cities of Augustine, transmuted through Bale's two churches, became two armies in Knox's writings.[29]

These two armies battled throughout history, but in Knox's time they were embodied in the Protestant and Catholic churches, namely, the "true" and "malignant" churches. As a man of the present, Knox focused his attention on the contemporary manifestation of this "evil" army—that is, the Roman papacy—which he labeled the antichrist. His denunciation

---

27. Firth, *The Apocalyptic Tradition,* 67–68.

28. Rupp, "The Europe of John Knox," in *John Knox: A Quatercentenary Reappraisal,* 3–5.

29. *Works,* 5:33, 398–99, 413; John Bale, "The Image of bothe churches" reprinted in *The English Experience* (Amsterdam: Theatrum Orbis Terrarum, Ltd., 1973), preface; Firth, *The Apocalyptic Tradition,* 124.

of the papacy as antichrist dwarfed all other apocalyptic considerations and became one of the major motifs of his thought.[30]

Also, in harmony with the apocalyptic mood of his century, Knox saw the return of Christ and the judgment as impending. Yet he was not obsessed with this line of thought for there remained the immediate task of establishing Protestantism in Scotland. Nevertheless, in speaking of an imminent end and the last days, Knox demonstrated the clear linear movement of history toward its divinely appointed conclusion.[31]

The Church and Covenant

To a lesser extent, Knox's concept of the church, the covenant, the puri-fication of religion also affected his historical thinking—though often as an extension of his providential and apocalyptic perspectives of history. The church of John Knox came in several forms, frequently in response to changes in the historical situation, but his themes of the continuous church and small flock related to his historical thought. Actually these themes can be regarded as an aspect of his apocalyptic thought. In an attempt to legitimize the Reformed kirk to a Jesuit in 1568, Knox argued that all aspects of the faithful "true" church of his day formed a continuous line with the faithful in Israel. On the other hand, Israel had its unfaithful, false prophets and idolaters, and such people formed a direct line with the Church of Rome in Knox's day.[32]

Knox's favorite expression of the visible church was the suffering small flock consisting primarily of the elect. At times the small flock was the historic church persecuted in every age. In other places the Protestant community was the small flock. Even after the establishment of Protestantism in Scotland, Knox spoke of the small flock as existing in an abused condition under Mary Stewart. At any rate, the suffering small

---

30. *Works*, 1:3, 81, 101, 190; 2:543; 3:24; 4:445, 470, 511, 513; 6:12, 192, 400–2; Hugh Watt, *John Knox in Controversy* (New York: Philosophical Library, 1950), 13; LeRoy E. Froom, The *Prophetic Faith of Our Fathers*, 4 vols. (Washington, D.C.: Review and Herald, 1948), 2:450–45.

31. *Works*, 3:231, 241–44, 288; 4:262, 303–5; 6:494–95.

32. *Works*, 3:31, 239; 4:481, 487, 513; 6:309, 311, 315; Richard Kyle, "The Nature of the Church in the Thought of John Knox," *Scottish Journal of Theology*, 37, no. 4 (1984): 486, 489–91.

flock was God's key instrument in the cosmic struggle throughout the ages and, as such, played a key role in Knox's apocalyptic view of history.[33]

Knox's concept of the covenant also related to his historical thought. The "Deuteronomic view of history" is used in Old Testament studies to refer to an interpretation of events as being either favorable or unfavorable to Israel in direct relationship to its faithfulness to the covenant with God. The translators of the *Geneva Bible*, in a similar manner, read into their annotations their own view of history. According to such a perspective, the English nation, in covenant with God, would be blessed or cursed just as Israel had been—that is, in direct correspondence with the nation's faithfulness and obedience to the laws of God.[34]

John Knox may have been one of these translators. At any rate, he maintained a view of history similar to these translators. In drawing analogies between Israel and either England or Scotland, Knox believed that these nations would be judged in accordance to their faithfulness to the covenant. He did not, however, regard either England or Scotland as "chosen" nations, and he was too much of an internationalist to limit the covenant obligations to these countries. In fact, Knox did not push extensively the idea of the covenanted nation.[35]

Knox viewed history largely as a perpetual conflict between two churches and two armies. The "true" church fought to exterminate idolatry and to purify religion. As a consequence Knox, portraying himself as a Hebrew prophet, depicted the Scottish reformation as a reenactment of Israel's struggle against idolatry. Not surprisingly, this theme of a vigorous conflict against idolatry (i.e. Catholicism)—whether implicit or overtly stated—permeated nearly every page of his *History* in many different and unrelated contexts.

Idolatry is often defined in the strict literal sense of substituting or worshipping a false god instead of the true God. Knox adopted a wider definition. He declared idolatry to entail not only the worship of a false god, but also to trust and honor anything besides the true God.[36] Thus

33. *Works*, 3:5; 4:263; 6:272, 569–70; Janton, *Concept et Sentiment*, 69–70, 94–95.

34. Dan G. Danner, "The Theology of the Geneva Bible: A Study in English Protestantism," (Ph.D. diss., University of Iowa, 1967), 85–96, 184–94.

35. Richard Greaves, "The Knoxian Paradox: Ecumenism and Nationalism in the Scottish Reformation," *Records of the Scottish Church History Society*, (Summer 1973): 96–97.

36. *Works*, 1:192, 194. For a discussion on Knox's struggle against idolatry, i.e. the

Knox's definition broadly encompassed most activities of the "malignant" church throughout history.

KNOX'S VIEW OF HISTORY AT WORK

It now remains to illustrate, from only a few key sources, Knox's philosophy of history at work in his writings. His philosophy of history, while found in many sources, is most prominent in *A Faithful Admonition*, his treatise concerning predestination, the *History of the Reformation in Scotland*, and in *An Answer to Tyrie*. Knox's historical thought was not highly developmental, that is, it did not show significant growth towards a more advanced state. Rather, most components, especially his providential and apocalyptic views of history, were in place early. At times certain motifs became ascendant, but these shifts portrayed few significant changes.

A Faithful Admonition

A Faithful Admonition (1554), contained much of importance in respect to Knox's historical thought: it illustrated clearly his use of historical analogies that came close to being historical equations and his pattern of church history. In this tract, Knox recalled his last sermon preached before King Edward VI in 1553. This sermon, which condemned Edward's VI's ungodly ministers, paralleled the wicked ministers of David and Hezekiah with the hidden papists in Edward's ministry. In the story, Old Testament Israel equaled England; Edward compared to David; Achitophel equated Dudley, Edward's minister; and Shobna corresponded with the Marquess of Winchester, Edward's treasurer.[37]

Also in a *Faithful Admonition*, Knox for the first time clearly described his perspective of church history. The church's history had a definite pattern of development: the church started out well and then encountered serious difficulties and persecutions. God delivered Israel out of Egypt, but then the false believers faltered in the wilderness. Knox illustrated this pattern by the story of the disciples in a storm at sea. When the disciples set out to sea in obedience to Christ's commandment, the weather was fair, but suddenly a storm arose. If the storm had existed from the begin-

---

Catholic mass, see Richard Kyle, "John Knox and the Purification of Religion: The Intellectual Aspects of His Crusade Against Idolatry," *Archiv für Reformationsgeschichte*, 77 (1986): 265–80.

37. *Works*, 3:280f.

ning, few would have ventured out. But then the seas were moved by a vehement and contrary wind that blew against the disciples' boat. Knox compared the wind to Satan, for neither the wind nor Satan can be seen, but their results can be observed and felt.

The reformer applied this analogy to the entire scope of the church's history. With only a boat for transportation in this unstable world, the early church began well. But about 800 A.D., which was at mid-sea, the doctrine of transubstantiation developed. Knox saw this entire storm as brought by Satan. Furthermore, he transferred the sea analogy specifically to the Church of England where the English Reformation through Edward VI was seen as the calm phase of the voyage—followed by the storm under Mary Tudor and the return of the infamous transubstantiation doctrine. Satan's instruments again perverted the gospel and persecuted the saints. Yet, as in the original parable, the true disciples of Christ did not perish because God shall continue to protect his elected and afflicted church until the final victory at the end of the world.[38]

Predestination Treatise

Knox's 1559 treatise concerning predestination intermixed his providential and apocalyptic views of history as clearly and as sharply as did any of his writings. Nowhere does the reformer articulate the militant dichotomy between the Catholic and "true" Christian church as he does here. Knox took Augustine's division of the two cities and transformed them into two churches and then into two armies. In God's counsel a difference existed between human beings, but all were in one lump mass. From this mass God appointed two seeds to come forth, and these two seeds represented the two churches. From the seed of Eve came the individual elect, which composed the church of Christ, and from the seed of the serpent sprang the reprobate and church of Satan.[39]

Knox extended Augustine's doctrine of two cities—God appointed two companies of people from the beginning to do battle. One army was the church of God, the elect spouse of Christ; the other was the malignant synagogue of Satan. This battle would not end until Christ's second com-

---

38. Ibid., 3:273–89, 322.

39. *Works*, 5:61–62. For a discussion on Knox's doctrine of predestination see Richard Kyle, "The Concept of Predestination in the Thought of John Knox," *Westminster Theological Journal*, 46, no. 1 (1984): 53–77; Greaves, *Theology and Revolution*, 25–43.

ing, which would usher in the judgment.[40] Thus Knox's historical thought evidenced a dynamic linear movement toward an appointed end.

History of the Reformation in Scotland

Knox's convictions regarding God's sovereign control of history and the division of the world into two armed camps remained with him and became the dominant motifs of his *History*. Although Knox emphasized the themes of persecution and martyrdom in his description of the early years of the Reformation in Scotland, he did not model his *History* solely upon the martyrologies of Jean Crespin and John Foxe. Rather, because of his interest in contemporary religion and politics, Knox had more in common with the approach of John Sleidan. When Knox wrote the preface to his *History*, he echoed the purpose declared by Sleidan in his introduction to the *Commentaries*. Each man wrote a history of religion demonstrating the conflict between Protestantism and Catholicism and touched upon political and military activities only to the extent that they engaged the subject of religion.[41]

Despite the same approach, Knox's *History* reads very differently from Sleidan's. In part, this variance developed because of differing versions of the prophetic tradition. Sleidan hoped that the Reformation would be accomplished by a great emperor whose reign was prophesied for the last age of the world.[42] Following Bale and Foxe, Knox put his faith not in princes but in the small congregation of the elect. Emphasizing his prophetic role, Knox told a story of two armies locked in an apocalyptic struggle.[43]

Knox wrote his *History* in the framework of the pattern of the church's history that he previously established in *A Faithful Admonition*. The church throughout history has started out well and then encountered serious difficulties and persecutions. Along this line, the Scottish church began well. But after its victory many apostates within the church sank it into depression and idolatry. Knox's *History* established this theme: books

---

40. *Works*, 5:62, 407, 413. At the close of his work on predestination, Knox utilized and recommended the history of John Sleidan, entitled the *Commentaries*, a work that the Scottish reformer would also use in his *History*. *Works*, 5:423f.

41. *Works*, 1:3–5; John Sleidan, *A Famouse Cronicle of oure time, called Sleidanes Commentaries*, trans. John Daus (London, 1560), Preface. The English edition published in 1560 is too late to have been used by Knox.

42. Sleidan, *Commentaries*, Preface; Firth, *The Apocalyptic Tradition*, 128.

43. *Works*, 2:281; Firth, *The Apocalyptic Tradition*, 128.

one to three describe the victory of the godly, while book four tells of the decline from the purity of God's Word.[44] Within this wide pattern, Knox told a story of the Scottish Reformation that focused on his providential and apocalyptic view of history.

Knox's concept of history emerged in his description of detailed events, personal affairs, political developments, and military battles. In his *History*, Knox did not characterize the great issues of the day (Protestantism versus Catholicism, monarchy versus the people, church versus state, revolution versus reaction, future versus the past) as political problems. Rather, the reformer subordinated every issue to the struggle between the Roman church and the gospel of Christ.[45] This struggle became a grim, merciless battle between the forces of light and the forces of darkness. Knox first opposed the Queen Regent, and later he resisted her daughter Mary Queen of Scots. In this dramatic struggle—which Knox's *History* described in epic fashion—Satan's attack on the gospel aroused God himself: "Thus ceased not Satan by all means, to maintain his kingdom of darkness, and to suppress the light of Christ's Evangel. But potent is he against whom they fought, for when they waged war in greatest security, then God began to show his anger."[46]

In this war God's hand manifested itself in all events. In one place a journey may be postponed to the disappointment of those waiting in ambush, while in another, the heart of a bitter opponent may be moved.[47] During the confrontation at Cupar Muir (1550), "God did so multiply our number, that it appeared as men had rained from the clouds."[48] Knox also attributed the episode of the ordinance at Haddington (1548) to a similar miracle: here God conducted the French attack so that more than a hundred of their bullets fell as only two shots.[49]

Knox understood this development well because he believed that the same God who had razed the walls of Jericho and had divided the waters of the Red Sea was still at work. The God who punished sin by the flood could still display anger at wickedness in Scotland. In every natural disas-

44. *Works*, 2:266. See Lee, "Knox and His History," 86–87.

45. *Works*, 1:4; William Croft Dickinson, *The Scottish Reformation and Its Influence upon Scottish Life and Character* (Edinburgh, St. Andrew Press, 1960), 19–20.

46. *Works*, 1:119.

47. Ibid., 1:131–32.

48. Ibid., 1:351.

49. Ibid., 1:223.

ter, Knox saw a wrathful God punishing sin. Famine and plagues were not accidents. Rather, they represented God's visitation upon Scotland for sin. Knox saw plagues as God's favorite means of punishment.[50]

He attributed defeat in battle not to the enemy's superiority, but to God's direct intervention. The English victory at Solway Moss (1542) was due to "the hand of God, fighting against [the] pride . . . of his own little flock."[51] Furthermore, Knox reacted in anger when the Scots attributed victory to their own strength. The defenders of the Castle of St. Andrews (1547) bragged of the thickness of their walls, and Knox responded by prophesying that the walls "should be but egg shells" and "you shall be delivered in your enemy's hands."[52] Likewise, he did not see the Queen Regent's death in terms of natural causes, but rather in the sense of divine punishment.[53]

Answer to Tyrie

In his *Answer to Tyrie*—written by 1568 but not published until 1572— Knox continued his previous ideas, but gave them some new directions. Knox rejected the priest's claim that Romanism had fulfilled the promise of a universal church found in the second chapter of Isaiah. In this debate, he pointed out that the conditions prophesied by Isaiah for the last times were still unrealized, and thus implied that the world would not end immediately.

Actually Knox, writing in good Augustinian fashion, said the last days had begun with Christ's Incarnation and would continue until his return in judgment. The last days included the first preaching of the gospel, the defection from it during the Middle Ages (approximately 800 A.D.), and its restoration in the world. Knox saw himself living in the recovery stage, which had begun during the Reformation, but was not yet complete.[54] This model of church history, introduced in Knox's earlier writings, continued to reflect a linear pattern that approximated the past millennial schemes of some Protestant writers—which either spiritualized the golden age or believed that it had already occurred.[55]

50. Ibid., 1:270–72; 2:417.
51. Ibid., 1:89.
52. Ibid., 1:205.
53. Ibid., 1:220.
54. *Works*, 6:494–95.
55. Ibid., 6:508.

In the debate with Tyrie, Knox utilized other historical sources—especially Aventinus' history of Bavaria, which recounted the vices and crimes of popes during the Middle Ages and the prophecies of antichrist found in the commentary of Joachim of Fiore. Knox used these writings and others to support his contention that the Apocalypse of John applied to the Roman church alone and not the Roman Empire. The reformer quoted Joachim as identifying the whore of Revelation with the false church in Rome, which contrasted so completely with the poor pilgrims who made up the "true church."[56] Herein can be found the basis of Knox's uncompromising condemnation of Rome and his supremely partisan approach to the writing of history.

THE VALUE OF KNOX'S HISTORY

John Knox vigorously pursued his vocation of preaching God's Word—an undertaking that clearly works its way into his historical thought. Though the reformer possessed a clear-cut concept of history, he made no major contributions to historical thought. Pre-Reformation historical thought was not devoid of any sense of divine purpose. Nevertheless, the generally static nature of medieval thought diminished such a focus. And the Reformation helped restore the profundity of Augustine's conception of history as the work of God, instilling several generations of Protestants with a fresh interpretation of the past and a vivid sense of historical destiny. John Knox had a part in this unfolding. This contribution notwithstanding, the primary value in discussing Knox's concept of history is that it opens another window to the thought world of this prominent Scottish reformer and offers a striking illustration of Protestant historical thought.

A sixteenth-century writer can be excused for not employing the methods of modern historians. Still, Knox's interpretation of the past, in many ways, must be regarded as theology rather than history. Though Knox saw the present in the light of the past, particularly from the vantage point of the Old Testament, he was primarily a man of the present. Consequently, he used past events, whether in his polemical writings or *History*, for the purpose of promoting "true" religion as he perceived it. Past events to Knox were worth transcribing only to glorify God and to show his handy work

---

56. *Works*, 6:505–7; Marjorie Reeves, *Joachim of Fiore and the Prophetic Future* (New York: Harper and Row, 1976), 136–37. Knox cited Joachim's Exposition to condemn the Roman Church but showed no interest in the Abbott's predictions of a future age.

and the futility of opposing him. As a result, Knox's concept of history not only reflected his religious faith and his personal experiences, but also became a powerful force in his thinking—prompting him to contend for the Reformed faith in an exceedingly vigorous manner.

8

Knox in Zion:
The Reformation in Scotland (1559–1572)

T HE DEATH OF QUEEN Mary Tudor in November 1558 and the secession of her half-sister Elizabeth held significant ramifications for the
English speaking exile community living in Geneva. The large refugee
population of Protestants wished to leave Geneva, and some were particularly anxious to reform the church in England. In January 1559, the city
council of Geneva granted their request, and Pastor John Knox soon found
himself without a congregation and without work. Knox also dreamed
of reform—not in England, but in his native Scotland. He left his family in the care of his best friend Christopher Goodman, and in February
1559, Knox headed for Scotland. From the city of Dieppe, he sought a
passport which would permit him to pass through England and visit his
former congregations in Newcastle and Berwick en route to Scotland. He
sent four urgent letters to his old friend William Cecil, Queen Elizabeth's
Secretary of State, requesting permission to pass through England while
at the same time alternately encouraging, lecturing, and even insulting
Cecil and the Queen.[1]

It is unlikely that Cecil ever passed the letters on to the Queen. Knox
came to understand that his vehement treatise—*The First Blast of the
Trumpet Against the Monstrous Regiment of Women*—rendered him and
everything associated with the city of Geneva odious to the Queen. In a
letter to Mrs. Anne Locke in April, Knox mentioned that his *First Blast*

---

1. *Calendar of State Papers*, Foreign Series of the Reign of Elizabeth, Joseph Stevenson,
ed.(London: Her Majesty's Stationery Office, 1863 reprint ed., 1966), 1:208–9. This letter
to Cecil, dated April 10, 1559 is Knox's third request for a license to pass through England
to visit his former congregations in Northern England. Knox continued his requests to
visit them even after he returned to Scotland. Hereafter cited as CSP.

"hath blown from me all my friends in England." He went on to say, "*The Second Blast*, I fear, shall sound somewhat more sharp."[2] Queen Elizabeth ordered a house to house search in London of anyone in possession of the odious book.[3] Without the needed passport, Knox bypassed England and arrived in Scotland in May of 1559 and became the natural leader of a fledgling movement to reform the Scottish kirk.

Knox returned to a country divided by both politics and religion. In April of 1558, Scotland and France linked their future with the marriage of Mary Queen of Scots and Francis, the son of King Henry II of France. King Henry had cleverly manipulated Mary of Guise, the Queen Regent, into French hands. Before the wedding, Mary signed three secret treaties with the French, which transferred Mary Stewart's rights to the thrones of England and Scotland if she died without heir.[4] The very real fear of a French takeover actually aided the Protestant party in Scotland. John Knox would soon learn that many Scots supported the Protestant cause without any theological convictions but purely out of antagonism to France.[5]

Knox's preaching tour of Scotland in 1555–1556 and his subsequent encouragement, counsel, and chastening through his letters were instrumental in establishing the machinery used to secure the reformation in Scotland. His condemnation of the cooperation between the Queen Regent and some Protestant Lords led to the formation of the so-called "Congregation" or "Lords of the Congregation,"—a mutual alliance with its roots in the Scottish practice of banding.[6] The Earl of Argyle was the most powerful noble in the Congregation, while Knox would subsequently provide spiritual leadership.[7] Some of the Scottish nobility and local lairds formed a series of bands or covenants. In these agreements, they

2. John Knox, *The Works of John Knox*, 6 vols. ed. David Laing (Edinburgh: Printed for the Bannatyne Club, 1846–1864) reprint ed., (New York: AMS Press, 1966), 6:14. Hereafter cited as *Works*.

3. Ibid.

4. Elizabeth Whitley, *Plain Mr. Knox* (Richmond: John Knox Press, 1960), 102–3.

5. Ian B. Cowan, *The Scottish Reformation: Church and Society in Sixteenth-Century Scotland* (London: Weidenfeld & Nicolson, 1982), 111–12.

6. Richard Greaves, *Theology and Revolution in the Scottish Reformation* (Grand Rapids: Christian University Press, 1980), 116–17.

7. John Guy, *Queen of Scots, the True Life of Mary Stuart* (New York: Houghton Mifflin Company, 2004), 104.

vowed to stop Catholic idolatry and replace it with a church reformed according to Scripture.

In May of 1556—during Knox's preaching tour in Scotland—the gentlemen of Mearns requested that he lead them in the Lord's Table, after which they banded themselves together to promote the gospel.[8] Using Old Testament models, Knox successfully blended the Scottish band and the Old Testament covenant, which signified mutual obligations between God and his people. In his 1558 treatise, titled the *Appelation*, Knox linked the nobility and magistrates into a covenant with God to reform religion and punish idolatry.[9] In the same month as his return to Scotland, the Congregation signed a band welcoming the important nobles—Archibald Campbell, the fifth Earl of Arglye, and Lord James Stewart—to the reforming movement.[10] Knox became the natural leader of a group he created through his pen and his powerful preaching.

Knox arrived in the midst of a growing storm. His preaching immediately rallied Protestants, but the mixed motives of what Knox calls the "rascal multitude" worried him. His preaching in Perth, May 1559, produced riots and massive destruction of church properties.[11] In June of 1559, Knox preached in St. Andrews, the ecclesiastical center of Scotland, and thus fulfilled a prediction he made as a slave aboard a French galley ship ten years earlier.[12]

In late June, Knox preached in St. Giles church in Edinburgh.[13] Within a week, a large number of Protestant burgesses publicly called Knox to become the minister at St. Giles in Edinburgh—a position he would hold until his death in 1572.[14] The Protestants prevailed in Perth and Stirling, but their triumph in Edinburgh proved short-lived. The Congregation quickly retreated in the face of the Queen Regent's superior

---

8. John Knox, *John Knox's History of the Reformation in Scotland*, ed. William Croft Dickinson, 2 vols. (Edinburgh: Thomas Nelson and Sons, Ltd. 1949), 1:122. Hereafter cited as Knox, *History*. See also F. Bardgett, "John Erskine of Dun: A Theological Reassessment," *Scottish Journal of Theology* 43 (January 1990): 64f.

9. *Works*, 4:465–520.

10. Ibid., 1:344–45.

11. Knox, *History*, 1:162. See Mary Verschuur, *Politics or Religion?: The Reformation in Perth 1540–1570* (Edinburgh: Dundedin Academic Press, 2006).

12. Ibid., 1:182.

13. Cowan, *The Scottish Reformation*, 117.

14. W. Stanford Reid, *Trumpeter of God: A Biography of John Knox* (New York: Charles Scribner's Sons, 1974), 176.

forces, and the Catholic Mass was restored in St. Giles and in seven burghs throughout Scotland.[15] We cannot accurately label these conflicts "war" or even as battles, but episodes limited primarily to marching and counter-charging without any contact. The Queen Regent depended on a small force of trained French soldiers, while the largely untrained "army" of the Congregation found its strength among local lairds.

LETTERS CHIEFLY RELATING TO THE PROGRESS OF THE REFORMATION IN SCOTLAND

It soon became apparent the Scots could not expel the French and establish a Reformed Church without English help. A large number of the letters, found in volume six of the *Works,* relate to the diplomatic correspondence between Knox and Secretary William Cecil and other principal parties involved in securing an Anglo-Scottish alliance. David Laing, Knox's nineteenth-century editor, labels these, "Letters Chiefly Relating to the Progress of the Reformation in Scotland, 1559-1562." The content of the letters from volume six will be considered as they fall into certain themes or topics.

Knox, the Anglo-Scottish Union, and the Politics of Reform

Even decades prior to the Protestant Reformation, many of the Scottish nobility looked for some way of bringing order into the chaos which prevailed in Scotland. One Scot writing in the sixteenth century claimed that every English king since the Norman Conquest "aimed to unite the two kingdoms."[16] For centuries, England sought to impose the union through military invasion, conquest or by dynastic marriage.

---

15. Cowan, *The Scottish Reformation*, 117.

16. Thomas Craig, De vione regnorum Britanniae (Scottish Historical Society), 242, quoted in Gordon Donaldson, "Foundations of Anglo-Scottish Union," 282, in *Elizabethan Government and Society, Essays Presented to Sir John Neale*, S.T. Bindoff, ed., (London: The Atholone Press, 1961), 282–314. See also, Jane E. A. Dawson, "Anglo-Scottish Protestant Culture and Integration in Sixteenth-Century Britain," in S. Ellis and S. Barber, eds., *Conquest and Union: The Formation of the British State, 1485–1725* (London: 1995), 87–114; William Ferguson, *Scotland's Relations with England: A Survey to 1707* (Edinburgh: John Donald Publisher Ltd., 1977), 51–96, and Roger A. Mason, "The Scottish Reformation and the Origins of Anglo-British Imperialism," in *Kingship and the Commonwealth. Political Thought in Renaissance and Reformation Scotland* (East Lothian, Scotland: Tuckwell Press, 1998), 242–69.

From the accession of King James I in 1406 until the middle sixteenth century, every Scottish monarch came to the throne as a minor.[17] The Roman Catholic Church in Scotland filled this power vacuum by dominating the crown. The church owned over half the land and its annual income was nearly twenty times that of the crown.[18] Prospects for union improved when Margaret Tudor married King James IV of Scotland in 1503, but died with James on the battlefield at Flodden in England.

The Scottish crown, however, increased its power somewhat. King James V used leverage against the Pope by threatening to follow the example of his uncle, King Henry VIII of England, through the confiscation of church property.[19] Henry, in fact, offered his nephew an alliance in 1539 and in 1541 and advised the capture of Scottish monasteries. The appearance of Protestantism in England provided some Scottish nobles with a potential weapon to battle both crown and church. Accurate or not, most Scots considered King Henry a strong defender of Protestants and believed that linkage with England could assure a Protestant victory in Scotland.[20] In 1541 King Henry convinced James of the need to meet and discuss an alliance. King James agreed and then reneged to meet his uncle Henry in York.

The biographer Jasper Ridley says every Protestant historian in the sixteenth century considered James' failure to appear at York as a watershed event, one which explains all of Scotland's misery for the next thirty years.[21] The Anglo-Scottish union suffered a temporary, but serious setback. The horror Knox and other reform minded Scots faced at the time of his return to Scotland was not merely the absence of a Protestant Anglo-Scottish union, but the strength of the Catholic Franco-Scottish alliance. Any hope of a genuine reformation of religion in Scotland rested on a Protestant alliance with England to force the removal of the French military, political, and religious hegemony in Scotland.

In promoting an alliance with England, Knox repeatedly used the language of the covenant on behalf of the Lords of the Congregation. He substituted the specific word, "covenant" with related words—such

17. Reid, *Trumpeter of God*, 7.

18. Ibid.

19. William Croft Dickinson, *Scotland from the Earliest Times to 1603* (New York: Thomas Nelson & Sons, Ltd., 1961), 30.

20. Jasper Ridley, *John Knox* (New York: Oxford University Press, 1968), 30.

21. Ibid.

as perpetual concord, contract, or league—to describe the relationship the Congregation wished to formalize with England.[22] Writing for the Congregation, Knox repeatedly identified two goals: (1) "For the glory of God, ... the true preaching of Jesus Christ, and (2) that the liberties, laws, and privileges of both these realms may remain inviolate of any ... foreign power."[23] Knox assured the English the Congregation wished for "nothing but the reformation of religion."[24] In a letter to Sir Henry Percy, Knox explained the Scots "mean neither sedition, nor rebellion against any just and lawful authority, but only the advancement of Christ's religion and the liberty of this poor realm."[25] He admitted to William Cecil that in removing idolatry from the Roman Church in Scotland, "the Reformation is somewhat violent."[26] In short, for Knox, "reformation" was a verb.

Perhaps Knox could not specifically use the word covenant in his letters to English officials because Scotland itself was not yet a covenanted nation. Some of its leaders had made a covenant with Christ, but Scotland did not formally become a covenanted nation until the Reformation Parliament of August 1560.[27] It is only after this point Scotland formally offered a marriage proposal. Only then could Israel (Scotland) and Judah (England) formalize a New Covenant relationship into a United Kingdom like the Old Testament people of God.

When Knox began his requests for a passport from Dieppe to England, he left tantalizing hints of a secret message he wished to communicate to Secretary William Cecil in person. His fervent requests continued from Scotland about the importance of a secret message he needed to deliver.[28] Because he had poisoned the waters with his *First Blast*, his requests were routinely ignored, and the message was delivered instead by a Scot named Alexander Whitelaw to William Cecil.

---

22. CSP, For. Elizabeth, 1:339–40, 1:430–32, 1:445–46. A very important secondary source for this point is Roger A. Mason, "Covenant and Commonwealth: The Language of Politics in Reformation Scotland," in *Church, Politics and Society: Scotland 1408–1929*, Norman MacDougall, ed., (Edinburgh: John Donald Publishers Ltd., 1983), 97–126.

23. CSP, For. Elizabeth, 1 431.

24. Ibid., 1:349–50.

25. Ibid., 1:351.

26. *Works*, 6:31.

27. Jane E. A. Dawson, "The Two John Knoxes: England, Scotland and the 1558 Tracts," *Journal of Ecclesiastical History* 42 (October 1991): 570–72.

28. *Works*, 6:31.

What Knox wished to communicate was a plan to unite the two countries through a marriage between Queen Elizabeth and a Scot, James Hamilton III, Earl of Arran. Knox apparently convinced the Congregation of the wisdom of this scheme. This idea appears in the diplomatic correspondence in the summer of 1559, but Arran's father—the rather weak and vacillating Duke of Chatelherault—had promoted the union some years earlier.[29] To be sure, the Lords did not promote the marriage exclusively for religious reasons. It must be noted they supported Knox's plan in part because they hoped to gain ecclesiastical property at the expense of the Roman Church.

The Elizabethan Moment

Historians refer to the so-called "Edwardian Moment." This prospect developed when King Henry VIII of England proposed a union of England and Scotland through an arranged marriage between Edward, the infant son of Henry, and the infant Mary who would become the Queen of Scots. The Edwardian moment failed for a number of reasons, but now the two countries faced another opportunity to redress an old failure. Knox was promoting an "Elizabethan Moment" through a royal marriage.

It is tempting to argue that Knox and the Earl of Arran privately designed the marriage scheme during their exile from Scotland. The lives of the two men crisscrossed throughout Scotland and Europe. The facts allow us to construct plausible scenarios in which the two men personally, or through common friends, influenced each other. Admittedly, documenting "influence" is an enterprise fraught with problems. We do know Arran's father hired as his chaplain Protestant preachers Thomas Guilliame and John Rough in 1542. Knox said he first heard the gospel from Guilliame, and we might mark his conversion to the evangelical faith from this event.[30] Arran would have been eight or nine years old when the Castilians, who captured St. Andrews Castle, held him hostage. Knox may even have taught him at the castle along with his other charges. Knox, of

---

29. As early as 1545, the Scottish Governor proposed a marriage between Mary Stewart and the Prince of the Realm, James, the Governor's eldest son. See, Marguerite Wood, "The Imprisonment of the Earl of Arran," *Scottish Historical Review* 24 (January 1927): 119.

30. David Calderwood, *The History of the Kirk of Scotland*, 4 vols., ed., T. Thompson, (Edinburgh: The Wodrow Society, 1842–1843), 1:155f.

course, became the chaplain to the Castilians in 1547 and inaugurated his preaching career.

The French seized the castle and forced the Castilians into prison or as galley slaves. French King Henry II took young Arran hostage in France where he lived for a decade. When Arran's father consented to the marriage of Mary Stewart and Francis, the dauphin of France, he was rewarded with the Dutchy of Chatelherault, which provided a residence for Arran.[31] Some evidence suggests Arran, disguised as a servant, entered Geneva in July 1556 traveling with John Knox.[32] In February 1559, Arran formed a Protestant church in Chatelherault and secured a pastor. The date of Arran's conversion to Protestantism is not clear, and some believe his evangelical fervency "developed suspiciously after the wedding of Mary [Stewart] and the accession of Elizabeth."[33]

We pick up Arran's trail again in May of 1559 when the English Ambassador, Sir Nicholas Throckmorton, assumed his duties in France. Apparently the fervency of Arran's Protestantism alarmed King Henry II, who requested his presence at Court.[34] Arran, however, fearing for his safety, eluded Henry's men and escaped with the help of Throckmorton. The English wished for Arran's return to Scotland so that he might provide the rebellion a show of legitimacy and provide leadership. Queen Elizabeth even suggested an escape route for Arran through the Jersey Islands.[35] The Lords of the Congregation arranged for Arran to flee France for Geneva, Zurich, and Lusanne by traveling in disguise as Monsieur Beaufort.[36] Knox suggests that Calvin and Arran knew each other and exchanged letters.[37] In Zurich, Peter Martyr was Arran's host. Writing to

31. John Durkan, "James, Third Earl of Arran: The Hidden Years," *Scottish Historical Review* 62 (October 1986): 135.

32. Ibid., 158.

33. R. K. Hannay, "The Third Earl of Arran and Queen Mary," *Scottish Historical Review* 18 (July 1921): 263.

34. J. B. Black, *The Reign of Elizabeth 1558–1603* (Oxford: The Clarendon Press, 1936, 2nd ed., 1965), 42.

35. Hannay, "The Earl of Arran and Queen Mary," 265.

36. Durkan, "James, Third Earl of Arran," 163–64. The Foreign Calendar notes Arran lived off fruit and hid in the woods for two weeks to escape his captors. See CSP, For. Elizabeth, 1:416. The letter is dated July, 1, 1559.

37. Hannay, "The Earl of Arran and Queen Mary," 265. See for example, John Calvin, *Letters of John Calvin* 3 vols., Jules Bonnet, ed., (New York: Burt Franklin Reprints), 3:453–56.

John Jewel in England, Martyr used coded names for Arran and Thomas Randolph, an English agent and guide. Queen Elizabeth mentioned that influential Protestants in both England and Scotland were promoting a marriage between Arran and herself.[38]

Alexander Whitelaw (who communicated Knox's secret marriage scheme to Cecil) arrived in London from France in late June bearing dispatches from Ambassador Throckmorton. It is interesting that Knox promoted the marriage plan before his return to Scotland. His letters to Secretary William Cecil promoting the marriage originated in France, not in Scotland.[39] The Protestants in Scotland who supported the marriage arrangement seemed not to possess any specific details and knew of it only in general terms.[40] The circle of men privy to the marriage scheme included Knox, Arran, and Whitelaw. It seems likely these men devised the marriage plan as the centerpiece of a plan to reform the Scottish kirk and relayed only hints of it to the Protestant leaders in Scotland.

All of the covert diplomacy paid off as Arran successfully eluded French agents. Arran arrived in London from Antwerp in late August and conferred with Cecil and Elizabeth behind closed doors.[41] The meeting between Arran and the Queen was merely a prelude to the "Elizabethan Moment." A formal marriage proposal would not come until the following year, long after Knox was removed from his diplomatic post. The Earl of Arran initially captivated the English government for two reasons. He was not only a possible suitor for Elizabeth, but they also believed his military experience was crucial to the success of the Protestant rebellion in Scotland. While living in France, Arran had gained notoriety for his military leadership on behalf of the Huguenots.[42] It became clear to Elizabeth that Arran was not a suitable match, however. His name also surfaced later as a potential suitor for Mary Stewart when the widow returned to Scotland after the death of her husband, Frances II the King of

---

38. John Jewel, *The Works of John Jewel Bishop of Salisbury* (Cambridge, 1801), 4:1224, 1226, 1228, 1235–36, 1240 cited in Durkan, "James, Third Earl of Arran," 163.

39. *Works*, 6:20.

40. CSP, For. Elizabeth, 1:335–56. The letter dated June 23, 1559 was written by William Kirkcaldy of Grange to William Cecil suggesting Elizabeth should avoid a hasty commitment to marriage.

41. Ibid., 1:482–3 and 508–9.

42. W. Forbes Leith, *The Scots Men-at-Arms and Guard Life in France* (Edinburgh: 1882), 1:189–93, cited in Durkan, "James, Third Earl of Arran," 160.

France. Arran's insanity led to his confinement from 1562 until his death in 1609. There would be no "Elizabethan Moment" involving the Queen and the Third Earl of Arran.

The Knox-Locke Letters

Mrs. Anne Locke deserves a special place in the life and memory of John Knox. Thirteen of Knox's letters to Mrs. Locke survive from the years 1556 to 1562, testifying to the special bond between them. On the basis of the letters' content, some students of Knox believe no one, in fact, occupied a closer place in Knox's heart than Anne Locke.[43] Robert Louis Stevenson argued in his essay, "John Knox and His Relations with Women," that John Knox loved Anne Locke more than any other woman in his life.[44] Patrick Collinson even suggests the two might have wed under the right circumstances.[45]

Anne, the eldest daughter of Stephen Vaughan, grew up in a household increasingly attracted to Protestantism. Mr. Vaughan engaged in international trade and performed diplomatic duties for Henry VIII and worked closely with Thomas Cromwell. Henry's government sent Stephen Vaughan to find William Tyndale and to persuade him to return to England in order to use his writing abilities on behalf of Henry's divorce efforts. Vaughan met Tyndale on three occasions with the translator repeating the same message. He refused to return to England until the king allowed the printing and distribution of the Bible in the English language.[46]

Anne Vaughan married Henry Locke, a Protestant engaged in the sale of expensive fabrics.[47] We first meet Anne in Knox's correspondence when he informed Mrs. Bowes, his future mother-in-law, of his living arrangements in late 1553. Knox lived with the Locke family before he joined the Marian exile in 1554. Knox wrote to Mrs. Locke on two occasions, imploring her to move to Geneva where she could worship in freedom and safety. He argued two points in his letters: she should not at-

43. Patrick Collinson, "The Role of Women in the English Reformation Illustrated by the Life and Friendship of Mrs. Anne Locke," *Studies in Church History* (1956): 2:261.

44. Ibid., 2:264.

45. Reid, *Trumpeter of God*, 141. Professor Reid expressed his skepticism regarding Patrick Collinson's claims.

46. David Daniell, *William Tyndale: A Biography* (New Haven: Yale University Press, 1994), 209–12.

47. Collinson, "The Role of Women in the English Reformation," 263.

tend the Church in England as it evolved under Mary Tudor, and Geneva provided a spiritual haven for Protestant exiles.

In his letter dated December 9, 1556 Knox used a phrase describing Geneva repeated in biographies and history books for the past 450 years. Knox's description of Geneva as the most perfect school of Christ since the days of the Apostles referred to the four-fold structure of church governance as they related to church and civic affairs. Mrs. Locke must have found Knox's arguments compelling because she arrived in Geneva with her two infant children and a maid, but without her husband in May of 1557.[48]

The first letter Knox wrote to Mrs. Locke after he left Geneva for Scotland is very revealing. At some length Knox assured Anne of his friendship and care. Neither time nor physical separation could diminish the bond they shared. With a hint of annoyance, he repeated his criticism of the Church in England as it developed along Elizabethan lines. The preaching and sacraments still reflected what Knox called the "dregs of papistry."[49] It was, according to Knox, a "bastard religion" with a liturgy containing "mingle mangle."[50] He also lowered his guard somewhat regarding the fallout from his infamous treatise, *The First Blast of the Trumpet*. Following his own metaphor, he admitted that his "First Blast" blew all his friends away.[51]

Safely back in London, Anne Locke provided a kind of clearing house dispensing information to reformers and co-religionists and assisted Knox in the Reformation in Scotland. Knox desperately needed the assistance of Christopher Goodman in Scotland. On several occasions, Knox wrote to Anne with messages for Goodman. He also asked Anne to relay messages to Miles Coverdale, the Bible translator, and John Bodley, who would later hold the printing rights for the *Geneva Bible*.[52]

---

48. Reid, *Trumpeter of God*, 140–41.

49. *Works*, 6:12.

50. Ibid., 6:83.

51. Ibid., 6:14.

52. *Works*, 6:30, 78, 108–9. See also F.F. Bruce, *The English Bible: A History of Translations* (London: Lutterworth Press, 1961), 91.

Help Us!

Knox asked Anne for both money and books. As the Scottish Protestants and sympathizers battled the French Catholics, Knox sought money for the soldiers. He asked Anne Locke to raise money for this godly cause in Scotland or face potentially dire consequences in England. He told Anne if France were not stopped in Scotland, the road to London was wide open and vulnerable.[53] In December of 1559, Knox asked Anne to send him Calvin's sermons on Isaiah and the revised edition of the *Institutes of the Christian Religion*. Anne had a vested interest in the dissemination of Calvin's literature because while in Geneva, she translated some of Calvin's sermons on Isaiah.[54]

The Knox letters to Anne Locke provide valuable information regarding the progress of the Reformation in Scotland. He shared with Anne his need for courage to face the French when they arrived in full force.[55] The early days of the struggle witnessed considerable destruction of church property including altars, vestments, statues, and abbeys. Knox told Locke the reformation of religion was not the destruction of icons, nor merely the removal of surplices and other religious paraphernalia. The reformation of religion included the ministry of the Word of God, the administration of sacraments, and the suppression of idolatry.[56] Knox reported how God had intervened on the behalf of the Scots. The French army moved within six miles of St. Andrews, but rapidly retreated when the English navy appeared off shore.[57] For Knox, this was nothing less than the hand of God at work.

After the eventual French defeat and withdrawal of both the French and English forces, the Scottish Parliament outlawed the Mass and other Catholic practices. The fragile coalition in Scotland formed to battle the French began to crumble. Some of the nobility, who initially stood with the Lords of the Congregation, began to see opportunities for wealth without regard to the future financial stability of the infant Reformed Church. When the young widow Mary Stewart arrived from France—following

53. *Works*, 6:100.

54. Ibid., 6:100, 108. See also Collinson, "Women in the English Reformation," 265.

55. *Works*, 6:21.

56. Ibid., 6:22–26.

57. Ibid., 6:105. Compare Knox's retelling of this same story on page 108. In the retelling a few of the details become shaky.

the death of her husband King Francis II—to assume her rightful place as the Queen, some nobles ignored her illegal celebration of the Mass in her private chapel. Knox once more found himself engaged in a religious war against superstition.

The reformer poured out his heart to Anne Locke about the hypocrisy of the nobility.[58] Knox thundered against the Queen's Mass from the pulpit of St. Giles, but without success.[59] In his letter he repeated the biblical pattern for worship, warning against adding anything or diminishing anything prescribed in the Bible. As Scotland once more tolerated the Mass, Knox predicted the mercy of God was their only hope.[60] He despaired for his life, but ended the letter in a forward thinking manner. He sent Anne a copy of the *Scots Confession of Faith,* produced at the request of the Reformation Parliament.[61]

The last letter of Knox to Anne Locke dated May 6, 1562 is likewise revealing. The first sentence shows sorrow, even the despair Knox faced after the personality clashes between the Earl of Arran and the Earl of Bothwell. Knox reluctantly intervened and the two men embraced only to renew the hostility days later. Knox no doubt wondered, with friends like these, who needed enemies?[62]

The "Cecilian" Connection

William Cecil, Queen Elizabeth's Secretary of State, provided essential support for the Reformed party in Scotland and was a friend of John Knox. The oft strained relationship between the two men dated to 1549 when Cecil used his influence to liberate Knox from French confinement. Knox then served the English crown as a preacher, chaplain to Edward VI, and advisor of sorts to Archbishop Cranmer. The Knox-Cecil correspondence stretched for ten years. The bulk of the letters date from Knox's official role as the Secretary of the Lords of the Congregation and relate to his efforts on behalf of the Reformed cause.

Even while Knox requested a favor from Sir William Cecil for a passport, he admonished him for cowardice during the reign of Mary Tudor.

---

58. Ibid., 6:130.
59. Ibid., 6:129.
60. Ibid., 6:84.
61. Ibid., 6:130.
62. Ibid., 6:140–41.

Cecil's silence made him an accomplice in the death of nearly three hundred martyrs ordered by Mary. "You are worthy of hell," he told Cecil.[63] He asked the Secretary to deliver a message to the Queen regarding the extraordinary mercy extended to her by God. If Cecil failed to deliver this message, Knox threatened to expose Cecil to the whole world for his personal failure.[64] After repeated letters, in which Knox requested the right to travel and preach in Northern England, he finally received an answer of sorts in late July 1559. Cecil explained to Knox that all of the letters finally reached him. He could not explain how or why they were delayed.[65]

Beginning in the late summer of 1559, Knox pressed his case for English support of the Congregation against French and Catholic forces in Scotland. Without funding, the unpaid soldiers of the Congregation might very well desert. The French were also attempting to purchase the loyalties of the Congregation's soldiers. Knox's forecast was grim. If England stood by in a neutral position, the Reformed cause would be lost.[66] In a November 18, 1559 letter, Knox admitted or explained that William Maitland of Lethington would replace him as the Secretary for the Congregation. In the end everyone, including Knox, recognized his gifts were better used in the pulpit than in a quasi-diplomatic position.[67]

After Queen Mary returned to Scotland, Knox thundered from the pulpit in St. Giles—warning of the potential dangers of tolerating the celebration of the mass in the Palace of Holyrood. Word quickly traveled to London, and Knox defended the content of his preaching in a letter to Cecil. Knox explained he was guided by experience. He knew that failure to attack the demon-inspired Mass allowed Satan to grow increasingly bold.[68] Knox also learned to his consternation that the Queen claimed John Calvin as an ally of sorts. She claimed Calvin argued ministers did not have the right to interfere with her religious practice. Knox told Calvin he had tried to correct this false rumor but with little success. In an interesting moment of self-disclosure, Knox confessed to Calvin: "I am a continual

---

63. Ibid., 6:16. For an excellent source on the relationship between Cecil and Knox see Conyers Read, *Mr. Secretary Cecil and Queen Elizabeth* (London, 1955).

64. *Works*, 6:19.

65. Ibid., 6:55–56.

66. Ibid., 6:68–69, 6:98.

67. Ibid., 6:99, cf. 6:94.

68. Ibid., 6:131.

trouble to you, and I have no other to whom I can confide my anxieties."[69] Even some of Knox's friends sided with Mary because of his hostile words in the pulpit. William Maitland wrote to Cecil: "you know the vehemence of Knox's spirit which cannot be bridled."[70] Maitland wished Knox had extended a more gentle approach when dealing with the young Queen.

THE REASONING BETWEEN THE ABBOT OF CROSSRAGUEL AND JOHN KNOX CONCERNING THE MASS

The Parliament in Scotland, known as the "Reformation Parliament," formally embraced the principles of Protestantism in August of 1560. They banned the Catholic Mass and the church in Scotland slowly began to take the shape of a Reformed kirk. Some steps included removing the altars from the Communion table and making the pulpit the central feature of worship. The newly established church faced serious challenges even from the beginning. Perhaps its most formidable challenge surfaced when news reached Scotland of the death of King Francis II of France, husband of Mary. The new kirk would soon face an additional threat with the return of Mary Queen of Scots from her French exile.

Mary and her entourage arrived in Edinburgh in August of 1561. When their worst fears about the Queen's religion became apparent, the General Assembly commissioned John Knox to shore up Protestant support by way of a preaching tour in the West country near Kyle and Galloway.[71] His preaching accomplished its intended goal and inspired 78 lairds to sign a band or covenant, pledging themselves to support and defend the ministers of the Reformed kirk against its enemies.[72]

In addition to preaching, Knox also led people in the celebration of the Lord's Supper. Without conceding the claims of historians like Gordon Donaldson—who was to make Knox something of a closet Anglican—it is fair to affirm Knox's belief in the importance of the sacrament of Holy Communion. Biographer Eustace Percy, in fact, claimed Knox restored

---

69. Ibid., 6:133–34.

70. Ibid., 6:136–37.

71. Hugh Watt, *John Knox in Controversy* (London: Thomas Nelson and Sons, Ltd., 1950), 49.

72. Margaret H. B. Sanderson, *Ayrshire and the Reformation: People and Change, 1490–1600* (East Lothian, Scotland: Tuckwell Press, 1997), 121.

the sacrament for the nation of Scotland.[73] This explains in part Knox's revulsion to the Catholic Mass. For one, it was indefensible from Scripture and was invented by human thinking. In Knox's mind, creativity in worship apart from the express warrant of Scripture constituted idolatry. The Mass not only involved a sacrilege of a re-sacrifice of Christ, it also cut people off from the means of grace the Lord Jesus intended in the Lord's Supper. Knox's forceful preaching and teaching of these points cheered his supporters but also stirred the anger of Quintin Kennedy, the Abbot of Crossraguel, from the pulpit in Kirkoswald.

Like Knox, Kennedy studied at St. Andrews, but completed his education at the University of Paris. He earned a reputation for his scholastic learning.[74] Kennedy gained his position as Abbot at the monastery following his brother's death. Professor Hugh Watt relates the remarkable means whereby the Kennedy clan later stole the monastic property. The Commendator of Crossraguel was slowly roasted over a fire until the property was ceded to the Kennedys.[75]

Never one to shrink at the opportunity to preach or ignore a commendation of the gospel, Knox and some lairds attended the church of Kirkoswald the following Sunday. Knox intended to listen to the Abbot and then ask for the opportunity for rebuttal. In the Abbot's absence, Knox preached and explained why the Mass was an abomination in God's sight. As he stepped down from the pulpit a note from the Abbot was handed to Knox. The letter accepted Knox's challenge to a debate to be held eight days later. This led to several rounds of correspondence working out the details and logistics of a face to face debate between John Knox and Qunitin Kennedy, the Abbot of Crossraguel. Knox lobbied for a larger venue and more observers. Both men appeared eager to debate and were equally confident of victory.[76]

The debate held at the Provost's manse in Maybole lasted three days, beginning September 28, 1562. Both men had prepared orations they delivered for the occasion. They also moved beyond the prepared texts and spoke directly to each other. In the negotiations, Knox challenged the Abbot to

---

73. Watt, *John Knox in Controversy*, 50.

74. *Works*, 6:153–54.

75. Watt, *John Knox in Controversy*, 52–53.

76. *Works*, 6:176–84. See also Watt, *John Knox in Controversy*, 56.

defend the Mass directly from the Word of God. In turn the Abbot claimed he could rebut Knox's claim that the Mass was not based on Scripture.[77]

The Abbot's Scriptural Basis for the Mass

The Abbot of Crossraguel defended the Mass from the shadowy figure of Melchizadek, the priest and King of Salem mentioned only briefly in Scripture. In Genesis chapter 14, Melchizadek brought bread and wine to Abraham and his army. According to the Abbot, Melchizadek offered an oblation and sacrifice of bread and wine unto the Lord. Christ is identified in Hebrews as a priest after the order of Melchizadek. The Abbot interpreted Christ's actions in the Last Supper as an oblation, substituting his body and blood with bread and wine. Failure on Christ's part to follow the sacrificial practice would have contradicted the Scripture's claim that Jesus was a priest after the order of Melchizadek.[78]

Knox's rebuttal unfolded slowly. He used the occasion to question not merely the biblical basis of the Mass, but in fact the entire arsenal of Roman doctrine. Neither the Mass, nor purgatory, nor praying to saints, celibacy nor erecting images are biblically defensible.[79] He rejected the name "Mass" and everything related to it: the action occurring in transubstantiation, the interpretation or opinion of its value, and the role of the priest involved in the sacrifice.[80] Knox was in good company. He and his fellow reformers faced the same challenges as the prophets in the Old Testament. He saw a direct continuity between the Old Testament prophets and himself. God raised up these biblical prophets to rebuke people for their sin, admonish priests for their negligence, and condemn their idolatry in times of widespread spiritual corruption. Similarly, God raised up "Zwinglians, Oecolampadians and Calvinists" to perform the same spiritual duties in the sixteenth century.[81]

On the first day of the debate Knox insisted on a definition of terms. What exactly did the Abbot mean by the word sacrifice? What kind of sacrifice was it? Was it *eucharistica*, a thanksgiving? Was it *propiciatorium*,

---

77. *Works*, 6:186.

78. Ibid., 6:186, 196.

79. Ibid., 6:189, 192.

80. Ibid., 6:199.

81. Ibid., 6:190.

a satisfaction made to the justice of God?[82] The Abbot intended the latter understanding of the Mass as a sacrifice. Knox quickly widened the gap when he insisted on a distinction between the Lord's Supper and the Mass. The Lord's Supper was not a re-sacrifice of Christ, but rather a sacrament of thanksgiving. In modern language, the Lord's Supper was a means of sanctifying grace, not a means of saving grace.

After hearing the Abbot's novel defense of the Mass from the example of Melchizadek, Knox asked for a reading of Genesis 14 and noted the text made no mention of a sacrifice of bread and wine. Only by inference could an oblation be found. The text was silent on that crucial point. The Abbot insisted Knox explain what happened to the bread and wine mentioned in the text. Knox speculated Abraham and his army used the food and drink for nourishment. The Abbot, however, showed from the text that Abraham and his army feasted on the spoils of war. This altogether fruitless exchange took up two of the three days of debate.[83]

Late in the debate the Abbot believed he caught Knox in a trap. Knox insisted that everything find its warrant in Scripture, yet his assertion that Abraham and his men consumed the bread and wine is not found in Scripture. Knox quickly pointed out the Abbot's misuse of the principle. Knox explained he merely offered an opinion at the Abbot's insistence. He refused to stand by it as the only valid interpretation of Scripture. More importantly, Knox noted that neither an article of faith nor doctrine of salvation were involved. The real issue involved whether Melchizadek offered a sacrifice to God, not the food eaten by Abraham and his army.[84]

It is unlikely the debate changed many minds. The Abbot of Crossraguel succeeded in introducing a novel defense of the Mass—one that was repeated for a time in Scottish Catholic history but did not move beyond the border. A few Catholic writers claimed the Church canonized the Abbot of Crossraguel, who died in July of 1564, only two years after the debate. In truth the Abbott was not canonized and his memory is perpetuated only in the writings of John Knox.[85]

---

82. Ibid., 6:198.

83. Ibid., 6:200–3.

84. Ibid., 6:217–18.

85. Ibid., 6:156. See also Watt, *John Knox in Controversy*, 67–68.

SERMON ON ISAIAH

Despite John Knox's image and reputation as a fiery preacher, it is ironic so few of his sermons have survived. One of the few surviving sermons was preached from Isaiah 26:13–21 on August 19, 1565 from his favorite pulpit in St. Giles Church. On this particular Sunday the congregation included a very notable dignitary.[86] Lord Darnley, who had become King of Scotland upon his marriage to Mary Queen of Scots, sat in a specially designed throne. The king attempted to satisfy the religious preferences of all his subjects by attending worship at Reformed Churches, as well as the Mass with his wife in the Holyrood Chapel.[87]

The king immediately took offense at Knox's sermon because of the numerous references to tyrannical rulers and the consequences promised to those who broke God's law with impunity. The king also became annoyed at the length of the sermon when Knox preached an hour longer than normal.[88] Darnley complained to his wife and like a spoiled child refused to eat his dinner. The Privy Council summoned Knox to appear that same afternoon to explain the nature of his offensive sermon. They forbade him to preach in St. Giles when the king and queen were in residence.[89] The king also demanded Knox be banned from preaching for a period of fifteen to twenty days.[90]

Knox defended himself and his exposition of the text claiming he simply quoted the Word of God. If the sermon offended the king, he took offense at God and his revealed word. Knox was merely the messenger. Knox did in fact abandon St. Giles for a time visiting churches on behalf of the General Assembly.[91] Ten days after Knox delivered the sermon he attempted to reconstruct it in writing. He took this course of action to defend himself against the allegations that his sermon unfairly targeted the king and queen of Scotland.

The prophet Isaiah foresaw the coming judgment by God against Jerusalem and Judah. The people would be scattered, the city razed, and

---

86. Richard Kyle, *The Ministry of John Knox: Pastor, Preacher, and Prophet* (Lewiston, New York: The Edwin Mellon Press, 2002), 93–94.

87. *Works*, 6:223.

88. Knox, *History*, 2:159.

89. *Works*, 6:230.

90. Knox, *History*, 2:160.

91. *Works*, 6:224–25.

the ark of the covenant and the temple burned.[92] Knox raised two pre-liminary questions concerning this impending judgment. Who or what is the ultimate authority and how does God use earthly rulers for his own ends? The text was unambiguous. There is no power but of God.[93] From this biblical truth and Knox's comments, the king of Scotland began to take offense. Kings and queens are nothing special by nature of their birth. They merely serve a role by God's good pleasure.[94] Earthly rulers honor God by living out the counsel of Joshua found in chapter one, verses seven and eight. God expected kings and queens to revere the book of the law and not let it depart from their mouths. They were expected to mediate on it day and night. Knox's implication was clear. If kings and queens failed to live by this godly counsel, they could expect rebuke from God.

Secondly, kings and queens cannot take the law into their own hands for their own selfish purposes. Only God has absolute power. Earthly monarchs are subject to God and their power is strictly limited. Drawing from the example of God's people in the Babylonian Captivity, Knox believed Scotland stood ripe for God's judgment. Knox warned of God's condemnation if the king and queen in Scotland suppressed bibli-cal preaching and abolished the sacraments.[95] The people of God found themselves in captivity because of their mocking and stubborn refusal to heed the prophets' warnings. Knox delivered a bold statement here linking himself with the same authority as the biblical prophets. Knox claimed to possess secrets given him by God, known to no human being. God appointed him to prophesy and forewarn nations, kings, and queens of the fatal consequences for disobedience.[96]

When Knox defended his sermon before the Privy Council, his words were somewhat disingenuous. He claimed only to quote the Word of God and thus allow his listeners to make the application. In fact, his explicit references to Scotland, to Scotland's king, and the certainty of the punishment of Edinburgh left little to the imagination. Linking Judah and Jerusalem with Scotland and Edinburgh, Knox quoted the prophet Jeremiah. Every nation similarly disobeying God "shall be likewise pun-

---

92. Ibid., 6:234.

93. Ibid., 6:235.

94. Ibid., 6:236.

95. Ibid., 6:238–39.

96. Ibid., 6:230, 240–41.

ished."[97] Like Israel, Scotland deserved God's wrath because the leaders abandoned justice and rebelled against God. They engaged in fraud and violence in their course of governance. If Darnley's blood pressure was elevated at this point, Knox's next point made him livid. Using Isaiah chapter three, Knox showed how God removed Judah's prophets, heroes, and judges and in their place appointed mere children to govern them and women to rule over them.[98] Knox now angered both the king and queen. Such tyrants who oppressed God's people shall perish in shame "without hope of resurrection."[99]

The last major point of Knox's sermon involved the distinction between God's rebuke of the reprobate versus punishment of his elect. How may we distinguish between the reprobate and the elect? Knox said the worldly princes feed their souls with the liquor of pride, ambition, and lust.[100] When God rebukes the reprobate, they ignore him and stubbornly refuse to change. By contrast, when the elect are chastened, they repent of their sin and cry out to God in humble submission.[101] All of Knox's listeners could prove their status as either reprobate or elect by their response to his prophetic admonition. The king immediately demonstrated his true colors when he bitterly complained of the challenge he heard at St. Giles on Sunday morning, August 19, 1565.

AN ANSWER TO A LETTER OF A JESUIT NAMED TYRIE

In 1567 a Jesuit named James Tyrie wrote a number of letters aimed at refuting the Reformed faith. Some were addressed to his eldest brother— David Tyrie of Drumkilbo, Scotland—who had left the Church of Rome for Protestantism. David Tyrie asked Knox to answer one of the letters. He received the letter in 1568 and produced a hasty rebuttal to Tyrie. He was not entirely satisfied with his response to Tyrie and decided to suppress it. Some three years later during his brief exile in St. Andrews, Knox wrote a more thoughtful reply titled a *Vindication of the Reformed Religion in Answer to a Letter Written by Tyrie, a Scottish Jesuit.* In a letter to Sir J. Wishart of Pittarrow (July 19, 1572), the ailing Knox explained, "I have set

97. Ibid., 6:241–42.
98. Ibid., 6:242, cf. Isaiah 3:2, 4 and 12.
99. Ibid., 6:244, 263.
100. Ibid., 6:252–53.
101. Ibid., 6:256.

forth an answer to a Jesuit who long hath railed against our religion."[102] This brief work was Knox's last published treatise.

Knox answered Tyrie by reprinting each charge or question followed by his own response. The first charge Tyrie made involved the antiquity of the Roman Church versus the novelty of the Reformed Church in Scotland. If you cannot point to your church 300 or 1000 years ago, it follows that you have no church, Tyrie charged. The true church, Knox countered, is found in the knowledge of God and in his son Jesus Christ our savior. The true church is the body of Christ. The true church is found wherever the doctrines of the apostolic church are affirmed. Knox then went on the offensive. He noted you could find people 1000 years earlier who believed what the Church of Scotland affirmed in 1560, but the same was not true of the Roman Church. Rather, the Roman Church not the Reformed Church, embraced novel ideas. Rome no longer embraced apostolic doctrine and by definition ceased being a church.[103]

Tyrie also challenged Knox on the issue of succession and unity of the Roman Church. By contrast, Tyrie regarded the Reformers and their numerous sects as splintered and schismatic. Knox countered Tyrie with Scripture.[104] Jesus said in Mathew 11 "come unto me all ye that labor and are heavy laden." "All that the Father giveth me shall come to me . . . [and] I [shall] cast not away."[105] Using John six, Knox lectured Tyrie on the significance of Jesus' words. There was nothing in Jesus' words about lineal succession. The message was very simple Knox claimed, "the father giveth and the son receiveth."[106] Our church, Knox wrote, displays its unity in its insistence on apostolic teaching. We accept no ceremonies, practices, or rites not found in Scripture.[107]

Not only was Knox unwilling to concede any shred of legitimacy to Rome, the pope sometimes played the role of the antichrist. In light of

---

102. Ibid., 6:17.

103. John Knox, *Writings of the Rev. John Knox* (London: The Religious Tract Society, 1831), 267–76. This is volume 3 in an 8 volume series titled, The British Reformers, from Wycliff to Jewell. We are citing volume 3 here because the English translation is much preferred to the Laing edition of Knox's *Works.*

104. Ibid., 282, 296.

105. Ibid., 282.

106. Ibid.

107. Ibid., 283, 287.

such behavior—Knox argued popes had turned the temple of the Lord into Babylon, claimed inerrancy, and demanded to be worshipped.[108]

The exchange between Knox and Tyrie was remarkably cordial, each praying for the other and wishing the other well. Gone is the vituperative language sometimes found in Knox's polemical works.[109] Within a year Tyrie responded from Paris with a *Refutation*, published in 1573, some months after the death of John Knox.

LETTERS, DURING THE LATER PERIOD OF KNOX'S LIFE

The victory of Protestants in Scotland and the subsequent establishment of the Reformed Church in the Parliament of August 1560 proved short-lived. Word reached Scotland in December of the death of Francis II, King of France and husband of Mary Stewart. He died at age sixteen from an ear infection.[110] As a result of the king's death, the Guise family in France lost considerable influence and the real power shifted to the Queen mother, Catherine de Medici.[111] Francis' death also opened the door for Mary to return home and claim her crown as Queen of Scotland. Knox greatly feared the infant Reformed Church in Scotland might not survive because Mary could rally the sections of Scotland, which retained the "dregs of papistrie."[112] Years later when Knox's worst fears were realized, he poured his heart out in a public prayer following the murder of Regent Moray. Knox called Queen Mary the "mother of all mischief."[113]

Mary arrived with her French entourage and three of her uncles, including the Duke de Guise, in Edinburgh in August of 1561. The Queen's arrival, her efforts to restore Catholicism, and the extraordinary machinations surrounding her marriages provide the backdrop to Knox's letters through 1568. Perhaps Theodore Beza's descriptive letter to Knox is the best a writer could produce regarding the chaos in Scotland. He told Knox

108. Ibid., 295–96. Knox was referring to the way Pope Gregory VII dealt with French King Henry IV at Canosa. The Pope left the penitent King Henry barefoot in the snow for several days before accepting his apology.

109. Ibid., 297–98.

110. Knox, *History*, 1:347.

111. A. M. Renwick, *The Story of the Scottish Reformation* (London: Inter-Varsity Fellowship, 1960), 120.

112. Caroline Bingham, *The Stewart Kingdom of Scotland* 1371–1603 (London: Wedenfeld & Nicolson, 1974), 201f.

113. *Works*, 6:569.

Scotland suffered "with tragedies such as the whole of Greece never acted in its theatres."[114] Truth in Scotland was indeed stranger than fiction.

Mary wasted no time when she illegally celebrated the Mass the first Sunday after her arrival in Scotland. Lord James Stewart, Mary's half-brother, defended her right to have Mass in her private chapel in the Holyrood Palace.[115] The Queen's Privy Council settled on a compromise: it allowed the Queen's court to practice Catholicism in a country that officially embraced Protestantism and outlawed Catholic practice only a year earlier.[116] This compromise gave the Queen and her company a significant beachhead from which to battle Knox and the Reformed Church. James Stewart, the Earl of Moray, defended this arrangement for several years (1561–1565)—straining his once, strong friendship with Knox.

The nineteen year old widowed Queen sought to strengthen her government and her own power by finding a suitable husband. Through her courtier William Maitland, Mary entered into negotiations to marry Spain's Don Carlos, heir of Philip II.[117] Mary, however, was unaware of Catherine de Medici's and Queen Elizabeth's active lobbying against this marriage.[118] Such a union could have had grave consequences for the Reformed Church in Scotland, and Knox condemned the proposed marriage in strong language. He warned Mary of divine wrath resulting from an alliance with Catholic Spain.[119]

Knox used the pulpit at St. Giles to speak out against the Queen's Mass and her marriages. On four occasions, Knox's comments led to face-to-face meetings demanded by Queen Mary who resented his intrusion into her private affairs. For the past 450 years, various accounts of John Knox making the young Queen cry have shaped the popular perception of Knox as a bigot, brute, and bully. A closer examination of the events and details of their interviews reveal two stubborn leaders starting with irreconcilable presuppositions.

---

114. Ibid.

115. Guy, *Queen of Scots*, 137.

116. Renwick, *The Story of the Scottish Reformation*, 124–25.

117. Guy, *Queen of Scots*, 165–68. See also, W. E. Blake, "Knox and Lethington: A Lesson in Religious and Political Alienation," *Scotia* 5 (1981): 9–20.

118. Guy, *Queen of Scots*, 168.

119. Knox, *History*, 2:82.

Mary's Marriage Woes

Having failed for years to find a suitable husband, Queen Mary married her cousin Henry Stewart—Lord Darnley, a Catholic, and the son of the Earl of Lennox. Like Mary, Darnley was a great grandchild of Henry VII and in the line of succession to the throne of England. They were secretly married in April 1565 and publicly married in late June.[120] The marriage to Darnley and the rise of David Rizzio, an Italian court musician, also meant the decline of the influence of James Stewart, the Earl of Moray.[121] Rizzio essentially assumed the role of a foreign secretary and controlled the Queen's correspondence.[122] The jealousy of Darnley and the unbounded arrogance of Rizzio led to the Italian's murder in short order. Several Protestant leaders—including the Earls of Moray, Morton, and Glencairn and Lords Lindsay and Ochiltree—concocted a plan to remove Rizzio from power.[123]

In 1564 the widowed John Knox shocked many of his closest friends when he married the seventeen year old daughter of Lord Ochiltree. Despite the close friendship between Knox and Lord Ochiltree, there is no suspicion of Knox's involvement in the murder plot.[124] Rizzio was stabbed to death on March 9, 1566, when he was pulled from a room in the palace of Holyrood where he dined with the Queen. The band of murderers acted on Darnley's command and used his dagger in the murder and left it in the body. Despite his obvious involvement in the deed, Mary outwardly feigned her love for Darnley. She used him for her own political advantage but inwardly despised him.[125]

In June 1566 Mary gave birth to a son James, who nearly four decades later would claim his dual thrones in Edinburgh and London. The news of the Queen's newborn son generated great joy in Scotland and

120. Renwick, *The Story of the Scottish Reformation*, 142–43. Gordon Donaldson describes Rizzio, (also spelled Riccio) as both morally and intellectually worthless. See Donaldson, *Scotland, The Making of a Kingdom, James V—James II* (Edinburgh: Mercat Press, 1990), 120.

121. Hume Brown, *History of Scotland* 2 vols. (Cambridge: Cambridge University Press, 1912), 2:100.

122. Ibid., 2:104.

123. Ibid., 2:105.

124. Donaldson, *Scotland, The Making of a Kingdom*, 122. Donaldson says Knox heartily applauded the murder of Rizzio.

125. Renwick, *The Story of the Scottish Reformation*, 147.

equally great consternation by Queen Elizabeth because of her own barren womb.[126] Estranged from Darnley, Mary turned to James Hepburn, the fourth Earl of Bothwell, for political advice and soon for physical and emotional support. In the end, Mary's marriage to Bothwell sealed her tragic place in history.[127]

Historians cannot agree on the exact alliances and precise motives resulting in the murder of Lord Darnley.[128] In the early morning of February 10, 1567 the small house in the kirk-of-field, next to the city wall, was blown up by a large cache of gunpowder. Darnley's body was found in the garden, unharmed by the explosion, but strangled to death.[129] Bothwell and Mary were both widely suspected as the masterminds of Darnley's murder.[130] Lennox, the father of Darnley, demanded Bothwell be brought to justice. The trial in the Tolbooth was so packed with Bothwell supporters, Lennox and his supporters could not attend.[131] Some weeks later Bothwell was able to procure a separation from his wife through the Archbishop of St. Andrews, who annulled his current marriage. Queen Mary and Bothwell were married in a Protestant ceremony at Holyrood May 15, 1567.

The marriage generated a popular uproar and forced Mary to raise an army for her own defense. Her army proved of little consequence as many soldiers defected in the face of battle. On June 15, only a month after her unpopular marriage, the Queen's army lost the battle at Carbery Hill near Pinkie. Through the offices of William Kirkaldy, Mary had arranged for Bothwell to escape the battle and flee for freedom.[132] Mary surrendered to the Confederate Lords and was forced to abdicate the throne in favor of her year old son James.[133] John Knox preached the sermon at the

---

126. Brown, *History of Scotland*, 2:107.

127. Jenny Wormald, *Court, Kirk, and Community, Scotland 1470–1625* (Edinburgh: Edinburgh University Press, 1981), 143.

128. Donaldson, *Scotland The Making of a Kingdom*, 126–27; Guy, *Queen of Scots*, 269f. Thomas Duncan labeled Darnley a "hopeless Degenerate." See T. Duncan, "The Relations of Mary Stuart with William Maitland of Lethington," *Scottish Historical Review* 5 (January 1908): 156.

129. Renwick, *The Story of the Scottish Reformation*, 152.

130. Brown, *History of Scotland*, 2:110–11.

131. Donaldson, *Scotland The Making of a Kingdom*, 128.

132. Guy, *Queen of Scots*, 335.

133. Donaldson, *Scotland The Making of a Kingdom*, 131.

coronation of the infant prince at Stirling on July 29. The Earl of Moray, the Queen's half-brother, was summoned from his self-imposed exile in France and arrived in Edinburgh in August and was named Regent.

Scotland and the Reformed Kirk after Mary

At the same time as Mary's abdication, the General Assembly was scheduled to meet in late June. Knox returned from England in order to participate in the proceedings of the Assembly, his last major contribution to the Reformed party.[134] Moray called for Parliament to meet in December. The body approved nearly all the recommendations of the General Assembly and finally ratified the Reformation Acts of 1560—marking 1567 as perhaps the true date of the legal establishment of the Reformation in Scotland.[135]

Mary made one final effort to regain her royal position. She escaped from her confinement in Loch Leven Castle and gathered a considerable assembly of earls, bishops, lords, abbots, and barons pledging themselves in a bond for her defense. At Langside, south of modern day Glasgow, Mary witnessed the Regent's army slaughter her army in a battle lasting less than an hour. She fled south and arrived in England on May 16, 1568. It was a remarkable irony that she sought refuge in a country where only a few years earlier she claimed to be the rightful queen. Mary was later involved in several plots to overthrow Elizabeth and establish herself on the English throne. She spent the next nineteen years of her life in confinement until her execution, February 8, 1587.

In Scotland Regent Moray battled Mary's faithful supporters as well as the powerful Hamilton family. The Hamiltons successfully conceived and carried out the assassination of Regent Moray in February of 1570. The Hamiltons were motivated by greed and a lust for power that strengthened the families claim in the line of succession to the Scottish throne.

The Earl of Lennox, father of the late Lord Darnley, succeeded Moray as Regent. Because of his long residence in England and his cordial relations with Queen Elizabeth, over the years Lennox had unwittingly gathered a number of detractors in Scotland. Once more the Hamilton family schemed to replace the Regent in Scotland for their own political and financial benefit. The Civil War that ensued in 1570–1572 pitted the king's

---

134. Reid, *Trumpeter of God*, 248.

135. Renwick, *The Story of the Scottish Reformation*, 154.

men, the supporters of the infant James, against the queen's men. The later group continued to support Mary as the legitimate sovereign over both England and Scotland. Lennox's greatest triumph involved the capture of Dumbarton Castle, a stronghold of the Queen with a great store of war materials.[136] John Hamilton, the Archbishop of St. Andrews, was subsequently snared and charged with the murder of Darnley and conspiracy against the King. He was hanged in public in Stirling April 7, 1571. Regent Lennox, however, proved to be of no help to the Reformed Church when he scoffed at the request of the General Assembly for financial support of the ministers. One of the serious blows the Reformed Church suffered over the years was its lack of financial means.[137]

Kirkcaldy of Grange—Governor of the Castle of Edinburgh and defender of Queen Mary—hatched a fantastic plot to blow up the entire Parliament and king's party in September 1571 when they assembled in Stirling. The plot failed but in the chaos of the assault, Regent Lennox was shot in the back.[138] The new Regent, the Earl of Mar, held his new position in name only. The Earl of Morton held the real power in Scotland. The good offices of Queen Elizabeth secured a temporary truce between the king's men and the queen's men in the summer of 1572.

While the Civil War laid siege to Edinburgh, Knox's friends convinced him to move temporarily to the safer confines of St. Andrews. Frail and unsteady on his feet Knox still preached and delivered some lectures at the university. After the truce made Edinburgh safe again, the congregation of St. Giles summoned Knox to return. Knox returned to Edinburgh at the same time Scotland learned of the slaughter of 20,000 Huguenots in the St. Bartholomew's Day Massacre in France. This event perhaps more than any other destroyed Queen Mary's party of supporters.

As Knox lay dying, he left behind a nation and a people still divided over fundamental religious issues. He died in Edinburgh, November 24, 1572—not with the certainty of the triumph of the Reformed party in Scotland—but with a personal triumph. He died with a clear conscience that throughout his life he had faithfully proclaimed God's Word to a people in desperate need of hope.

---

136. Ibid., 158–59.

137. J. D. Mackie, *A History of the Scottish Reformation* (Edinburgh: Church of Scotland Youth Committee, 1960), 162–63.

138. Renwick, *The Story of the Scottish Reformation*, 161.

9

Views of Knox: Extreme Makeover

F EW THINGS ARE CERTAIN in life we like to say, except death and taxes.
From the perspective of a Reformation historian—who is ill equipped
to comment on thanatology or progressive fiscal policy—a third certainty
is the association, if not the equation, between John Knox and the Scottish
Reformation. John Knox, however, has lately been dethroned from his
historic perch.

The purpose of this chapter is to trace the changing status of Knox
in the Reformation narrative. In the world of marketing and reality TV,
we will attempt to trace the "extreme makeover" of the Scots reformer. If
you prefer another network's version of reality TV, John Knox has been
"kicked off the island."

Knox faced many critics during the sixteenth century. This chapter,
however, is not about Knox's critics per se, but rather the changing perception of Knox's precise role. The fact Knox had so many critics in his
own day demonstrates in part that he held a preeminent position among
Protestants in Scotland from the middle 1500s. This chapter will offer a
modest analysis of selective Knox literature from the last two centuries.
And it will note how the popular biographies and histories contributed
to a "Knox mythology," which still enjoys widespread support. Finally, we
will briefly examine the conclusions of revisionist studies seeking to correct the Knox mythology.

THE WHIG HISTORIANS

Scottish writer Thomas Carlyle (1795–1881) was arguably one of the
most influential Knox interpreters. Though not without his own severe
critics, Carlyle influenced many subsequent biographers of Knox for gen-

erations.[1] Carlyle is best remembered for his stirring literary biographies, dramatic but factually flawed histories, and his literary criticism. Carlyle trained for the Christian ministry but abandoned it and Christianity after reading David Hume and Edward Gibbon. He could not totally embrace the rationalism of the *philosophes*. Instead he embraced romanticism as his personal creed and as a lens for what he considered the three great sources of revelation: the Bible, nature, and history.[2] If Carlyle lost his faith in traditional, biblical Christianity, he tried to find it in literature and in history. He created a "secular faith based on wonder, vitality, and imagination"—qualities he found in heroic leaders.[3]

His book *Heroes and Hero Worship* began as lectures published in 1840 and reveal his passion to find the "unconscious and mysterious forces that underlie the personalities of great men."[4] Carlyle found in John Knox a hero who overcame the challenges of Scotland's "barbarism," and one who turned the hearts of the people to God. Carlyle called his native Scotland "a poor barren country, full of continual broils, dissensions, massacring; a people in the last stage of rudeness and destitution . . . a country without a soul."[5] In his view, Knox resuscitated the corpse and nursed the country back to spiritual health.

1. This claim is based upon our own reading of biographies that praise Thomas Carlyle for his insights. See for example, William M. Taylor, *John Knox* (New York: A. C. Armstrong & Son, 1886), v., index, and Taylor Innes, *John Knox* (London: Oliphant Anderson & Ferrier), 39.

2. Keith C. Sewell, review of John D. Rosenberg, *Carlyle and the Burden of History* (Cambridge: Harvard University Press, 1985), in *Fides et Historia* 19 no. 3 (October 1987): 82–84. See also Trevor Hogan, "The Religion of Thomas Carlyle," in *Reinventing Christianity*, Linda Woodhead, ed., (Burlington, VT: Ashgate, 2001), 149–62.

3. Ann W. Engar, "Thomas Carlyle," in *Dictionary of Literary Biography* 144, Steven Serptin ed., (Detroit: Gale Research, Inc., 1994), 35f, hereafter cited as DLB.

4 Ibid., 40.

5. Thomas Carlyle, *Heroes & Hero Worship* (Boston: Dan Estes & Charles Lauriat, 1884), 369. This was also the conclusion of native son David Hume in his *History of England*. Hume saw "Scottish history as little more than an interplay of feudal anarchy and religious bigotry." Hume considered both Protestants and Catholics guilty of bigotry. Cited by Michael Fry, "The Whig Interpretation of Scottish History," 76–77 in Ian Donnachie and Christopher Whatley, ed., *The Manufacture of Scottish History* (Edinburgh: Polygon, 1992), 72–89. There is a growing body of scholarship that is correcting the barbarous image of Scotland found in many early histories. It argues that colonized people are always made to believe in the inferiority of their culture, and that this happened to Scotland in the union of 1707. According to this view, the "civilization" of Scotland began with the generous help of England in 1707. The Scottish Enlightenment occurred only

According to Carlyle, Knox became a hero not only for leading the Reformation in Scotland but also for working a miracle as both a physician and a moral reformer. "This is what Knox did for his nation. I say we may call it a resurrection as from death . . . The people began to live . . . ."[6] One interpreter called Carlyle a "Victorian sage or prophet to describe his immense influence on Britain in the nineteenth century."[7] In his study, *The History Men,* Professor John Kenyon calls Carlyle "a Victorian prophet in the Hebraic sense of the word, meaning self-styled gurus and teachers who denounced the sins of their generation and called for a return to older values or the substitution of the new."[8]

Ironically, this description of Carlyle is the identical one he used himself. Under the heading, "Priest as Hero," Carlyle described Knox as his hero.[9] In Carlyle's other extended essay on Knox entitled, "The Portraits of

---

because England rescued the country from its barbarous destiny. A growing number of Scottish scholars are committed to counter this "inferiorist mentality." See for example Craig Beveridge and Ronald Turnbull, *The Eclipse of Scottish Culture: Inferiorism and the Intellectuals* (Edinburgh: Polygon, 1989), 5f. This new historiography impinges on Knox scholarship because the common thread that unites his critics, blames him for leaving Scotland a cultural wasteland. According to this view Knox became a kind of Calvinist Ayatollah whose greatest triumph involved taking the fun out of life. This charge is a piece of the same cloth that blames the Puritans for anything their opponents dislike in Colonial New England. This is the thesis of Edwin Muir and Hugh MacDiarmid to name two authors. Muir for example, concluded his book by claiming that what "Knox really did was to rob Scotland of all the benefits of the Renaissance." See Edwin Muir, *John Knox: Portrait of a Calvinist* (New York: Viking Press, 1929), 316. This thesis is echoed in an essay titled, "Knox, Calvinism and the Arts," by the eminent Scots poet Hugh MacDiarmid. See Hugh MacDiarmid, Cabell Maclean and Anthony Ross, *John Knox* (Edinburgh: The Ramsay Head Press, 1976), 75–96. This attack rejects any positive Calvinist legacy in Scotland. The Scottish nationalists probably sour on Knox in part because of his promotion of the Anglo-Scottish union. In his book *On Scotland and the Scottish Intellect,* Henry Thomas called Calvinism "one of the most detestable tyrannies ever seen on earth . . . . Under its influence . . . the Scotch mind was thrown into such a state that, . . . the noblest feelings of hope, of love, and of gratitude, were set aside and were replaced by the dictates of a servile and ignominious fear." Quoted in Beveridge and Turbull, *The Eclipse of Scottish Culture,* 18–19.

6. Carlyle, *Heroes & Hero Worship,* 370.

7 Rosemary Jann, *The Art and Science of Victorian History* (Columbus: Ohio State University, 1985), 33.

8. John Kenyon, *The History Men: The Historical Profession in England Since the Renaissance* (Pittsburgh: University of Pittsburgh Press, 1984), 97. This prophetic motif is also the thesis of a biography by Julian Symons, Thomas Carlyle, *The Life and Ideas of a Prophet* (New York: Oxford University Press, 1952).

9. Carlyle, *Heroes & Hero Worship.*

John Knox," he depicts Knox as a prophet of God. "There is in Knox . . . the spirit of an Old-Hebrew prophet such as . . . in Moses in the desert at the sight of the burning bush,"—a larger than life hero who encountered God and in turn inspired others to a higher plane of living.[10]

History made of heroes became a religion for Carlyle and a chance to encounter his own "burning bush." For Carlyle, "the strongest force within a human being is unconscious and mysterious. God is in man, literature is a branch of religion, and the artist's goal is to represent the mysterious and God-like deliverances of his deepest unconscious."[11] Vicarious living through heroes like Knox sanctified Carlyle and allowed him to dwell, albeit briefly, in the heavens. The heroic acts of Knox became a means of grace for Carlyle. Almost at a loss of words to venerate the prophet, Carlyle offered these thoughts. "A . . . higher title than 'man of genius' . . . belong[s] to Knox." Rather, he regarded Knox as a "heaven-inspired seer . . . [whose] spiritual endowment is of the most distinguished class intrinsically capable of whatever is noblest in literature and in far higher things."[12]

Sir Herbert Butterfield of Cambridge once identified "Whig history" as the "tendency in many historians to write on the side of Protestants and Whigs, to praise revolutions provided they have been successful, to emphasize certain principles of progress in the past . . . ."[13] In its Scottish version, it included a strong aversion to the Stewart house for its hostility toward Protestantism and its alleged promotion of absolutism. By contrast, the Reformation was equated with freedom. Whig historians saw history as a cast of heroes and villains. They were expected to make judgments of their subjects and to pass them on to the reader.[14]

Carlyle, an untrained historian, writing within the Whig tradition was more concerned with narrative and vivid storytelling than in empirical evidence. Carlyle, in fact, grew contemptuous of exact scholarship and

10. Thomas Carlyle, "The Portraits of John Knox," in *Critical and Miscellaneous Essays*, 5 vols., (New York: Scribner's Sons, 1901), 356.

11. Thomas Carlyle, "Characteristics," *Edinburgh Review* (December 1831): cited in Engar, "Thomas Carlyle," 38.

12. Carlyle, "The Portraits of John Knox," 352.

13. Herbert Butterfield, *The Whig Interpretation of History* (London: G. Bell and Son, Ltd., 1931, reprinted 1950), v. See also Butterfield's, *Englishman and His History*, 1944. Regarding the political use of the Whig label and a commentary on Carlyle's lack of affinity for either Whigs or Tories see, John MacCunn, *Six Radical Thinkers* (New York: Russell & Russell, Inc., 1964), 142f.

14. Donnachie and Whatley eds., *The Manufacture of Scottish History*, 73, 76–77.

hated the drudgery of historical research.[15] Of all Victorian historians, Carlyle wrote with singular admiration for German culture and ideas, but like many of his colleagues, he ignored the "scientific" model of Leopold von Ranke.[16] Carlyle sought instead to identify from history those principles of heroism the historian could not verify through empirical means.

Thomas Carlyle did not a wear a perfectly tailored suit of Whig clothing, but his costume is close enough to let him hang in the same ideological closet with the Whigs. He credited Knox with the genius and catalyst behind a cultural Renaissance in Scotland, which produced "Scotch literature and thought, Scotch industry; James Watt, David Hume, Walter Scott, [and] Robert Burns . . . ." Moreover, Carlyle found "Knox and the Reformation acting in the heart's core of every one of these persons and phenomena; I find that without the Reformation they would not have been."[17] With notable exceptions, such conclusions became the stock-in-trade approach taken by biographers, until the late Victorian period and modified significantly in the 1960s.

Though separated by hundreds of years, Carlyle here committed the exact sin against which Butterfield warned. "The Whig historian," Butterfield noted, "stands on the summit of the twentieth century and organizes his scheme of history from the point of view of his own day . . . ."[18] Carlyle saw a direct line of liberty running from Knox to the Glorious Revolution and to America. "The Puritanism of Scotland became that of England, [and] of New England, a tumult in the High Church of Edinburgh spread into

15. Kenyon, *The History Men*, 106, and Heyck, *The Transformation of Intellectual Life*, 127. Such observations are not intended to denigrate the significant scholarship of all historians who might fit or are labeled "Whig" historians. Samuel Gardiner's multivolume work on the English Revolution, though dated, is perhaps unsurpassed in its exacting attention to detail. Whig historians are most vulnerable when they read into history the inevitable triumph of progress. Some Whig historians like Carlyle are blatant examples of promoting this error.

16. Kenyon, *The History Men*, 97. John D. Rosenberg notes Carlyle is frequently misquoted. "Passages often cited as 'straight' Carlyle are in fact spoken by one of his many quirky impersonations—Dryasdust, Smelfungus, Plugson of Undershot, [and] Sir Jabesh Windbag." To obscure the identity of the speaker is to lose half of what is said, for in Carlyle's view, no thought exists apart from the voice that utters it, just as no historical text exists apart from the conflicting chorus of voices that enacted it." See, Rosenburg, *Carlyle and the Burden of History* (Cambridge: Harvard University Press, 1985), 18, unnumbered footnote.

17. Carlyle, *Heroes & Hero Worship*, 370.

18. Butterfield, *The Whig Interpretation*, 13.

a universal battle and over all these realms . . . ." Rather, there developed "after fifty years of struggling, what we all call the 'Glorious Revolution' a Habeas Corpus Act, Free Parliament and much else!"[19]

While acknowledging the Whig tendencies in Carlyle, we must honestly address the simple question—so what? The Whig historian Thomas Babbington Macaulay once argued "the best portraits are those in which there is a slight mixture of caricature."[20] Views such as Macaulay's "led many Victorian historians to paint the past in artificially brilliant colors."[21] Carlyle's vivid portrait of Knox, in fact, featured garish day glow colors and a neon halo that illuminated the path followed by subsequent Victorian biographies.[22]

Some critics hoped Carlyle's words would die with him, and others wondered how he ever found a publisher. "The impenetrability of Carlyle's writing—his bizarre vocabulary, his contorted syntax and rhetorical violence—not to mention the wild exaggeration with which most of his views were expressed" did not derail his literary career.[23] One modern critic said Carlyle's ideas might be "dangerous if turned into the vernacular."[24] In fact, subsequent biographers did turn Carlyle's heroic image of Knox into the vernacular, and fortified the Knox mythology which has only recently been challenged.

The "demythology" of Knox did not begin until the late Victorian period when English historians pursued more "scientific" models—a trend increased significantly by revisionists beginning in the 1960s. In England this important shift from history written by men of letters to academic history took two paths. Books like H.T. Buckle's *History of Civilization* echoed positivists—such as John Stuart Mill and August Comte—who argued historians should synthesize learning from many fields of study,

19. Carlyle, *Heroes & Hero Worship*, 370.

20. Thomas Babbington Macaulay, "Machiavelli," *Critical and Historical Essays* (London, 1883), 50, quoted in Heyck, *The Transformation of Intellectual Life*, 125.

21. Heyck, *The Transformation of Intellectual Life*, 125.

22. Robert S. Rait claims "a belief in Knox's infallibility became almost an article of faith in the Free Church." See, Rait, "John Knox and the Scottish Reformation," *The Quarterly Review 205* (July and October, 1906): 174.

23. Kenyon, *The History Men*, 97.

24. James Pope-Hennessey, *Monckton Milnes: The Years of Peace (1949)*, 184, quoted in Kenyon, *The History Men*, 116–18.

identify the laws of human behavior, and write a science of society.[25] By contrast, the scientific school motivated by Ranke demanded a passionate yet disinterested dedication to archival research. Such an approach dismissed both the didactic role of history and the amateur men of letters.

LATE VICTORIANS AND "PHILISTINES"

By the late nineteenth century, the intellectual stage was set for a new critical biography of Knox written by a trained historian. In this setting, Professor Peter Hume Brown was a transitional figure between men of letters and professional historians, and in 1895 he wrote the first critical biography of Knox.[26] Brown denied Knox any intellectual legacy and credited him instead with fearless preaching and motivational leadership. Absent is the pious warbling found in the earlier Victorian portraits of Knox. Brown announced his respect for Thomas M'Crie's work, the first important biography of Knox, but also noted how subsequent scholarship occasionally rendered M'Crie's judgments unsound.[27] Brown also stung Thomas Carlyle for accepting tradition over contradictory evidence and relegated some of Carlyle's flawed findings to an appendix.[28] Brown's biog-

---

25. Heyck, *The Transformation of Intellectual Life*, 133–36.

26. Peter Hume Brown, *John Knox: A Biography*, 2 vols., (London: Adam and Charles Black, 1895). See also C. H. Firth, "In Memoriam: Peter Hume Brown," in *Scottish Historical Review 16* (January 1919): 153. For a definition and a history of men of letters and their magazines see John Gross, *The Rise and Fall of the Men of Letters* (New York: Collier Books, 1970. R. G. Cant also includes P. Hume Brown as a Whig interpreter of Scottish history. See Cant, *The Writing of Scottish History in the Time of Andrew Lang* (Edinburgh: Scottish Academic Press, 1978), 9.

27. Brown, *John Knox*, see for example, 1:158, 167. M'Crie (1772–1835) was a Presbyterian church historian who wrote notable biographies of Knox and Andrew Melville in the early 1800s. His biography of Knox advanced the cause of the evangelical branch of The Church of Scotland. He is also credited with writing one of the first scholarly studies of the Scottish Reformation. See S. Ibell, S.V., "Thomas M'Crie," in the *Dictionary of Scottish History and Theology*, Nigel M. de S. Cameron, et al. ed., (Downers Grove, IL: InterVarsity Press, 1993), 506–7. For a modern interpretation of M'Crie's *Life of John Knox* (1811) see Ian Henderson, "Reassessment of the Reformers," 34–41, in Duncan Shaw, ed., *Reformation and Revolution: Essays Presented to the Very Reverend Principal Emeritus Hugh Watt* (Edinburgh: Saint Andrew Press, 1967).

28. Brown, *John Knox*, 1:11, 2:320–22. In appendix G. Brown explains why Carlyle's preference for the "Sommerville" portrait of Knox is groundless. In his research Brown used a letter from Sir Peter Young in Edinburgh to Theodore Beza that vindicates the accuracy of the portrait in *Icones*, (1580). Late in his career, Carlyle sought the assistance of his friend David Laing, the editor of Knox's collected *Works*, to raise money for a

raphy built on the work of David Laing and Peter Lorimer, but most importantly, he incorporated new materials discovered in foreign archives.[29] Brown is most provocative, but also most vulnerable to overstatement when he claims Knox was a reformer of "European importance." In a superficial sense this is true, but Knox's vagabond status in Europe certainly limited his actual contributions to the reformed cause in France, Frankfurt, and Geneva. Brown's biography received generally positive treatment in the major new journal, the *English Historical Review*.

Founded in 1885, the so-called Germanophile academic historians categorically disassociated their journal from Victorian literary publications.[30] James Bryce, one of the founders, identified the goals of the journal in the first issue: "to set forth the facts ... without any hint of partisanship. [The] main reliance will be on the scientific spirit which we shall expect from contributors."[31] Professor Brown brilliantly captured this very commitment to avoid the partisanship that dominated the M'Crie biography.

In 1905 a score of biographies appeared to commemorate what was mistakenly thought to be the four hundredth anniversary of Knox's birth.[32] Academic historians largely ignored the date while popular writers filled the vacuum. Most of the writers bypassed the critically constructed bridge

---

bronze statue of Knox in Edinburgh. The collaboration between the two men broke down because Carlyle refused to accept the traditional portraits of Knox. A statue of Knox was later erected and stood on a prominent place on the Mound. It was subsequently moved to a much less public place in the New College Quad. Carlyle would not have approved of this image of Knox.

29. John Knox, *The Collected Works of John Knox*, ed., David Laing, 6 vols, (Edinburgh: Printed for the Bannatyne Club, 1846–1864), reprint edition, (New York: AMS Press, 1966), and Peter Lorimer, *John Knox and the Church of England* (London, 1875). For a discussion of the discovery of Knox materials in foreign archives see Brown, *John Knox*, 2:320f.

30. Heyck, *The Transformation of Intellectual Life*, 149.

31. James Bryce, *English Historical Review* 1 (1895): 1–6. Brown went on to write a multivolume history of Scotland, edited 15 volumes of the Register of the Privy Council, was elected to the Fraser chair of Ancient History and Palaeography at Edinburgh University in 1908, and to the office of the Historiographer Royal of Scotland. He was also labeled by the author as "a proponent of 'higher whiggery.'" See, Michael Fry, *The Whig Interpretation of Scottish History*, 84–86.

32. For a review of the popular biographies aimed at a general reading audience see, Benjamin B. Warfield, "Historical Theology," *Princeton Theological Review* 3 (1905): 688–94. For a review of the Knox biographies from the perspective of a Scottish historian see, Robert S. Rait, "John Knox and the Scottish Reformation," *Quarterly Review* 205 (July 1906): 169–95.

erected by P. Hume Brown and instead fortified the "Knox mythology" designed by the early Victorian architects. Only a very few authors attempted to debunk the Knox mythology, which sold well to popular audiences.

Andrew Lang was among the most important interpreters of Knox in the early twentieth century. He studied at St. Andrews, Glasgow, and Balliol College, Oxford, and possessed the training to write a solid, academic biography of Knox. In an amazing career, Lang wrote or edited 270 books and wrote over 5,000 essays, articles, and reviews.[33] Ill health cut short Lang's academic career after holding the Open Fellowship at Merton College, Oxford for seven years.[34] His distinguished literary career included editing an extensive fairy book series for children. He also contributed articles for the ninth ed., of the *Encyclopedia Britannica* on the topics such as "apparitions, crystal-gazing, mythology, poltergeist, psychical research and Scotland."[35]

Like P. Hume Brown, Lang sought to "demythologize" the Knox mythology. He believed the ghost of Knox haunted Scotland, and the biographer's task demanded they aim a penetrating spotlight on their subject to vaporize the apparition. In the preface, Lang informed readers of his effort to "get behind the Tradition . . . of the Reformer."[36] Lang disdained the sentimental party in Scotland which "musters under the banner of the Covenant and sees scarcely a blemish in Knox." With such sentiment, Lang argued, "reason is thrown away."[37]

---

33. Roger Lancelyn Green, *Andrew Lang* (New York: Henry Z. Walck, Inc., 1962), 78. P. Hume Brown wrote a highly laudable obituary of Andrew Lang in the *Proceedings of the British Academy* 5 (1922–1912): 552–58.

34. Eleanor De Selms Langstaff, *Andrew Lang*, (Boston: Twanye Publishers, 1978), 28–29.

35. G. S. G. "Andrew Lang (1844–1912)," in the *Dictionary of Literary Biography*, 1912–1921, 320.

36. Andrew Lang, *John Knox and the Reformation* (London: Longmans Green and Company, 1905), ix. Robert S. Rait says in his review that Lang's biography "provoked more pious indignation in Scotland than any work since Mr. Henley's 'Essay on Burns.'" See, Rait, "John Knox and the Scottish Reformation," 181. Rait's statement supports our contention that a strong and passionate mythology surrounded the memory of Knox in Scotland. Rait believed that Lang's work is sound scholarship and "unquestionably a great book . . . in many ways a work of genius," 183. On the topic of Knox as a popular hero in Scotland see also, Robert S. Rait, "Scotland and John Knox," *The Fortnightly Review* 84 (July 1, 1905): 95f. Rait also delivered the annual Andrew Lang lecture at the University of St. Andrews in 1930. See Rait. *Lang as Historian* (Oxford: The Clarendon Press, 1930).

37. Lang, *John Knox and the Reformation*, x–xi.

While Lang resolved to write accurate, critical history, he found himself at odds with the lifeless, technical style of the new "scientific history." Lang penned an essay, titled "History as She Ought to Be Wrote," in which he defended the old but eminently readable popular histories of James Anthony Froude and Macaulay.[38] Lang argued that good history should stir people. He wrote, "without style no book will endure." "Style," he argued, "is the salt of literature."[39] Lang found the strict no salt diets of the scientific historians completely unpalatable.

Andrew Lang defended the old histories from what one of the doctors of history diagnosed as "Froude's disease," that is, "chronic inaccuracy."[40] As a carrier of this disease, Lang preferred it to the cure which he called "paralysis."[41] He argued that without imagination it was impossible to write good history.[42] Lang, in fact, used large doses of both imagination and biting sarcasm in his *History of Scotland* and in his biography of Knox. Lang's biography contains thorough critiques of Knox's demeanor and his inaccuracy as a historian, but he never challenged Knox's unrivalled leadership in the Scottish Reformation. Despite the numerous and damaging critiques, Lang was not the academic historian who would ultimately challenge the Knox mythology.

St. Andrews' historian D. Hay Fleming found Andrew Lang's writing contemptible and labeled his review, "Knox in the Hands of the Philistines."[43] For twenty years Fleming and Lang nurtured an unortho-

---

38. Andrew Lang, "History as She Ought to Be Wrote," *Blackwood's Magazine* 166 (August 1899): 266–74. Lang's first effort at writing history involved a university history of St. Andrews in 1893. Lang wrote only from secondary sources and critics had a field day with his schoolboy errors. As a result of this stinging criticism, Lang resolved that he would henceforth rely only on manuscripts and archival records.

39. Ibid., 269.

40. Ibid., 273. See also, Matthew A. Fitzsimons, Alfred G. Pundt and Charles E. Nowell, eds., *The Development of Historiography* (Harrisburg, PA: The Stackpole Company 1967), 202–3.

41. Lang, "History as She Ought to Be Wrote," 273.

42. Ibid., 267.

43. D. Hay Fleming, "John Knox in the Hands of the Philistines," *The British Weekly* 33 (February 19, 1903): 493–94, and (February 26, 1903): 517–18. Fleming also reviewed and included William Law Mathieson, *Politics and Religion*, 2 vols., 1902 among the "Philistine" authors. See also D. Hay Fleming, *Critical Reviews Relating to Scotland* (London: Hodder and Stoughton, 1912), 188–204. This is a valuable book because it collects over one hundred of Fleming's book reviews in magazines that are now difficult to find. It includes reviews from publications such as *The Athenaeum, The Bookman, The*

dox friendship, each rigidly partisan though from opposite perspectives. Lang once referred to Fleming as his "friend and constant trouncer."[44] "Trouncing" is an apt description of Fleming's reviews of Lang's *History of Scotland* and subsequent biography of Knox. Fleming believed Lang's scholarship would not help his reputation, nor "remove the reproach that he is one of the most careless of critical writers."[45]

Fleming demonstrated the chronic distortions of Knox's words that allowed Lang to hold the reformer up for ridicule. Fleming also regretted that for all Lang's lip service to truth, he was in fact guided by partisanship and expediency.[46] Despite such criticism, the two men frequently discussed their work and bore no personal grudges. Near the end of his life, Lang wrote Fleming a letter summarizing their friendship. "You have been rather the Freeman to my Froude, but I hope there has never been an

---

Bulwark, Fife Herald, Speaker, The Union Magazine and the *Original Secession Magazine*. The D. Hay Fleming Reference Library in the second floor of the public library in St. Andrews is a repository for much of Fleming's personal library. Another thorough critique of Lang is T.D. Wanliss, *The Muckrake in Scottish History or Mr. Andrew Lang Re-criticized* (Edinburgh: W. J. Hay, 1906). With his tongue firmly planted in his cheek, Wanliss wrote, "I heartily wish him [Lang] a long life—so that he may have plenty of time for amendment. And above all, when in the future, he pursued his historical labours, I most sincerely wish that he may always have near him, a judicious friend to correct his proof-sheets!" 46.

44. Henry M. Patton, *David Hay Fleming, Historian and Antiquary* (London: Oliver and Boyd, 1934), 61.

45. D. Hay Fleming, "Mr. Lang's 'John Knox,'" *The British Weekly* (June 22, 1905): 257–58.

46. Ibid., 258. We fully appreciate that reference to D. Hay Fleming fits into the category of politically incorrect. Some Scottish reviewers discredit any piece of scholarship merely for referencing him as a source. For many years Hay Fleming was a "card carrying" officer in the Knox club which existed in large part to thwart Roman Catholicism in Scotland. The Knox Club began in 1909 and formed branches in Aberdeen, Glasgow, and Belfast. The list of Knox Club publications reveals a preoccupation with the "menace" of Roman Catholicism. A collection of the club's publications is found in the D. Hay Fleming Reference Library in St. Andrews. Despite this attitude toward Catholicism, Hay Fleming deserves recognition for his careful scholarship. This is also the judgment of Ian B. Cowan, see "Regional Aspects of the Scottish Reformation," (London: The Historical Association, 1978), 39. We must acknowledge a faculty member of the University of Glasgow (who shall remain nameless) brought this to our attention and also showed us how Knox was thought of at the university. Our host showed us a portrait of Knox that hangs in a prominent place at the University—directly over the men's toilet in the Divinity Building!

unkind thought on my side, nor an unsportsmanlike criticism on yours, which is very rare among men of letters."[47]

Lang's work deserves attention because it attempted to debunk the prevailing sentimental hagiography and questioned the accuracy of Knox's *History*. In his attempt to demythologize Knox, however, Lang helped create a new mythology which contained as many errors as the original. In the new makeover, Knox is still the leader of the Scottish Reformation, but his character was now besmirched. Once Lang applied the new stage makeup on Knox, the reformer came across as petty, mean-spirited, and inflexible. Subsequent critics of Knox learned this lesson well from Lang. From this point Knox's legacy was regularly portrayed as Scotland's Puritan killjoy. Students of Knox would have to wait patiently for another makeover artist—not a Philistine author of fairy tales like Lang.

EXTREME MAKEOVER: JOHN KNOX AND THE REVISIONISTS

In 1960 on the 400th anniversary of the Scottish Reformation, Professor Gordon Donaldson challenged the traditional interpretation of Knox and the Scottish Reformation and shifted the scholarship to a fundamentally new footing.[48] The old view maintained that Scotland in the early sixteenth century suffered an acute case of spiritual dry rot, and the people sought a thorough reformation of the church and the ecclesiastical bureaucracy. This view further argued that when Knox and the Lords of the Congregation promoted a new and improved approach to worship, there was both widespread and popular support. Donaldson rejected what has been called "the irretrievable decay of the Catholic Church and the irresistible rise of Protestantism."[49]

---

47. Paton, *David Hay Fleming*, 62. Freeman was a "scientific" historian who delivered ruthless critiques of Froude's writing.

48. Gordon Donaldson, *The Scottish Reformation* (Cambridge: Cambridge University Press, 1960). If Knox was a defender of haggis and all things Scottish, Donaldson, (always a fish and chips man) changed the menu in favor of a more Anglo oriented cuisine.

49. Roger Mason, "Covenant and Commonweal: The Language of Politics in Reformation Scotland," in Norman MacDougal, ed., *Church, Politics & Society: Scotland 1408–1929* (Edinburgh: John Donald Publishing Ltd., 1983), 97. See also, Jenny Wormald, *Court, Kirk and Community, Scotland 1470–1625* (Edinburgh: Edinburgh University Press, 1981), 75, 109–21, 200–1.

Two years later a group of (mostly) Catholic scholars also commemorated the fourth centenary of the Scottish Reformation in two issues of *The Innes Review*, which were subsequently collected into book form. These scholars ably demonstrated the reformation of the Catholic Church began long before Knox and well before his enthusiastic followers engaged in looting and image breaking. They further argued that the violent upheaval and material destruction of churches and monasteries could have been avoided if the Catholic led reforms had been allowed to play out.[50]

Such arguments while plowing new ground are not entirely convincing nor accurate. The conciliar movement in the Scottish Church made friendly gestures toward Protestantism, and some of the proposed "reforms" went far beyond the most blatant examples of clerical immorality. The Catholic councils at the very least promoted an Erasmian, humanist style reform of the Catholic Church. They were less forthcoming with fundamental biblical, exegetical, and theological reforms.

Alec Ryrie has argued persuasively, however, that in the end, it was not Protestant radicals who doomed the success of the Catholic reform movement. Rather, it was the political machinations of Queen Regent Mary of Guise who short-circuited the Catholic reform movement. Not wishing to alienate Protestants in her realm, Mary refused to vigorously enforce the heresy laws. Her failure of nerve ironically doomed Archbishop Hamilton's reform efforts and ensured the Protestant survival and subsequent victory.[51]

Additional scholarship that challenge the old mythologies are the regional studies of the Reformation in Scotland.[52] Sweeping generaliza-

50. David McRoberts, ed., *Essays on the Scottish Reformation* (Glasgow: John S. Burns & Sons, 1962). The essays were prepared for the fourth centenary of the Scottish Reformation and appeared in two issues of *The Innes Review*, the journal of the Scottish Catholic Historical Association. It was later decided to collect the essays into book form. The forward reads in part, "the story which emerges from the following pages is much more involved, much more human, exciting and real, and therefore much more credible, than the uncomplicated and ingenious tales of our grandfathers," vi. In so many words, it is aimed at correcting what we have called the "Knox mythology."

51. Alec Ryrie, "Reform Without Frontiers in the Last Years of Catholic Scotland," *The English Historical Review* 119 (February 2004): 480f. We are indebted to Dr. Ryrie for kindly bringing this essay to our attention.

52. Ian B. Cowan, *The Scottish Reformation: Church & Society in Sixteenth-Century Scotland* (London: Weidenfeld & Nicolson, 1982, and "Regional Aspects of the Scottish Reformation." Other regional studies include, Frank D. Bardgett, *Scotland Reformed, The*

tions have given way to a more complex and sophisticated analysis. In the regional studies, the Scottish Reformation is depicted as a variegated pattern. The traditional view has, according to Roger Mason, "at long last [been] consigned to oblivion."[53]

If the Scottish Reformation is "peculiarly myth-ridden," John Knox stands in the center of the mythology.[54] Revisionist scholarship has not only attempted to reverse the traditional interpretation of the Scottish Reformation, but dethrone John Knox as well. Professor Jenny Wormald writes in effect that Knox was a legend only in his own mind. "Only in the autobiographical and propagandist pages of Knox's *History of the Reformation* does Knox appear as the Luther, Zwingli and Calvin of Scotland." She contends, "In practice, inspiring though he was, he fell short of these towering figures of the Reformation, partly because he was a considerable embarrassment to the secular leaders of the movement."[55]

Wormald is quite right regarding Knox's image among the secular leaders, but her point holds up only if the Scottish Reformation is viewed in political terms. The Reformation represented a complex brew of political, nationalistic, economic, and religious motives. Knox's own brand of genius was his ability to blend the political ambitions of many of the Lords with religious aspirations.[56] Knox's leadership in producing the major documents of the Scottish Reformation is powerful evidence of his leadership.

Furthermore, in the chronology of events leading to 1559 and 1560, Professor Wormald does not grant Knox his due in bullying the Lords and lairds into forming the first Covenant of the Lords of the Congregation

---

Reformation in Angus and the Mearns (Edinburgh: John Donald Publishers Ltd., 1989) and Margaret H.B. Sanderson, *Ayrshire and the Reformation: People and Change 1490–1600* (East Lothian, Scotland: Tuckwell Press, 1997). Margaret Sanderson and James Kirk will soon publish a new edition of Knox's *History* with T&T Clark International, and Professor Jane Dawson is working on a new biography of Knox. We thank the late Professor David Wright of Edinburgh for providing us with news of current scholarship by scholars in Scotland.

53. Mason, "Covenant & Commonwealth," 97.

54. W. Ian P. Hazlett, "Settlements: The British Isles," in Thomas A. Brady Jr., Heiko Oberman and James Tracy, eds., *Handbook of European History, 1400–1600, Late Middle Ages, Renaissance and Reformation*, 2 vols., (Leiden: E.J. Brill, 1995), 2:473. See also a valuable work by Hazlett, "The Reformation Movement in Scotland: A Survey and Literature Published from 1978 to 1984," *Pacific Theological Review* 17 no.3 (1984): 33–39.

55. Wormald, *Court, Kirk and Community*, 110.

56. Ian B. Cowan, "John Knox and the Making of the Scottish Reformation," *Proceedings of the Conference on Scottish Studies 1* (1973): 26–27.

in December of 1557.[57] His language and tactics were not admirable per-haps, but the force of his personality that translated into blunt leadership is undeniable. His desire to return to Scotland—not long after his expul-sion and after the burning of Knox in effigy—speaks more to his courage than the "ivory tower" image of Geneva depicted by Wormald.[58]

Though not a specialist of the Scottish Reformation, perhaps the most sweeping revisionist example is Euan Cameron's book, *The European Reformation* published by Oxford University Press in 1991. In his cover-age of the Scottish Reformation, Knox's role is not diminished, it is simply eliminated. The very few references to Knox include him with a list of pamphleteers on the topic of resistance theory and a passing reference to the disgruntled exiles in Frankfurt.[59]

One of the most interesting of the recent books on the Scottish Reformation is Linda J. Dunbar's *Reforming the Scottish Church*, pub-lished in 2002. Dunbar writes of John Winram—one of the other five "Johns" who wrote the *Scots Confession* and the *Book of Discipline*. She is convincing when she debunks the old charge that Winram was a vac-illating pragmatist or a two-faced hypocrite supporting Catholics or Protestants as it proved politically expedient. Dunbar also succeeds in promoting Winram's stock as a leader in the Reformed Church, serving as a Superintendent of the Fife from 1560 to 1582. She does not, however, make a convincing case for replacing John Knox with John Winram as the leader of the Scottish Reformation.[60]

Collectively, the revisionist literature helps to detract from Knox's leadership, but the extreme makeover of the Scottish Reformation and the changing face of John Knox are to this point still a work in prog-ress. The best the revisionists can tell us is that the leader of the Scottish

---

57. Wormald, *Court, Kirk and Community*, 111–12.

58. Ibid., 113.

59. Euan Cameron, *The European Reformation* (Oxford: Clarendon Press, 1991), 355–56, 386. The index incorrectly references Knox to page 385. The Scottish Reformation is "covered" on pages 289–91 without a single reference to Knox. Jonathan Zophy, an-other popular author of texts on the Reformation, and a nonspecialist of Scotland ap-parently didn't get the memo about Knox. He identifies Knox as the "greatest hero of the Reformation in Scotland." See, Jonathan W. Zophy, *A Short History of Renaissance and Reformation Europe* (Upper Saddle River, NJ: Prentice-Hall, 1999), 251.

60. Clare Kellar, *Scotland, England, and the Reformation 1534–1561* (Oxford: Oxford University Press, 2003). See the review of Kellar, in the *Sixteenth Century Journal* 37 no. 1 (Spring 2006): 244–46.

Reformation was not John Knox: the real leader is in fact "to be announced." In a letter to John Ruskin, James Anthony Froude once related a conversation where he told a man that in a thousand years, only two Scots would be known to humankind—John Knox and Thomas Caryle.[61] If Froude is correct, Knox's staying power will continue to frustrate the revisionists who wish to throw him off the island. If "Froude's disease," that is, "chronic inaccuracy," is a correct diagnosis, reports of Knox's death are not mere exaggerations.

61. Helen Gill Vildoen, *The Froude-Ruskin Friendship* (New York: Pageant Press, 1966), 11.

Bibliography

PRIMARY SOURCES:

Knox, John. *History of the Reformation in Scotland.* 2 vols. W.C. Dickinson, ed. Edinburgh: Thomas Nelson and Sons, Ltd. 1949.

———. *Selected Practical Writings of John Knox, Public Epistles, and Treatises, and Expositions to the Year 1559.* Kevin Reed, ed. Dallas: Presbyterian Heritage Publications, 1995.

———. *The Works of John Knox.* 6 vols. David Laing, ed. Edinburgh: Printed for the Bannatyne Club, 1846–64.

———. *Writings of the Rev. John Knox.* London: The Religious Tract Society, 1831.

SECONDARY SOURCES

Balke, William. *Calvin and the Anabaptist Radicals.* Grand Rapids: Eerdmans,1981.

Bardgett, Frank D. *Scotland Reformed: The Reformation in Angus and the Mearns.* Edinburgh: John Donald Publishers, Ltd. 1989.

Bell, M. Charles. *Calvin and Scottish Theology.* Edinburgh: The Handsel Press, 1985.

Blake, W.E., "Knox and Lethington: A Lesson in Religious and Political Alienation." *Scotia* 5 (1981): 9–20.

Breslow, Marvin A. ed., *The Political Writings of John Knox.* Cranbury, NJ: Associated University Press, 1994.

Brown, K.M., "In Search of the Godly Magistrate in Reformation Scotland." *Journal of Ecclesiastical History* 40 no. 4 (1989): 553–81.

Brown, P. Hume. *John Knox.* 2 vols. London: Adam and Charles Black, 1894.

Burleigh, J.H.S. *A Church History of Scotland.* London: Oxford University Press, 1960.

Burns, J.H., "John Knox and Revolution." *History Today* 8 (August 1958): 565–73.

———. "The Political Ideas of the Scottish Reformation." *Aberdeen University Review* 36 (1955-56): 251–68.

Cameron, James K. ed. *The First Book of Discipline.* Edinburgh: St. Andrew Press, 1972.

———. "Aspects of the Lutheran Contribution to the Scottish Reformation, 1528–1552." *Lutheran Theological Journal* 19 (1985): 12-20.

Cassidy, John. "The Quest for Godly Rule: The Development of Resistance Theory in Reformation Scotland." *Scottish Tradition* 14 (1988): 1–10.

Christianson, Paul. *Reformers and Babylon: English Apocalyptic Visions from the Reformation to the Eve of the Civil War.* Toronto: University of Toronto Press, 1978.

Collinson, Patrick. "The Authorship of a Brief Discourse of the Troubles Begun at Frankfort." *Journal of Ecclesiastical History* 9 (October 1958): 188–208.

Cowan, Henry. "When was John Knox Born?" *Records of the Scottish Church History Society* 1 (1926): 217–28.

Cowan, Ian B., "John Knox and the Making of the Scottish Reformation." *Proceedings of the Conference on Scottish Studies* 1 (1979): 22-20.

———. *The Scottish Reformation: Church and Society in Sixteenth-Century Scotland.* New York: St. Martin's Press, 1982.

D'Assonville, V.E. *John Knox and the Institutes of Calvin.* Durban, South Africa: Drakensberg Press, 1968.

Dawson, Jane E., "The Two John Knoxes: England, Scotland and the 1558 Tracts." *Journal of Ecclesiastical History* 42 no. 4 (1991): 555–76.

Dickens, A.G. *The English Reformation.* New York: Schocken Books, 1969.

Dickinson, William Croft. *Andrew Lang, John Knox and Scottish Presbyterianism.* Edinburgh: Thomas Nelson and Sons, Ltd. 1952.

———. *Scotland from the Earliest Times to 1603.* New York: Thomas Nelson and Sons, Ltd. 1961.

———. *The Scottish Reformation and Its Influence upon Scottish Life and Character.* Edinburgh: St. Andrew Press, 1960.

Donaldson, Gordon. *Scotland: James V to James VII.* Edinburgh: Oliver and Boyd, 1965.

———. *The Scottish Reformation.* Cambridge, UK: Cambridge University Press, 1960.

Durkan, John. "Scottish Reformers: The Less than Golden Legend." *The Innes Review* 45 no. 1 (1994): 1–28.

Firth, Katherine R. *The Apocalyptic Tradition in Reformation Britain, 1530–1545.* Oxford: Oxford University Press, 1979.

Frankforter, A. Daniel. "Correspondence with Women: The Case of John Knox." *Journal of Rocky Mt. Medieval and Renaissance Association* 6 (1985): 159-72.

———. "Elizabeth Bowes and John Knox: A Woman and Reformation Theology." *Church History* 56 (September 1987): 333–47.

Gill, Stewart D., "He Made My tongue a Trumpet. . . ." *The Reformed Theological Review* 51 (1992): 102–10.

Gray, John R., "The Political Theory of John Knox." *Church History* 8 (June 1939): 132–47.

Greaves, Richard L., "Calvinism, Democracy and the Political Thought of John Knox." *Occasional Papers of the American Society of Reformation Research* 1 (1978): 81–92.

———. "John Knox and the Covenant Tradition." *Journal of Ecclesiastical History* 24 (January 1973): 23–32.

———. "John Knox and the Ladies, or the Controversy over Gynecocracy." *Red River Valley Historical Journal* 2 (Spring 1977): 6–16.

———. "John Knox, The Reformed Tradition, and the Development of Resistance Theory." *The Journal of Modern History* 58 (September 1976): 1–31.

———. "The Knoxian Paradox: Ecumenism and Nationalism in the Scottish Reformation." *Records of the Scottish Church History Society* (Summer 1973): 85–98.

———. "The Nature of Authority in the Writings of John Knox." *Fides et Historia* 10 no. 2 (Spring 1978): 30–51.

———. *Theology and Revolution in the Scottish Reformation.* Grand Rapids: Christian University Press, 1980.

Guy, John. *Queen of Scots, the True Life of Mary Stuart.* New York: Houghton Mifflin Company, 2004.

Hargrave, O.T., "The Predestinarian Offensive of the Marian Exiles at Geneva." *Historical Magazine of the Protestant Episcopal Church* 42 (1973): 111–23.

Healey, Robert M., "Waiting for Deborah: John Knox and Four Ruling Queens." *Sixteenth Century Journal* 25 no. 2 (1994): 371–86.

Horst, Irvin Buckwalter. *The Radical Brethren: Anabaptism and the English Reformation to 1558*. Nieuwkoop, Netherlands: De Graff, 1972.

Janton, Pierre. *Concept et Sentiment de l'Eglise Chex John Knox: le reformateur ecossaise*. Paris: Presses Universitaries de France, 1972.

———. *John Knox: L 'homme et l' oeuvre*. Paris: Didier, 1967.

Johnson, Dale W. "Marginal at Best: John Knox's Contribution to the Geneva Bible." In *Adaptions of Calvinism in Reformation Europe*, ed. Mack P. Holt, 241–48. Aldershot, UK: Ashgate Publishing Company, 2007.

———. "Serving Two Masters: John Knox, Scripture and Prophecy." In *Religion and Superstition in Reformation Europe*, eds. Helen Parish and William G. Naphy, 133–53. New York: Manchester University Press, 2002.

Johnson, Dale W. and James Edward McGoldrick, "Prophet in Scotland: The Self-Image of John Knox." *Calvin Theological Journal* 33 no. 1 (April 1998): 76–86.

Kellar, Clare. *Scotland, England, and the Reformation 1534–1561*. New York: Clarendon Press, 2003.

Kirk, James. "The Influence of Calvinism on the Scottish Reformation." *Records of the Scottish Church History Society* 18 (1974): 157–79.

———. *Patterns of Reform: Continuity and Change in the Reformation Kirk*. Edinburgh: T and T Clark, 1989.

———. ed. *The Second Book of Discipline*. Edinburgh: St. Andrew Press, 1980.

Knappen, M. M. *Tudor Puritanism*. Chicago: The University of Chicago Press, 1939.

Kyle, Richard. "The Christian Commonwealth: John Knox's Vision for Scotland." *The Journal of Religious History* 16 no. 3 (1991): 247–59.

———. "John Knox: A Man of the Old Testament." *Westminster Theological Journal* 54 no. 2 (1992): 65–78.

———. "John Knox and Apocalyptic Thought." *Sixteenth Century Journal* 15 no. 4 (1984): 449–69.

———. "John Knox and the Purification of Religion: The Intellectual Aspects of His Crusade Against Idolatry." *Archiv für Reformationgeschicte* 77 (1986): 265–80.

———. "John Knox and the Care of Souls." *Calvin Theological Journal* 38 no. 1 (2003): 133–44.

———. "John Knox Confronts the Anabaptists: The Intellectual Aspects of His Encounter." *Mennonite Quarterly Review* 75 (October 2001): 493–515.

———. "John Knox: The Main Themes of His Thought." *Princeton Seminary Bulletin* 4 no. 2 (1983): 101–12.

———. "The Church-State Patterns in the Thought of John Knox." *Journal of Church and State* 30 no. 1 (Winter 1988): 72–81.

———. "The Concept of Predestination in the Thought of John Knox." *Westminster Theological Journal* 46 no. 1 (1984): 53–77.

———. "The Divine Attributes in John Knox's Concept of God." *Westminster Theological Journal* 48 no. 1 (1986): 161–72.

———. "The Hermeneutical Patterns in John Knox's Use of Scripture." *Pacific Theological Review* 17 no. 3 (1984): 19–32.

———. "John Knox's Concept of History: A Focus on the Providential and Apocalyptic Aspects of His Religious Faith." *Fides et Historia* 18 no. 2 (1986): 5–19.

———. "John Knox's Concept of Providence and Its Influence on His Thought." *Albion* 18 no. 3 (1986): 395–410.

———. "John Knox's Methods of Biblical Interpretation: An Important Source of His Intellectual Radicalness." *Journal of Religious Studies* 12 no. 2 (1985): 57–70.

———. *The Mind of John Knox*. Lawrence, KS: Coronado Press, 1984.

———. *The Ministry of John Knox: Pastor, Preacher, and Prophet*. Lewiston, NY: The Edwin Mellen Press, 2002.

———. "The Nature of the Church in the Thought of John Knox." *Scottish Journal of Theology* 37 no. 4 (1984): 485–501.

———. "Prophet of God: John Knox's Self-Awareness." *The Reformed Theological Review* 61 no. 2 (2002): 85–101.

———. "The Thundering Scot: John Knox the Preacher." *Westminster Theological Journal* 64, no. 1 (2002): 135–49.

Lang, Andrew. *John Knox and the Reformation*. London: Longmans, Green and Co., 1905.

———. "Knox as Historian." *Scottish Historical Review* 2 (January 1905): 113–30.

Lee, Maurice. "John Knox and His History." *Scottish Historical Review* 45 (April 1966): 69–78.

Lorimer, Peter. *John Knox and the Church of England*. London: Henry S. King & Co., 1875.

Lynch, Michael. *Edinburgh and the Reformation*. Edinburgh: John Donald Publishers, Ltd. 1981.

MacCulloch, Diarmaid. *Thomas Cranmer*. New Haven: Yale University Press, 1996.

MacDougall, Norman. ed. *Church, Politics and Society: Scotland 1408–1929*. Edinburgh: John Donald Publishers, Ltd. 1983.

MacGregor, Geddes. *The Thundering Scot: A Portrait of John Knox*. Philadelphia: Westminster Press, 1975.

Mackie, J.D. *A History of the Scottish Reformation*. Edinburgh: Church of Scotland Youth Committee, 1960.

Marshall, Sherin. ed. *Women in Reformation and Counter-Reformation Europe: Public and Private Worlds*. Bloomington, IN: Indiana University Press, 1989.

Mason, Roger. *John Knox on Rebellion*. Cambridge: Cambridge University Press, 1994.

———. *Kingship and the Commonwealth, Political Thought in Renaissance and Reformation Scotland*. East Lothian, Scotland: Tuckwell Press, 1998.

———. "Knox, Resistance and the Moral Imperative." *History of Political Thought* 1 (1980–81): 411–36.

———. ed. *John Knox and the British Reformations*. Aldershot, UK: Ashgate Publishing Company, 1998.

M'Crie, Thomas. *The Life of John Knox*. 2 vols. Edinburgh: William Blackwood, 1818.

McEwen, James S. *The Faith of John Knox*. Richmond: John Knox Press, 1961.

McGoldrick, James Edward. *Luther's Scottish Connection*. Cranbury, NJ: Associated University Presses, 1989.

———. "Patrick Hamilton: Luther's Scottish Disciple." *Sixteenth Century Journal* 17 (1986): 81–88.

McRoberts, David. ed. *Essays on the Scottish Reformation*. Glasgow: John H. Burns and Sons, 1962.

Merriman, Marcus H., "The Assured Scots: Scottish Collaborators with England During the Rough Wooing." *Scottish Historical Review* 47 (April 1968): 10–34.

Muir, Edward, *John Knox: Portrait of a Calvinist.* Edinburgh: J. and J. Gray, 1929.

Parker, T.M. *The English Reformation to 1558.* Oxford: Oxford University Press, 1966.

Percy, Lord Eustace. *John Knox.* John Knox Press, 1966.

Rait, R.S. "John Knox and the Scottish Reformation." *Quarterly Review* 205 (July 2006): 169–95.

———. "Scotland and John Knox." *The Fortnightly Review* 78 (July-December 1905): 95–108.

Read, Conyers. *Mr. Secretary Cecil and Queen Elizabeth.* Alfred A. Knopf: London, 1955.

Reed, Kevin. *John Knox: The Forgotten Reformer.* Dallas: Presbyterian Heritage Press, 1997.

Reid, W. Stanford. "John Knox and His Interpreters." *Renaissance and Reformation* 10 no. 1 (1974): 14–24.

———. "John Knox, Pastor of Souls." *Westminster Theological Journal* 40, no. 1 (1977): 1–21.

———. "John Knox's Theology of Political Government." *Sixteenth Century Journal* 19 no. 4 (1988): 529–40.

———. "The Lollards in Pre-Reformation Scotland." *Westminster Theological Journal* 11 (1942): 269–83.

———. "Lutheranism in the Scottish Reformation." *Westminster Theological Journal* 6 (1944–45): 91–111.

———. "The Middle Class Factor in the Scottish Reformation." *Church History* 16 no. 3 (1947): 137–53.

———. *Trumpeter of God.* New York: Scribner's, 1974.

Renwick, A.M. *The Story of the Scottish Reformation.* London: Inter-Varsity Fellowship, 1960.

Ridley, Jasper. *John Knox.* New York: Oxford University Press, 1968.

Russell, E., "John Knox as a Statesman." *The Princeton Theological Review* 6 (January 1908): 1–28.

Ryrie, Alec. *The Origins of the Scottish Reformation.* Manchester, UK: Manchester University Press, 2006.

———. "Reform Without Frontiers in the Last Years of Catholic Scotland." *The English Historical Review* 119 (February 2004): 480f.

Sanderson, Margaret H.B. *Ayrshire and the Reformation: People and Change, 1490–1600.* East Loathian, Scotland: Tuckwell Press, Ltd. 1977.

Shaw, Duncan. *Reformation and Revolution.* Edinburgh: St. Andrew Press, 1967.

———. "Zwinglian Influences on the Scottish Reformation." *Records of the Scottish Church History Society* 22 pt. 2 (1985): 119–39.

———. ed. *John Knox: A Quatercentenary Reappraisal.* Edinburgh: St. Andrew Press, 1975.

Shearman, J., "The Ordination of John Knox: A Symposium." *Innes Review* 6 (1955): 99–106.

Shephard, Amanda. *Gender and Authority in Sixteenth-Century England.* Keele, UK: Keele University Press, 1994.

Spotiswoode, John. *The History of the Church and State of Scotland.* London: R. Roystan, 1677.

Sutherland, N.M., "The English Refugees at Geneva, 1555–59." *History Today* 27 (December 1977): 779–87.

Torrance, Iain R., "Patrick Hamilton and John Knox: A Study in the Doctrine of Justification." *Archiv für Reformationgeschicte* 65 (1974): 171–84.

Verschuur, Mary. *Politics or Religion?: The Reformation in Perth 1540–1570.* Edinburgh: Dunedin Academic Press, 2006.

Watt, Hugh. *John Knox in Controversy.* Edinburgh: Thomas Nelson and Sons, Ltd. 1950.

Wendel, Francois. *Calvin: The Origins and Development of His Religious Thought.* New York: Harper and Row, 1963.

Whitley, Elizabeth. *Plain Mr. Knox.* Richmond: John Knox Press, 1960.

Wilkinson, J., "The Medical History of John Knox." *Proceedings of the Royal College of Physicians of Edinburgh* 28 (1998): 81–101.

Wormald, Jenny. *Court, Kirk, and Community: Scotland 1470–1625.* Toronto: University Press, 1982.

Subject Index